Mario Andretti

Mike O'Leary

MBI Publishing Company

Dedication

Only one person knows how much time and effort went into writing *Mario Andretti*. This book is dedicated to my wife, Sandi, who has always been there with support and ideas. You're the brass ring, babe.

First published in 2002 by MBI Publishing Company, Galtier Plaza, Suite 200, 380 Jackson Street, St. Paul, MN 55101-3885 USA

The information in this book is true and complete to the best of our knowledge. All recommendations are made without any guarantee on the part of the author or Publisher, who also disclaim any liability incurred in connection with the use of this data or specific details.

We recognize that some words, model names and designations, for example, mentioned herein are the property of the trademark holder. We use them for identification purposes only. This is not an official publication.

MBI Publishing Company books are also available at discounts in bulk quantity for industrial or sales-promotional use. For details write to Special Sales Manager at Motorbooks International Wholesalers & Distributors, Galtier Plaza, Suite 200, 380 Jackson Street, St. Paul, MN 55101-3885 USA.

Library of Congress Cataloging-in-Publication Data Available
ISBN 0-7603-1399-7

On the front cover: Right: Mario Andretti at the track. *David Nearpass*
Bottom: Mario races the Newman-Haas entry at Indianapolis in 1992. *David Nearpass*
Center: Mario at the Terre Haute Action Track in Rufus Gray's Gapco sprinter, circa 1964. *Ken Coles*

On the frontispiece: Mario before the 1974 Ontario Grand Prix. *Howard Koby*

On the title page: On his way to a second place finish, Mario leads Jacques Laffite during the 1978 Long Beach Grand Prix. *Howard Koby*

On the back cover: Top: Mario led two laps and finished behind Emerson Fittipaldi and Scott Pruett at Detroit in 1989. *Ken Coles* **Bottom:** Mario is shown here before the start of an October 1965 USAC National Championship race in Sacramento. *John Mahoney*

Edited by Peter Bodensteiner
Designed by Stephanie Michaud

Printed in China

Like many others, Mike O'Leary first fell in love with the excitement of motorsports when his father took him to Indianapolis and other Hoosier ovals as a youngster. He whetted his interest in writing while reading his dad's racing books and magazines. Today Mike reports sprint, midget and champ car events from those same race tracks for National Speed Sport News and writes the popular column, "Hoosier Pit Pass". He is also a frequent contributor to various motorsports periodicals.

When not writing, Mike is employed by an engineering firm in the defense industry. He and his wife Sandi live in the rolling hills of southern Indiana. They raised two children; Andy lives in Indianapolis with his wife Kasey and Erin lives and works in Oregon.

Contents

A Note Regarding the Data and Tables

Every effort has been made to ensure the completeness and accuracy of the data presented in Mario Andretti. Significant differences exist in the way various organizations compile and maintain data. For example, in road racing it is typical to only assign finishing positions to certain finishers, while those who dropped out of the event are simply listed as "DNF" or "retired." In American oval track racing, finishing positions are normally assigned to all starters. Keeping these differences in mind, I have made an effort to report the data in its original format as much as possible. The only translation that was made consistently was converting meters and kilometers into miles for the convenience of the predominantly American reading audience.

An interesting element of the average finish calculations is that they combine the results of the diverse range of tracks and competition where Mario competed into a single value. For example, the road courses include American championship and Grand Prix venues, endurance races, and the Pikes Peak Hill Climb while the paved oval category ranges from the temporary indoor oval in the Astrodome to the Indianapolis Motor Speedway. It should be noted that when calculating average finishing position where the finishing position was not listed, or was DNF or retired, the event was not included in the calculations.

Quick Facts about Mario Andretti

Personal

Full Name	Mario Gabriele Andretti
Born	February 28, 1940, Montona, Italy
Wife	Dee Ann
Children	Michael, Jeff, Barbie
Grandchildren	Marco, Marissa, Miranda, Isabella, Lucca
Residence	Nazareth, Pennsylvania

Career*

Number of USAC sprint car races before first victory	19
Number of USAC champ car races before first victory	17
Number of CART races before first victory	4
Number of F-1 races before first victory	10
Total number of race victories	100
Most consecutive race victories	3 (twice: 1966 8/27 Milwaukee, 8/28 Oswego, 9/4 Eldora; 1967 7/30 Langhorne, 8/6 St. Jovite (two races))
Most wins in a season	1966 – 14 wins, 8 champ car, 5 sprint, 1 midget
Highest percentage of wins in a season	1984 – 6 victories in 17 races, 35.3 percent
Number of poles won	117
Most poles in a season	1974 –11 poles
Highest percentage of poles in a season	1984 – 9 poles in 17 races, 52.9 percent
First sprint car victory	October 4, 1964, Salem, IN
First champ car victory	July 25, 1965, Indianapolis Raceway Park, IN
First champ dirt car/silver crown victory	September 10, 1966, Springfield, IL
First F-1 victory	March 6, 1971, South African Grand Prix
Last sprint car victory	July 16, 1967, Oswego, NY (2 wins same day)
Last champ car victory	April 4, 1993, Phoenix, AZ
Last champ dirt car/silver crown victory	September 2, 1974, DuQuoin, IL
Last F-1 victory	August 27, 1978, Dutch Grand Prix

*Does not include events prior to 1964

Mario had won Indy and a couple of national championships, and raced in Formula One when he buckled into his Silver Crown machine at DuQuoin in 1973. His victory in the 100-miler later that afternoon would be his second of the season in champ dirt cars. *Ken Coles*

Introduction

Career Overview

While life is not always fair, it is manageable. It is a matter of attitude and confidence.

Mario on the best advice he received from his parents
– from www.Andretti.com

It could have been a Hollywood movie, but the Hollywood powerbrokers might have deemed it too improbable or unrealistic. Yet Mario Andretti's story is factual, and it relates the achievement of the classic American dream as much as anyone else's life.

Mario grew up in a succession of refugee camps in Yugoslavia with his parents, his twin brother, Aldo, and sister, Anna Maria, in the years following World War II. As soon as he had the opportunity, Mario's father brought his young family to America. It was during these years that Mario developed a passion for very fast cars.

Nearly a half-century later, Mario Andretti has succeeded beyond his wildest teen-age imagination. The Formula One World Championship; three United States Auto Club (USAC) Indy car championships; another with Championship Auto Racing Teams (CART); a point title with USAC's Silver Crown division; and winning the Indianapolis 500, the Daytona 500, Pikes Peak, and the 12 Hours of Sebring: The list of Mario Andretti's accomplishments in racing is unparalleled. Mario is as versatile as any driver who ever donned a helmet. It is not surprising that one magazine recognized him as "Driver of the Century." Yet throughout his career, Mario's

Mario hasn't lost any of his popularity. Here, Mario and Wally Dallenbach sign autographs for young fans at California Speedway before the 2001 Marlboro 500. *Howard Koby*

At Michigan in 1974, Mario leans on Cale Yarborough and Benny Parsons during the drivers meeting before the IROC race. *Ken Coles*

greatest accomplishment remains his indisputable affinity with racing fans.

"Who do you think you are, Mario Andretti?" A clear indication of Mario's success is that to people around the world, his name has grown to signify something identifiable to us all. Mario Andretti has become symbolic of the top, the very elite of motorsports. Yet there is a sincerity that makes each of us confident that away from racing's high society, Mario Andretti will be approachable and good-

natured. The main character in my father's bad haircut story, the one he made up and has been telling for years, is Mario. The content of the story isn't important, but it just wouldn't be the same with Bobby Unser or Richard Petty. It naturally had to be Mario.

In a dramatic scene in the television show *NYPD Blue*, Andy Sipowicz' son Theo is sitting in a toy race car. Dr. Timmons says to Theo, "You look like Mario Andretti." In his hit song "Drive," singer Alan Jackson claims

that as a teen-ager, he felt like Mario Andretti when his father allowed him behind the wheel of the family car.

Years after his retirement from full-time competition, Mario Andretti remains symbolic in popular culture. He is still in demand as a spokesman in product endorsements and television and print advertisements. Let us consider some of the reasons for this enduring affinity.

One reason for this unwavering popularity may be a trademark of Mario's racing career.

Riverside got a facelift in the summer of 1969 and the Can-Am inaugurated the new facility. Mario followed Denny Hulme and Chuck Parsons at the finish. *Mike Smith*

Mario developed a strong fan following while in midgets and sprint cars. He raced in an indoor USAC midget event in the Astrodome in 1969. Here he rides into the oval with Bobby Unser, Mel Kenyon, and A. J. Foyt during the prerace ceremonies. *Ken Coles*

Through four decades he consistently accomplished what was considered improbable. While still teen-agers, he and his twin brother, Aldo, fashioned a racing car from a junked Hudson. After that, each step was forward: There was neither time nor reason to look back. How unlikely was it for the shy Italian teen-ager trying to knock down the fences at the rural Pennsylvania dirt track to race at the renowned Indianapolis Motor Speedway? How unlikely was it for Mario to progress from midgets, sprint cars, and the big championship cars on the mile-long fairground ovals to the inner circle of international paddocks with racing royalty? Not only unlikely, these feats were considered impossible by many. But no one explained that to Mario Andretti when he and Aldo were pushing forward to see the brutish machines thunder around Italy's Mille Miglia, or lingering tentatively in the pits at Langhorne in 1956.

The popularity that Mario has achieved is more than simple fan favoritism, and it is different from adulation. When the young Italian was hustling sprint cars around the Reading and Williams Grove dirt ovals, he began to develop a following. When he moved up to the Indy car circuit, the top series in the country at the time, Mario was perceived as an underdog, a David going head-to-head with Goliaths like A. J. Foyt and Parnelli Jones, and the number of people rooting for Andretti grew. When he headed across the ocean to compete in Formula One, he not only took his suitcase and helmet bag, but he carried the spirit of thousands of American racing fans. Previously, they may have had little interest in Grand Prix racing, but now they searched for news of Mario's progress. And when he returned to American racing full time, he did so as a hero and an international star, not unlike Lance Armstrong today, but on a larger scale.

Never satisfied with saying that he made the show, Mario excelled at every venue he

It was in the midgets that Mario earned his first racing headlines, but once he made it to USAC, he only ran a dozen midget events. His last midget appearance came in the 1969 Astro Grand Prix in Houston's Astrodome, billed as the richest midget race in the world. Teaming with midget champion Mel Kenyon, Mario finished seventh and eighth in the two 100-lap events. *Ken Coles*

The Hoosier Hundred at the Indiana State Fairgrounds has always been one of the most prestigious events on USAC's Silver Crown championship. In the last turn of the final race of the 1974 season, Jackie Howerton (42) is on his way to victory. Even though Mario (2) would win the season title with a third-place finish, this shot shows how hard he was working hard to get past teammate Al Unser (1). Unser finished second, but Mario earned the championship. *John Mahoney*

chose. For Mario, coming out of the Pennsylvania hills, USAC's sprint cars and midgets were a stepping stone. In 1967, he only ran three sprint car races, but he won two of them. Against the best in the country, he moved up to Indy cars and in his first full season won eight races and beat A. J. Foyt for the championship. The next year, he repeated that accomplishment. In stock cars, Mario won the Daytona 500 in his second attempt. His first F-1 victory came in his 10th race. Fans appreciate an underdog, but they really like one that wins.

Mario's popularity has grown like a large oak tree. Each time his career went in a different direction, the tree added new branches. And like a large tree, it grew stronger from many deep roots. Although he has been highly visible, he has avoided appearing difficult or unapproachable in an interview. In addition to a consistently positive presentation to the public, this has led to a strong relationship with the motorsports press.

Chris Economaki, publisher emeritus of *National Speed Sport News*, explains that in many ways Mario was the right person at the right time. "In addition to his driving abilities, Mario had a certain way in the give and take with the people who were around him, particularly the press. When he opened his mouth, he said something of substance. It was meaningful. Then and now, he's always had that quality. That was in the beginning when sponsors started sticking their head in the garage doors at Indianapolis. And you needed to have a driver that understood that. They needed were more than somebody who could just get in the car and turn the steering wheel and press the gas. Mario fit that need ideally."

Racers know that that there are many elements that contribute to success on the race track. The driver's skill and daring are only part of the equation. Good equipment and its mechanical preparation are also essential for success. But there is always one element that is constantly outside the grasp of drivers and crews alike—the affection of Lady Luck.

Usually, Mario's relationship with the fickle Lady was as good as any. Yet with the exception of one time early in his career, she seemed to abandon him whenever they returned to Indianapolis, the most prestigious

Victory lane was a familiar place for Mario. Here he's celebrating the victory in the 1975 California Grand Prix F5000 race, which earned him $19,450. *Howard Koby*

Mario may have hurt his career by staying with cars that weren't fully developed or as competitive as he needed. In contrast, the John Players Lotus 79 may have been the perfect car at the perfect time as Mario won the 1978 Formula One championship. *Howard Koby*

event of the season. While he was always on the sharp edge of his game and supported by the best teams and equipment, after 1969 something always happened to keep him from victory lane. Time after time, he would be firmly in a position to claim another victory when something broke or another car spun into his path. In one event, he was ruled the winner as the result of a postrace penalty levied by officials, only to have it overturned six months later. Watching Andretti's tribulations in the most covered motorsports event in the world only fueled his popularity.

One measure of Mario's career accomplishments is to consider the depth of the competition he faced. As you peruse this book, simply study the names of the drivers in the winner's column. Mario's first midget win came against Mark Donohue, whom he would continue to oppose for the next 10 years. When he joined USAC, he was learning the ropes in competition with the toughest veterans, men like Jud Larson and Don Branson. Perhaps his most frequent nemesis throughout his career was A. J. Foyt, whom he raced in sprints, Indy cars, stock cars, and sports cars. Very quickly he was up against Al and Bobby

Unser. Jacky Ickx was a formidable opponent in endurance racing as well as Formula One. On the Grand Prix circuit, Mario battled Jackie Stewart and Niki Lauda, then Emerson Fittipaldi. Later, Fittipaldi became a tough adversary in CART competition. For more than a decade, Mario's toughest competition included his own son, Michael, as well as the son of one of his toughest rivals, Al Unser, Jr. Much like the tip of an iceberg, these drivers are only a small sample of the many tough racers Mario lined up against in four generations of racing.

The teen-age dreams of the twin brothers have spawned a family firmly involved in motorsports. Mario's oldest son, Michael, has been one of the most successful and popular drivers in the CART series for 20 years. Like his father, he too tried his hand at Formula One, although with less success than he has achieved in the States. Mario's younger son, Jeff, raced for 10 years and has three Indianapolis 500 starts to his credit.

While twin brother Aldo shared Mario's dream of a racing career, it was cut short by injuries from a nasty wreck at Nazareth Speedway. Still, Aldo's son John followed the family's tradition. He has become a headliner with Richard Petty Team in Winston Cup. John also competed in CART, the Indianapolis 500, International Motor Sports Association (IMSA) GTP sports cars, National Hot Rod Assocation (NHRA) drag racing, and USAC, where he earned the midget division Rookie of the Year trophy in 1983.

For more than 30 years, Mario has held the imagination of American racing fans. No matter where Mario buckled his seatbelt, scores of Andretti fans filled the grandstands. And whether they first came to know him through sprinters and dirt cars, the Indy cars, Grand Prix racing, sports cars, or stockers, they were Andretti fans.

Mario has left performance records that will be a benchmark for every racer for generations to come. When he took the green flag at LeMans in 2000, he had competed during six decades. He is the only person to be named Driver of the Year in three different decades (1967, 1978, and 1984). Today Mario is enshrined in four Halls of Fame: the International Motorsports Hall of Fame, the Motorsports Hall of Fame of America, the Indianapolis Motor Speedway Hall of Fame, and the National Sprint Car Hall of Fame.

Isn't this the American dream?

Mario lifts the right front tire off the track during the IROC event at Riverside in 1977. After starting ninth, he finished second to Cale Yarborough. *Howard Koby*

CHAPTER 1

The Beginning

"You break your bones in that type of racing, I'll tell you. Sprint car racing is lethal, challenging racing. I love it. But I'm more conservative now. There was a certain plateau I reached in sprint car racing where I really didn't give a damn what happened or even what the car looked like – as long as it had four wheels and a steering wheel, man, I was gonna drive it!" *Mario, National Sprint Car Hall of Fame induction program, 1996*

ARDC Race Winners 1963 Season

March 31	Old Bridge, NJ	Len Duncan
April 21	Hagerstown, MD	Len Duncan
April 28	Hatfield, PA	"King" Carpenter
May 12	Owego, NY	Bill Randall
May 19	Thompson, CT	Ray Brown
May 24	Vineland, NJ	Ed "Dutch" Schaefer
May 25	Danbury, CT	Bert Brooks
May 30	Freeport, NY	Johnny Coy
June 1	New Egypt, NJ	Bobby Albert
June 8	Middletown, NY	Ray Brown
June 14	Freeport, NY	Johnny Kay
June 15	Hatfield, PA	Ed "Dutch" Schaefer
June 19	Menands, NY	Joe Csiki
June 21	Old Bridge, NJ	Joe Csiki
June 22	Danbury, CT	Ed "Dutch" Schaefer
June 23	Thompson, CT	Len Duncan
July 3	Old Bridge, CT	Tony Bonadies
July 4	Pleasantville, NJ	Johnny Mann
July 5	Freeport, NY	Ray Brown
July 6	Hatfield, PA	Ray Brown
July 13	Middletown, NY	Ray Brown
July 17	Norwood, MA	Joe Csiki
July 19	Freeport, NY	Johnny Mann
July 20	Danbury, CT	Len Duncan
July 27	**Lime Rock, CT**	**Mario**
July 28	West Haven, CT	Johnny Mann
August 2	Freeport, NY	Johnny Mann
August 16	Olivebridge, NY	"King" Carpenter
August 17	Danbury, CT	Tony Bonadies
August 18	Old Bridge, NJ	Bobby Albert
August 21	Norwood, MA	Bill Eldridge
August 24	Middletown, NY	Bert Brooks
August 29	Seekonk, MA	Joe Csiki
August 30	Essex Junction, VT	Jim Maguire
August 31	**Flemington, NJ**	**Mario**
August 31	**Hatfield, PA**	**Mario**
August 31	**Hatfield, PA**	**Mario**
September 1	Smethport, PA	Jim Shaffer
September 7	Rutland, VT	George Monson
September 8	Thompson, CT	Johnny Mann
September 15	Trenton, NJ	"King" Carpenter
September 27	Freeport, NY	Johnny Mann
September 28	Bloomsburg, PA	Hank Williams
September 28	Bloomsburg, PA	Len Duncan
October 13	Thompson, CT	Russ Klar
October 13	Thompson, CT	Ed "Dutch" Schaefer

Twin features were run on the same day: August 31, September 28 and October 13.

The Terre Haute Action Track is a demanding half-mile clay oval. In this 1964 photo, Mario's in the process of turning the second fastest qualifying lap of the afternoon in Rufus Gray's Gapco sprinter. *Ken Coles*

On February, 28 1940, twin boys were born to Gigi and Rina Andretti. Europe was in the early stages of what would explode into World War II. In the quiet city of Montona, near Trieste, life would quickly change for Gigi, a prosperous farmer, and his family, which included the boys, Aldo and Mario, and an older daughter, Anna Maria. Everything was taken from the Andrettis and when the war ended, they began life in a succession of

Yugoslavian camps established for those who survived the Nazi occupation.

When the twins were 14 they went to the Italian Grand Prix in Monza with friends, and the next spring, they saw the Mille Miglia. Both boys quickly fell in love with auto racing and decided that they wanted to become racing drivers. But Gigi was concerned with building a future for his family, and with the help of Rina's uncle in Nazareth, Pennsylvania,

decided to move the family from Italy to America. In the summer of 1955, the Andrettis emigrated, and while a new world was opening for the boys, they were afraid that they had seen their last motor race.

Like many eastern cities, Nazareth had a dirt oval that hosted weekly racing, and by coincidence, it was near where the Andretti family settled. The boys had always worked before, and they soon found jobs in a neighborhood gas sta-

When Bill and Ed Mataka hired Mario to drive their midget, he was looking for an opportunity that would provide him better equipment and allow him to race against better competition. Mario wears a bandage on his face as he poses for this photo before hot laps. *Bruce Craig, Gordon White Collection*

tion. In time, they saved enough money to buy a 1948 Hudson Hornet, and, they converted it into a stock car. Aldo and Mario took turns driving, and both won their first feature races. They were able to keep the knowledge of their racing from their father because of his inexperience with English, until Aldo was injured at the end of the summer in 1959.

At Nazareth, Mario won 20 feature races in local stock car competitions, and decided it was time to move to open wheel racing. He had a difficult time getting rides in the United Racing Club (URC) sprint cars where, as a young, slightly built foreign upstart, he was not welcomed by the established competitors. Today, Mario claims that this was the most challenging time in his whole racing career, "The biggest challenge was probably trying to convince the owners that I was physically strong enough and big enough to drive a race car. That was probably the most frustrating part, right at the beginning."

Interestingly, he drove his first URC race in *Beauty*, a machine owned and raced by the legendary Ted Horn a generation earlier. But by 1961, the 15 year-old car was fitted with a Cadillac engine and was no longer competitive. In that race at West Lebanon, New York on May 20, Mario finished fifth in the first heat and eighth in the 20-lap URC main event.

In his next two races, at Binghamton, New York, and Abbottstown, Pennsylvania, Mario finished 10th in the main events. At Abbottstown in August he drove the Markos Chevy, a Curtis that another Pennsylvanian, Al Herman, had raced to seventh place and the Rookie of the Year trophy at Indianapolis six years earlier. Mario ran in 20 URC sprint car races in 1961 and their records indicate that he received an "…award for ability under adverse conditions."

Mario knew that if he was going to break into racing on a larger scale, he would need more experience in the form of more racing laps. He would also have to put himself in position to be noticed by those with competitive cars in the bigger series. His next step was calculated to move closer to achieving these goals. He bought a three-quarter-size midget and began racing indoor events with the American Three-Quarter Midget Racing Association (ATQMRA) during the 1961–1962 winter. His first indoor win came at the tenth-mile Teaneck Armory, in Teaneck, New Jersey, in February 1962. That summer, he won again in his TQ midget, at Wall Stadium, a third-mile oval in Belmar, New Jersey.

Twenty-two years old, Mario stayed with the URC sprint cars, driving the Blair Chrysler machine several times. Records from 1962 show him finishing 13th in the main event on the banked third-mile mile oval at the new Quebec Modern Speedway in Val St. Michel, Canada, on July 15. Notes from another event simply say, "ANDRETTI - in box." With URC, Mario was driving a "____ box" more often than not. At season's end, he was listed

Mario raced the Mataka Brothers Kurtis Offy in 68 events during the 1962 and 1963 seasons. In 1963 he captured three feature wins in one day and set the course for the future. *Bruce Craig, Gordon White Collection*

Shangri-La Speedway in Oswego, New York on May 12. There was a runner-up finish in a 20-lap main at Danbury, Connecticut, on May 25, and a fourth at Marlboro Motor Raceway in Upper Marlboro, Maryland on October 13.

But Mario's real focus was in the 46 ARDC races he drove for the Mataka brothers. With their commitment and Mario's growing abilities, he finished the season third in points. And finally, he began to make some noise that the motor racing world would hear.

On July 27, he competed in his first road race, driving the Mataka midget in an ARDC event at Lime Rock, Connecticut, where he passed Mark Donohue on the last lap to earn the victory. Then, on August 31, he won a heat race and the main event during an afternoon program at the half-mile Flemington Speedway in New Jersey. As it was the Labor Day weekend, Hatfield had a double-header scheduled later that night, which included a make-up event. Mario claimed victories in match races and heats, and in both features, and quickly gained fame for winning three feature races in one day. For 40 years, the Mataka brothers have run their car with the number "3n1" in recognition of that achievement.

45th in the standings, with 157 points, 2,512 behind champion Earl Halaquist.

But Ed and Bill Mataka had been impressed with Mario's pluck and performance, and in July they decided to try him on the American Racing Drivers Club (ARDC) circuit in their Kurtis-Offy midget. The Mataka Brothers' car was known as a competitive ride, and it had sponsorship from a New Jersey paving contractor. This was Mario's first big break.

He raced in 22 ARDC midget features for the Matakas in 1962. Having racing only on dirt until this point, he quickly began developing a feel for pavement in the Mataka car. His first win came September 1 at Hatfield Speedway, a third-mile dirt oval in Pennsylvania.

In October, Mario and wife Dee Ann had their first child, Michael. That winter, Mario again campaigned his TQ in the ATQMRA competition. On January 26, he scored a victory at Island Gardens, a 0.1-mile track in West Hempstead, New York, leading the final 20 circuits of a 35-lap main event. The organization's hand-written file on Mario indicates that he was seventh in the final points.

During the summer of 1963, Mario continued to race with URC when he could fit it in. He had a third at Hagerstown, Maryland, on April 21 and a fourth-place finish at

1964

I had watched Mario from the day he took his first open cockpit drive. I wasn't privy to his stock car efforts. But he had a three-quarter midget that was famous because it had been built in California and it was the epitome of what a good three-quarter midget then should look like. I used to see him at places like the Teaneck Armory in New Jersey, and he had a certain style there that caught my eye. Of course, Mario tells the story of how I said that the day he won three features in one day, that was his ticket to the big time. He's never forgotten that. *Chris Economaki*

For 24-year-old Mario Andretti, 1964 would prove a pivotal year. The groundwork he had laid in the ARDC midgets, URC sprint cars and TQ midgets began to pay off. Opportunities in the form of better cars to drive were presented, and important people outside of the Northeast racing community began to take notice of the exciting young driver. Mario had a knack for fully exploiting every occasion to impress those who were beginning to open doors for him.

During the week before the Daytona 500, he was hired by Bruce Homeyer to drive his *Konstant Hot* midget in a series of NASCAR-promoted midget races at Daytona Municipal Stadium. Mario attracted some notice with the assignment, but he earned a lot more attention when he won the final night's big feature event.

Two months later, Mario ran with USAC's sprint cars at the historic Reading and Williams Grove ovals. He was given the opportunity to drive the Stearly Motor Freight roadster in his first USAC champ car race at Trenton on April 19. Despite a spin to avoid another car, he brought the machine home 11th. During the week before the Trenton race, a second son, Jeff, was born to Mario and Dee Ann.

In June, he drove Lee Glessner's Windmill Trucking (a Silnes chassis) at Langhorne. This was his first ride in the "big cars," which were used on the dirt tracks that made up a portion of the USAC national championship circuit. The car lacked power steering and was maintained by renowned sprint car racer Tommy Hinnershitz. Mario qualified eighth and finished ninth; Hinnershitz recalled thinking that if he had prodded Mario during the race, they would have finished higher. Hinnershitz helped him develop a feel for driving the big cars on the dirt, where he would soon excel.

Mario was hired by Rufus Gray to replace Jud Larson in his metallic blue number 83 Gapco sprint car, putting him in machinery capable of winning against USAC competition. As he worked his way up the racing ladder, important people like Chris Economaki and Clint Brawner began to notice him. When Brawner's regular driver was injured, Gray recommended Mario. Economaki also gave Andretti a high recommendation. After watching Mario race the Gapco sprinter at Terre Haute, Brawner hired him to pilot a new roadster, the Dean Van Lines Special, on the national championship circuit for the remainder of the year. Brawner and Jim McGee had built the machine, touted as a Blum chassis, as basically an ultralight copy of A. J. Watson's design. Hank Blum, who had worked with Watson, probably assisted in the design of this new roadster.

Running 20 events, Mario finished third in USAC sprint car points, trailing Don Branson and Jud Larson, who had battled each other all season long. He scored his first win against USAC competition driving the Gapco sprinter in the classic 100-lap Joe James—Pat O'Connor Memorial at Salem on October 4. While A. J. Foyt won his fourth national title, Mario was 11th in championship points after competing in 10 Champ car races.

Results By Track Type 1964

Event/Track	Number of Races	Average Finish	Best Finish	Track	Date	Division
Paved Ovals	15	8.42	1	Salem Speedway	10/4/64	USAC Sprint Car
Dirt Ovals	19	8.40	2 (twice)	New Bremen Speedway	5/31/64, 8/16/64	USAC Sprint Car
Road Courses	0					
Total	34	8.41	1			

Mario Andretti 1964 Record

Date	Event/Track	Qual	Finish	Entrant/Car/Number	Type Track	Sanction & Division	Distance	Laps Comp.	Race Winner	Comments
3/29/64	Reading Fairgrounds	7	5	Charlie Sachs #18	Dirt oval .5 mile	USAC Sprint Car	30 Laps		A J Foyt	
4/12/64	Williams Grove Speedway	15	11	Charlie Sachs #18	Dirt oval .5 mile	USAC Sprint Car	30 Laps		A. J. Foyt	
4/19/64	Trenton Speedway	16	11	Stearly Motor Freight Elder #28	Oval 1 mile	USAC Champ Car	100 Miles	92	A. J. Foyt	Running
5/3/64	New Bremen Speedway	4	4	Rufus Gray #83	Dirt oval .5 mile	USAC Sprint Car	30 Laps		Jud Larson	
5/29/64	Indianapolis Speedrome	14	18	Jake Vargo #17	Oval .2 mile	USAC Midget	100 Laps		Chuck Rodee	
5/31/64	New Bremen Speedway	6	2	Rufus Gray #83	Dirt oval .5 mile	USAC Sprint Car	30 Laps		Jud Larson	
6/13/64	Eldora Speedway	15	8	Jake Vargo #17	Dirt oval .5 mile	USAC Midget	40 Laps		Bob Wente	
6/14/64	Terre Haute Action Track	2	13	Rufus Gray #83	Dirt oval .5 mile	USAC Sprint Car	30 Laps		A. J. Foyt	
6/19/64	CNE Exposition Grounds	24	8	Jake Vargo #17	Oval .25 mile	USAC Midget	200 Laps		Ray Elliott	
6/21/64	Langhorne Speedway	8	9	Glessner Windmill Trucking Silnes #74	Dirt oval 1 mile	USAC Champ Car	100 Miles	95	A. J. Foyt	Running
6/28/64	Indianapolis Raceway Park	10	2	Rufus Gray #83	Oval .686 mile	USAC Sprint Car	100 Laps		Don Branson	
7/4/64	Salem Speedway	-	6	Charlie Alfater #10	Oval .5 mile	USAC Sprint Car	30 Laps		Bud Tingelstad	Car qualified by Mickey Shaw
7/5/64	Eldora Speedway	13	6	Rufus Gray #83	Dirt oval .5 mile	USAC Sprint Car	30 Laps		Jud Larson	
7/12/64	Winchester Speedway	8	9	Rufus Gray #83	Oval .5 mile	USAC Sprint Car	30 Laps		Bud Tingelstad	
7/18/64	Williams Grove Speedway	17	12	Rufus Gray #83	Dirt oval .5 mile	USAC Sprint Car	30 Laps		A. J. Foyt	
7/19/64	Trenton Speedway	8	11	Dean Blum Roadster #7	Oval 1 mile	USAC Champ Car	150 Miles	134	A. J. Foyt	Running
7/26/64	New Bremen Speedway	16	4	Rufus Gray #83	Dirt oval .5 mile	USAC Sprint Car	30 Laps		Jud Larson	
8/2/64	Salem Speedway	6	5	Rufus Gray #83	Oval .5 mile	USAC Sprint Car	30 Laps		Parnelli Jones	
8/9/64	Terre Haute Action Track	8	7	Rufus Gray #83	Dirt oval .5 mile	USAC Sprint Car	30 Laps		Don Branson	
8/15/64	Allentown Fairgrounds	1	13	Rufus Gray #83	Dirt oval .5 mile	USAC Sprint Car	30 Laps		Jud Larson	
8/16/64	New Bremen Speedway	5	2	Rufus Gray #83	Dirt oval .5 mile	USAC Sprint Car	30 Laps		Don Branson	
8/22/64	Illinois State Fairgrounds	9	6	Dean Kuzma Offy #7	Dirt oval 1 mile	USAC Champ Car	100 Miles	99	A. J. Foyt	Running
8/23/64	Wisconsin State Fair Park	9	3	Dean Blum Roadster #7	Oval 1 mile	USAC Champ Car	200 Miles	196	Parnelli Jones	Highest finishing roadster
8/29/64	Minnesota State Fairgrounds	7	5	Rufus Gray #83	Oval .5 mile	USAC Sprint Car	30 Laps		Don Branson	
8/30/64	Minnesota State Fairgrounds	2	2	Rufus Gray #83	Oval .5 mile	USAC Sprint Car	30 Laps		Jud Larson	
9/5/64	DuQuoin State Fairgrounds	-	17	Bob Nowicke #4	Dirt oval 1 mile	USAC Midget	100 Miles		A. J. Foyt	
9/6/64	Winchester Speedway	8	5	Rufus Gray #83	Oval .5 mile	USAC Sprint Car	30 Laps		Gordon Johncock	
9/7/64	DuQuoin State Fairgrounds	11	15	Dean Kuzma Offy #7	Dirt oval 1 mile	USAC Champ Car	100 Miles	45	A. J. Foyt	Wreck T3
9/26/64	Indiana State Fairgrounds	6	10	Dean Kuzma Offy #7	Dirt oval 1 mile	USAC Champ Car	100 Miles	97	A. J. Foyt	Running
9/27/64	Trenton Speedway	6	22	Dean Blum Roadster #7	Oval 1 mile	USAC Champ Car	200 Miles	54	Parnelli Jones	Spin T3
10/4/64	**Salem Speedway**	**4**	**1**	**Rufus Gray #83**	**Oval .5 mile**	**USAC Sprint Car**	**100 Laps**	**100**	**Mario**	**First USAC victory**
10/25/64	California State Fairgrounds	16	8	Dean Kuzma Offy #7	Dirt oval 1 mile	USAC Champ Car	100 Miles	99	A. J. Foyt	Running
11/7/64	Ascot Park	-	8	Babe Stapp #11	Dirt oval .5 mile	USAC Sprint Car	30 Laps		Bobby Unser	Car qualified by Steve Stapp
11/22/64	Phoenix International Raceway	3	18	Dean Blum Roadster #7	Oval 1 mile	USAC Champ Car	200 Miles	72	Lloyd Ruby	Broken torque arm

The Gapco sprinter worked as well on asphalt as on dirt. Mario hustled from fifteenth to second in a 100-lap USAC event on the oval at Indianapolis Raceway Park in 1964. Here he's working alongside Bud Tingelstad. *Ken Coles*

1965

I've been dreaming about coming to this place ever since I was 13 years old, back in Italy. Now I'm here. It certainly is the realization of a dream and I'm qualified. Now come race day, I'll be looking for the short way around. Mario, The History of the Indianapolis 500

As USAC's champ car division convened at Phoenix International Raceway for the first event of 1965, Mario was clearly an emerging star. He started the season in the Blum roadster and was leading in the opening race at Phoenix when a car looped in front of him, forcing him to spin. This relegated Andretti to a sixth-place finish. At the next champ car race in Trenton he ran second to Jim McElreath when the race was stopped by rain.

Ten years after arriving in America, Mario turned his first laps at Indianapolis. Brawner introduced a new tube-frame rear-engine Ford V-8-powered machine they had built that winter. Labeled a Brawner-Hawk, it had been based on the 1964 Brabham design. Mario earned the coveted Rookie of the Year trophy, finishing third behind Jimmy Clark and Parnelli Jones. He had set new track records in qualifying, which were surpassed by A. J. Foyt,

Clark, and Dan Gurney later in the day, and took the green flag from fourth.

Remembering his childhood dream of racing Grand Prix cars, he spent time with Clark and Lotus' Colin Chapman while at Indy in May, discussing the European racing scene. Providing a glimpse of the future, Mario notched his first champ car victory on the road course at Indianapolis Raceway Park, which wound through the track's infield, in July. After qualifying on the pole and leading 43 laps, Mario grabbed the win when Foyt ran out of fuel.

In 17 races on the national championship schedule, Mario scored a dozen top-five finishes. When he claimed the title with 2 events remaining, he became the first rookie national champion since Johnnie Parsons in 1949. He was also the youngest. Mario also finished 10th in the USAC sprint car standings, scoring a feature win at legendary Ascot Park in Gar-

dena, California.

Mario had had success on road courses, winning at Lime Rock in the Mataka midget, and at Indianapolis Raceway Park. As the season tapered off, he quickly took advantage of opportunities to do more road-course racing. In September, Mario drove in his first sports car race on New York's Bridgehampton road course for Luigi Chinetti's North American Racing Team. The clutch failed on the NART Ferrari 275P. A month later he joined Team Surtees in a Lola T70 Can-Am car at Riverside.

While Mario won the national championship, Johnny Rutherford was the USAC sprint car champion. Mario had competed in a dozen sprint car races and finished tenth in the points. He also raced in five USAC stock car events and was listed 12th in points.

Results By Track Type 1965

Track Type	Number of Races	Average Finish	Best Finish	Track	Date	Division
Paved Ovals	20	5.6	2 (6 times)	Trenton, Langhorne, Atlanta, Wisconsin, Salem, Phoenix	4/25, 6/20, 8/1, 8/14, 10/3, 11/21	USAC Sprint Car, USAC Champ Car
Dirt Ovals	13	7.15	1	Ascot	11/6	USAC Sprint Car
Road Courses	2	1*	1	IRP	7/25	USAC Champ Car
Total	40	6.06	1			

* In two races, Mario had one victory and one DNF.

USAC National Championship Points 1965

		Points	Wins
1.	**Mario**	3110	1
2.	A. J. Foyt	2500	5
3.	Jim McElreath	2035	3
4.	Don Branson	1875	3
5.	Gordon Johncock	2050	
6.	Joe Leonard	1415	1
7.	Bobby Unser	1402	
8.	Roger McCluskey	1060	
9.	Jud Larson	1028	
10.	Jim Clark	1000	1

Mario Andretti 1965 Record

Date	Event/Track	Qual	Finish	Entrant/Car/Number	Type Track	Sanction & Division	Distance	Laps Comp.	Race Winner	Comments
3/28/65	Phoenix International Raceway	3	6	Dean Blum Roadster #12	Oval 1 mile	USAC Champ Car	150 Miles	148	Don Branson	Running, led 63 laps
4/4/65	Reading Fairgrounds	12	-	Rufus Gray #3	Dirt oval .5 mile	USAC Sprint Car	30 Laps		Jud Larson	
4/18/65	Eldora Speedway	3	-	Rufus Gray #3	Dirt oval .5 mile	USAC Sprint Car	30 Laps		Jud Larson	
4/24/65	Reading Fairgrounds	10	8	Rufus Gray #3	Dirt oval .5 mile	USAC Sprint Car	30 Laps		Greg Weld	
4/25/65	Trenton Speedway	5	2	Dean Blum Roadster #12	Oval 1 mile	USAC Champ Car	100 Miles	87	Jim McElreath	Race stopped, rain
5/2/65	New Bremen Speedway	15	5	Rufus Gray #3	Dirt oval .5 mile	USAC Sprint Car	30 Laps		Red Riegel	
5/31/65	Indianapolis 500									
	Indianapolis Motor Speedway	4	3	Dean Van Lines Brawner/Hawk #12	Oval 2.5 miles	USAC Champ Car	500 Miles	200	Jim Clark	Rookie of the Year
6/6/65	Wisconsin State Fair Park	12	4	Dean Van Lines Brawner/Hawk #12	Oval 1 mile	USAC Champ Car	100 Miles	99	Parnelli Jones	Running
6/9/65	CNE Exposition Grounds	19	-	Bob Nagle #56	Oval .25 mile	USAC Midget	100 Laps			
6/20/65	Langhorne Speedway	1	2	Dean Van Lines Brawner/Hawk #12	Oval 1 mile	USAC Champ Car	100 Miles	100	Jim McElreath	Led 33 laps
6/27/65	Indianapolis Raceway Park	2	12	Rufus Gray #3	Oval .686 mile	USAC Sprint Car	100 Laps		Greg Weld	
7/4/65	Salem Speedway	-	4	Steve Stapp #4	Oval .5 mile	USAC Sprint Car	30 Laps		Don Branson	Car qualified by Gary Congdon
7/11/65	Winchester Speedway	22	-	Rufus Gray #3	Oval .5 mile	USAC Sprint Car	30 Laps		Johnny Rutherford	
7/17/65	Reading Fairgrounds	16	8	Rufus Gray #3	Dirt oval .5 mile	USAC Sprint Car	30 Laps		Johnny Rutherford	
7/18/65	Trenton Speedway	-	-	Dean Van Lines Brawner/Hawk #12	Oval 1 mile	USAC Champ Car	150 Miles	0	A. J. Foyt	Wrecked in practice
7/25/65	**Indianapolis Raceway Park**	**1**	**1**	**Dean Van Lines Brawner/Hawk #12**	**Road Course 1.875 miles**	**USAC Champ Car**	**150 Miles**	**80**	**Mario**	**First USAC Championship victory**
8/1/65	Atlanta Motor Speedway	8	2	Dean Blum Roadster #12	Oval 1.5 miles	USAC Champ Car	250 Miles	167	Johnny Rutherford	
8/7/65	Allentown Fairgrounds	13	13	Rufus Gray #3	Dirt oval .5 mile	USAC Sprint Car	30 Laps		Jud Larson	
8/8/65	Langhorne Speedway	3	4	Dean Blum Roadster #12	Oval 1 mile	USAC Champ Car	125 Miles	125	Jim McElreath	
8/11/65	Allentown Fairgrounds	12	6	Rufus Gray #3	Dirt oval .5 mile	USAC Sprint Car	30 Laps		Red Riegel	
8/14/65	Wisconsin State Fair Park	2	2	Dean Van Lines Brawner/Hawk #12	Oval 1 mile	USAC Champ Car	150 Miles	150	Joe Leonard	Led 1 lap
8/15/65	Wisconsin State Fair Park	22	4	Ray Nichels Zecol #4	Oval 1 mile	USAC Stock Car	200 Miles		Paul Goldsmith	
8/19/65	Wisconsin State Fair Park	10	16	Ray Nichels Zecol #4	Oval 1 mile	USAC Stock Car	100 Miles		Norm Nelson	
8/20/65	Illinois State Fairgrounds	11	7	Ray Nichels Zecol #4	Dirt oval 1 mile	USAC Stock Car	100 Miles		Bobby Issac	
8/21/65	Illinois State Fairgrounds	6	3	Dean Kuzma Offy #12	Dirt oval 1 mile	USAC Champ Car	100 Miles	99	A. J. Foyt	Running
8/22/65	Wisconsin State Fair Park	3	16	Dean Van Lines Brawner/Hawk #12	Oval 1 mile	USAC Champ Car	200 Miles	127	Gordon Johncock	Led 98 laps until mechanical failure
8/28/65	Minnesota State Fairgrounds	10	4	Rufus Gray #3	Oval .5 mile	USAC Sprint Car	30 Laps		Johnny Rutherford	
8/29/65	Minnesota State Fairgrounds	6	3	Rufus Gray #3	Oval .5 mile	USAC Sprint Car	30 Laps		Johnny Rutherford	
9/5/65	DuQuoin State Fairgrounds	-	19	Ray Nichels Zecol #4	Dirt oval 1 mile	USAC Stock Car	100 Miles		Paul Goldsmith	
9/6/65	DuQuoin State Fairgrounds	7	15	Dean Kuzma Offy #12	Dirt oval 1 mile	USAC Champ Car	100 Miles	14	Don Branson	Engine
9/18/65	Indiana State Fairgrounds	6	2	Dean Kuzma Offy #12	Dirt oval 1 mile	USAC Champ Car	100 Miles	100	A. J. Foyt	
9/19/65	Bridgehampton	6	DNF	NART Ferrari 275P #18	Road course 2.85 miles	USRRC	315 Miles		Hap Sharp	First sports car race, clutch failure
9/26/65	Trenton Speedway	4	13	Dean Van Lines Brawner/Hawk #12	Oval 1 mile	USAC Champ Car	200 Miles	168	A. J. Foyt	Running
10/3/65	Salem Speedway	1	2	Rufus Gray #3	Oval .5 mile	USAC Sprint Car	100 Laps		Bobby Unser	
10/24/65	California State Fairgrounds	2	3	Dean Kuzma Offy #12	Dirt oval 1 mile	USAC Champ Car	100 Miles	100	Don Branson	Led 25 laps
10/31/65	Riverside International Raceway			Surtees Lola T70	Road course 2.6 miles	LA Times GP	200.2 Miles	0	Hap Sharp	Crashed in heat race
11/6/65	**Ascot Park**	**2**	**1**	**Steve Stapp #4**	**Dirt oval .5 mile**	**USAC Sprint Car**	**30 Laps**	**30**	**Mario**	
11/7/65	Orange Show Speedway	11	8	Bob Weaver #32	Oval .25 mile	USAC Midget	50 Laps		George Benson	
11/13/65	Ascot Park	10	3	Steve Stapp #4	Dirt oval .5 mile	USAC Sprint Car	30 Laps		A. J. Foyt	
11/21/65	Phoenix International Raceway	1	2	Dean Van Lines Brawner/Hawk #12	Oval 1 mile	USAC Champ Car	200 Miles	200	A. J. Foyt	Led 183 laps, won championship
11/28/65	Hanford International Raceway	12	3	Kol Simon #1	Oval 1.5 mile	USAC Stock Car	200 Miles		Norm Nelson	

At Indy in 1965, Mario earned the Rookie of the Year trophy with his third place finish. *Ken Coles*

As a busy season winds down, Mario waits anxiously for the start of the Sacramento dirt car race in 1965. The fairground dirt tracks were an integral part of the national championship series until the 1970s. *John Mahoney*

Mario hustles out of the pits in the Dean Van Lines Hawk during the Indy 500. *Ken Coles*

Mario (9) battles with Don Branson at Eldora Speedway in Rossburg, Ohio, in April. Jud Larson won the 30-lap feature race. Mario won five features and finished second in points, while both Branson and Larson lost their lives before the season ended. *Ken Coles*

1966

Mario had been crashing about every week or so. He was a nobody then, but he won the first two races he ran for me in '66. The only scratch he ever put on my car was the last race he ran for me, at Manzanita, which he won. He just bent the rear bumper a little bit. Wally Meskowski, Indianapolis 500 Yearbook, 1976

Mario confers with a Firestone tire technician minutes before the start of the Hoosier Hundred. It would be the first of his two victories in the classic event. This is a good shot of the Offy-powered Dean Van Lines dirt car. *John Mahoney*

In his busiest year, Mario competed 49 times and, most importantly, claimed his second USAC national championship. In his second year in the Dean Brawner Hawk, Mario notched wins at Milwaukee (twice), Langhorne, Atlanta, IRP, the Indiana Fairgrounds, Trenton, and Phoenix. He won 9 pole positions, second only to A. J. Foyt's 10 the previous year. At Langhorne, he set a new track record and would have recorded his 10th pole position by more than three miles per hour if he hadn't wrecked on his second qualifying lap.

Driving Wally Meskowski's Wynn's Special, Mario had his best season in USAC sprint cars, finishing second to Roger McCluskey in the final points. He won races at Cumberland (Maryland), Oswego, Eldora, and Manzanita, and scored a second victory in the Joe James-Pat O'Connor Memorial at Salem.

Mario forged ties with Ford and Firestone, leading to opportunities that allowed him to expand his racing horizons. He competed in the first 24 Hours of Daytona endurance race with Ferrari before joining Ford's massive effort that won the 24 Hours of LeMans. Fulfilling his desire to continue to diversify his racing resume, Mario also competed in NASCAR's Daytona 500, with Smokey Yunick, and the Motor Trend 500 on the Riverside road course in Bill Stroppe's Ford.

USAC National Championship Points 1966

		Points	Wins
1.	**Mario**	3070	8
2.	Jim McElreath	2430	1
3.	Gordon Johncock	2050	
4.	Joe Leonard	1275	
5.	Al Unser	1260	
6.	Bobby Unser	1210	1
7.	Don Branson	1135	1
8.	Chuck Hulse	1030	
9.	Billy Foster	930	
10.	Bud Tingelstad	870	1

Results By Track Type 1966

Track Type	Number of Races	Average Finish	Best Finish	Track	Date	Division
Paved Ovals	16	8.63	1 (9 times)	Wisconsin (twice), Langhorne, Atlanta, Berlin, Oswego, Trenton, Salem, Phoenix	6/5, 6/12, 6/26, 7/8, 8/27, 8/28, 9/25, 10/2, 11/20	USAC Sprint Car, USAC Midget, USAC Champ Car
Dirt Ovals	20	6.00	1 (4 times)	Cumberland, Eldora, Ind. Fairgrounds, Manzanita	7/31, 9/4, 9/10, 11/27	USAC Sprint Car, USAC Champ Car
Road Courses	6	11.83	1	IRP	7/24	USAC Champ Car
Total	42	7.83	1			

Mario Andretti 1966 Record

Date	Event/Track	Qual	Finish	Entrant/Car/Number	Type Track	Sanction & Division	Distance	Laps Compl	Race Winner	Comments
1/9/66	Ft. Wayne Memorial Coliseum	16	-	Higman #64	Indoor	USAC Midget	100 Laps		Chuck Rodee	
1/23/66	Riverside International Raceway	25	16	Stroppe Ford Fairlane #71	Road course 2.6 miles	NASCAR Stock Car	500 Miles	154	Dan Gurney	Involved in a wreck
2//66	24 Hours of Daytona									
	Daytona International Speedway	4	4	NART Ferrari 365P2 #21	Road course 3.56 miles	WSCC	24 Hours	664	Ken Miles/ Lloyd Ruby	Co-drove with Pedro Rodriguez
2/26/66	Daytona 500									
	Daytona International Speedway	39	37	Yunick Chevrolet Chevelle #13	Oval 2.5 mile	NASCAR Stock Car	500 Miles	13	Richard Petty	Accident
3/20/66	Phoenix International Raceway	1	15	Dean Van Lines Brawner/Hawk #1	Oval 1 mile	USAC Champ Car	150 Miles	48	Jim McElreath	Accident with Foyt
3/26/66	12 Hours of Sebring									
	Sebring International Raceway	9	31	NART Ferrari 365P2 #26	Road course 5.2 miles	WSCC	12 Hours	188	Ken Miles/Lloyd Ruby	Accident, fire in pits
3/27/66	Reading Fairgrounds	10	5	Meskowski Wynn's #9	Dirt oval .5 mile	USAC Sprint Car	30 Laps		Jud Larson	
4/3/66	Eldora Speedway	7	7	Meskowski Wynn's #9	Dirt oval .5 mile	USAC Sprint Car	30 Laps		Arnie Knepper	
4/17/66	Eldora Speedway	10	8	Meskowski Wynn's #9	Dirt oval .5 mile	USAC Sprint Car	30 Laps		Larry Dickson	
4/24/66	Trenton Speedway	1	4	Dean Van Lines Brawner/Hawk #1	Oval 1 mile	USAC Champ Car	150 Miles	101	Roger Ward	Running, Led 64 laps, stopped after 102 laps because of rain
5/30/66	Indianapolis 500									
	Indianapolis Motor Speedway	1	18	Dean Van Lines Brawner/Hawk #1	Oval 2.5 miles	USAC Champ Car	500 Miles	27	Graham Hill	Led 16 laps, engine
6/5/66	**Wisconsin State Fair Park**	**1**	**1**	**Dean Van Lines Brawner/Hawk #1**	**Oval 1 mile**	**USAC Champ Car**	**100 Miles**	**100**	**Mario**	**Led all 100 laps**
6/11/66	Reading Fairgrounds	3	4	Meskowski Wynn's #9	Dirt oval .5 mile	USAC Sprint Car	30 Laps		Bobby Unser	
6/12/66	**Langhorne Speedway**	**1**	**1**	**Dean Van Lines Brawner/Hawk #1**	**Oval 1 mile**	**USAC Champ Car**	**100 Miles**	**100**	**Mario**	**Led all 100 laps**
6/19/66	24 Hours of LeMans	12	DNF	Holman & Moody Ford Mk II #6	Road Course 8.36 miles	ACO WSCC	24 Hours	97	Bruce McLaren/ Chris Amon	Co-drove with Lucien Bianchi, retired with a blown head gasket
6/26/66	**Atlanta Motor Speedway**	**1**	**1**	**Dean Van Lines Brawner/Hawk #1**	**Oval 1.5 mile**	**USAC Champ Car**	**300 Miles**	**200**	**Mario**	**Led all 200 laps**
7/4/66	Firecracker 400									
	Daytona International Speedway	8	31	Owens Dodge Charger	Oval 2.5 miles	NASCAR Stock Car	400 Miles	77	Sam McQuagg	Blown engine
7/8/66	**Berlin Raceway**	**13**	**1**	**Caves #1**	**Oval .33 mile**	**USAC Midget**	**50 Laps**	**50**	**Mario**	
7/15/66	Lakeside Speedway	16	3	Meskowski Wynn's #1	Dirt oval .5 mile	USAC Sprint Car	30 Laps		Arnie Knepper	
7/16/66	Tulsa Fairgrounds Speedway	6	4	Meskowski Wynn's #1	Dirt oval .375 mile	USAC Sprint Car	40 Laps		Larry Dickson	
7/17/66	Muskogee Speedway	9	2	Meskowski Wynn's #1	Dirt oval .5 mile	USAC Sprint Car	30 Laps		Roger McCluskey	
7/24/66	**Indianapolis Raceway Park**	**2**	**1**	**Dean Van Lines Brawner/Hawk #1**	**Road Course 1.875 miles**	**USAC Champ Car**	**150 Miles**	**80**	**Mario**	**Spun on first lap, came back to lead 38 laps and win**
7/30/66	Mosport Park	12	3	Nichels #31	Road course 2.459 miles	USAC Stock Car	125 Miles	50	Don White	
7/30/66	Mosport Park	-	16	Nichels #31	Road course 2.459 miles	USAC Stock Car	125 Miles		Sal Tovella	
7/31/66	**Cumberland Speedway**	**3**	**1**	**Meskowski Wynn's #1**	**Dirt oval .5 mile**	**USAC Sprint Car**	**30 Laps**	**15**	**Mario**	
8/5/66	Nazareth Raceway	11	18	Caves #1	Dirt oval .5 mile	USAC Midget	40 Laps		Larry Dickson	
8/6/66	Allentown Fairgrounds	29	-	Caves #1	Dirt oval .5 mile	USAC Midget	50 Laps		Don Meacham	
8/6/66	Reading Fairgrounds	5	3	Meskowski Wynn's #1	Dirt oval .5 mile	USAC Sprint Car	30 Laps		Roger McCluskey	
8/7/66	Langhorne Speedway	20	21	Robbins Vollstedt #66	Oval 1 mile	USAC Champ Car	100 Miles	33	Roger McCluskey	Set new track record on first qualifying lap, wrecked on second lap; reassigned to Jim Robbins backup car
8/14/66	Allentown Fairgrounds	5	4	Meskowski Wynn's #1	Dirt oval .5 mile	USAC Sprint Car	30 Laps		Dick Atkins	
8/20/66	Illinois State Fairgrounds	4	2	Dean Van Lines Offy #1	Dirt oval 1 mile	USAC Champ Car	100 Miles	100	Don Branson	Running
8/27/66	**Wisconsin State Fair Park**	**1**	**1**	**Dean Van Lines Brawner/Hawk #1**	**Oval 1 mile**	**USAC Champ Car**	**200 Miles**	**200**	**Mario**	**Led 159 laps**
8/28/66	**Oswego Speedway**	**3**	**1**	**Meskowski Wynn's #1**	**Oval .625 mile**	**USAC Sprint Car**	**100 Laps**	**100**	**Mario**	
9/4/66	**Eldora Speedway**	**5**	**1**	**Meskowski Wynn's #1**	**Dirt oval .5 mile**	**USAC Sprint Car**	**50 Laps**	**50**	**Mario**	
9/5/66	DuQuoin State Fairgrounds	5	15	Dean Kuzma Offy #1	Dirt oval 1 mile	USAC Champ Car	100 Miles	28	Bud Tingelstad	Engine
9/10/66	**Indiana State Fairgrounds**	**2**	**1**	**Dean Kuzma Offy #1**	**Dirt oval 1 mile**	**USAC Champ Car**	**100 Miles**	**100**	**Mario**	**Led 3 laps**
9/11/66	Terre Haute Action Track	3	15	Meskowski Wynn's #9	Dirt oval .5 mile	USAC Sprint Car	50 Laps		Roger McCluskey	
9/18/66	Winchester Speedway	7	3	Meskowski Wynn's #1	Oval .5 mile	USAC Sprint Car	100 Laps	100	Al Smith	
9/24/66	Reading Fairgrounds	18	7	Meskowski Wynn's #1	Dirt oval .5 mile	USAC Sprint Car	30 Laps		Larry Dickson	
9/25/66	**Trenton Speedway**	**1**	**1**	**Dean Van Lines Brawner/Hawk #1**	**Oval 1 mile**	**USAC Champ Car**	**200 Miles**	**200**	**Mario**	**Led 199 laps, set new 200 mile track record**
10/2/66	**Salem Speedway**	**4**	**1**	**Meskowski Wynn's #1**	**Oval .5 mile**	**USAC Sprint Car**	**100 Laps**	**100**	**Mario**	
10/9/66	Mt. Fuji International Speedway	-		Dean Van Lines Brawner/Hawk #1	Road course 2.7 miles	USAC Champ Car	216 Miles	0	Jackie Stewart	Burned piston in practice
10/23/66	California State Fairgrounds	3	10	Dean Kuzma Offy #1	Dirt oval 1 mile	USAC Champ Car	100 Miles	95	Dick Adkins	Contact with Snider while leading – broke gears, Led 64 laps
10/29/66	Ascot Park	8	-	Meskowski Wynn's #1	Dirt oval .5 mile	USAC Sprint Car	30 laps		Roger McCluskey	
10/30/66	Riverside International Raceway	13	DNF	Mecom T70 Lola Ford #1	Road course 2.6 miles	Can-Am	62 laps	37	John Surtees	Blown engine
11/12/66	Ascot Park	16	9	Meskowski Wynn's #1	Dirt oval .5 mile	USAC Sprint Car	30 laps		Roger McCluskey	
11/13/66	Stardust International Raceway	20	DNF	Mecom T70 Lola Ford	Road course 3 miles	Can-Am	70 laps	1	John Surtees	Gearbox
11/20/66	**Phoenix International Raceway**	**1**	**1**	**Dean Van Lines Brawner/Hawk #1**	**Oval 1 mile**	**USAC Champ Car**	**200 Miles**	**200**	**Mario**	**Led 153 laps**
11/27/66	**Manzanita Park**	**7**	**1**	**Meskowski Wynn's #1**	**Dirt oval .5 mile**	**USAC Sprint Car**	**30 Laps**	**30**	**Mario**	

1967

In 1967, Mario continued to sharpen his skills as he competed in six different series, driving champ cars, stock cars, sprinters, and sports cars. He began the year with victories in the Daytona 500 and the 12-hour endurance classic at Sebring. At Sebring, he was teamed with Bruce McLaren in one of Ford's fleet of Mk IVs.

Then he turned his attention to the USAC National Championship where he waged a season-long battle with Foyt, winning 8 of 21 races. Mario appeared to have the final event at Riverside in hand for his third consecutive title. But with six laps remaining, the Brawner/Hawk ran out of fuel, and he was forced into the pits. Foyt had been involved in a wreck early in the race and took over Roger McCluskey's car, finishing fifth. Even though Mario hustled to a third-place finish, he trailed Foyt by 60 points for the title.

Although Mario only competed in three USAC sprint car events, he won two of them, both at Oswego. He was driving a new Ford-powered machine for A. J. Watson. He finished fifth in the third race.

He competed in his first Pikes Peak Hill Climb in one of Brawner's Hawk Indy cars. And late in the season, Mario ran three Can-Am races in Paul Newman's Honker II, but with little success.

Results By Track Type 1967

Track Type	Number of Races	Average Finish	Best Finish	Track	Date	Division
Paved Ovals	16	11.87	1 (7 times)	Daytona, Trenton, Oswego (twice), Langhorne, Wisconsin,	2/26, 4/23, 7/16, 7/30, 8/20	NASCAR, USAC Sprint Car, USAC Champ Car
Dirt Ovals	7	6.28	1	Indiana State Fairgrounds	9/9	USAC Champ Car
Road Courses	16	9.06	1 (5 times)	Sebring, IRP, Mosport, St. Jovite (twice)	4/1, 7/23, 7/29, 8/6	USAC Champ Car
Total	40	9.72	1			

USAC National Championship Points 1967

		Points	Wins
1.	A. J. Foyt	3440	5
2.	**Mario**	**3360**	**8**
3.	Bobby Unser	3020	2
4.	Gordon Johncock	2690	2
5.	Al Unser	2505	
6.	Lloyd Ruby	2090	2
7.	Jim McElreath	1750	
8.	Roger McCluskey	1620	
9.	Joe Leonard	1575	
10.	Bud Tingelstad	965	

Mario Andretti 1967 Record

Date	Event/Track	Qual	Finish	Entrant/Car/Number	Type Track	Sanction & Division	Distance	Laps Compl	Race Winner	Comments
1/22 – 29/67	Riverside International Raceway	16	9	Holman Moody Ford #114	Road course 2.6 miles	NASCAR Stock Car	500 Miles	164	Parnelli Jones	Motor Trend 500; After 40 laps, delayed by rain until 1/29
2/5/67	24 Hours of Daytona Daytona International Speedway	5	DNF	Holman & Moody Ford GT40 Mk II #5	Road course 3.56 miles	WSCC	24 Hours	298	Lorenzo Bandini/Chris Amon	Co-drove with Richie Ginther, clutch failure
2/26/67	Daytona 500 Daytona International Speedway	12	1	Holman & Moody/Stroppe Ford #11	Oval 2.5 miles	NASCAR Stock Car	500 Miles	200	Mario	Outran Fred Lorenzen
4/1/67	12 Hours of Sebring Sebring International Raceway	1	1	Ford GT40 Mk IV #1	Road course 5.2 miles	WSCC	12 Hours	238	Mario with Bruce McLaren	Debut of new Ford Mk IV
4/9/67	Phoenix International Raceway	-	-	Dean Van Lines Brawner/Hawk #1	Oval 1 mile	USAC Champ Car	150 Miles	0	Lloyd Ruby	Wrecked in practice, then wrecked Robbins car after qualifying
4/23/67	Trenton Speedway	1	1	Dean Van Lines Brawner/Hawk #1	Oval 1 mile	USAC Champ Car	150 Miles	150	Mario	Led all 150 laps, set new qualifying and 150 mile race records
5/27/67	Indianapolis Raceway Park	3	2	Holman & Moody/Stroppe Ford #11	Oval .686 mile	USAC Stock Car	300 miles		Parnelli Jones	
5/30/67	Indianapolis 500 Indianapolis Motor Speedway	1	30	Dean Van Lines Brawner/Hawk #1	Oval 2.5 miles	USAC Champ Car	500 Miles	58	A. J. Foyt	Lost wheel in turn 1
6/4/67	Wisconsin State Fair Park	-	-	Dean Van Lines Brawner/Hawk #1	Oval 1 mile	USAC Champ Car	100 Miles	0	Gordon Johncock	Wrecked in practice
6/11/67	24 Hours of Le Mans, Le Mans	3	24	Ford GT40 Mk IV #3	Road course 8.36 miles	ACO WSCC	24 Hours	188	Dan Gurney/A. J. Foyt	Wreck when brakes locked, suffered broken ribs
6/18/67	Langhorne Speedway	6	3	Dean Van Lines Brawner/Hawk #1	Oval 1 mile	USAC Champ Car	100 Miles	100	Lloyd Ruby	
6/24/67	Indiana State Fairgrounds	12	28	Holman & Moody/Stroppe Ford #11	Dirt oval 1 mile	USAC Stock Car	100 Miles		Don White	
6/25/67	Pikes Peak Hill Climb	6	14	Leader Cards/Rislone Lotus 24 Chevy #1	12.42 mile hill climb	USAC Champ Car	12.42 miles	1	Wes Vandervoort	First Pikes Peak attempt
7/1/67	Mosport Park	15	21	Dean Van Lines Brawner/Hawk #1	Road Course 2.459 miles	USAC Champ Car	100 Miles	3	Bobby Unser	Broke half shaft
7/1/67	Mosport Park	20	11	Dean Van Lines Brawner/Hawk #1	Road Course 2.459 miles	USAC Champ Car	100 Miles	6	Bobby Unser	Halted at 6 laps, rain
7/4/67	Firecracker 400 Daytona International Speedway	9	27	Holman & Moody/Stroppe Ford #11	Oval 2.5 miles	NASCAR Stock Car	400 Miles	20	Cale Yarborough	mechanical problem
7/9/67	Wisconsin State Fair Park	4	4	Holman & Moody/Stroppe Ford #11	Paved 1 mile	USAC Stock Car	200 Miles		Don White	
7/16/67	Oswego Speedway	2	1	Watson Ford #2	Oval .625 mile	USAC Sprint Car	50 Laps	50	Mario	
7/16/67	Oswego Speedway	1	1	Watson Ford #2	Oval .625 mile	USAC Sprint Car	50 Laps	50	Mario	
7/22/67	Eldora Speedway	19	5	Watson Ford #2	Dirt oval .5 mile	USAC Sprint Car	30 Laps		Rollie Beale	
7/23/67	Indianapolis Raceway Park	2	1	Dean Van Lines Brawner/Hawk #1	Road Course 1.875 miles	USAC Champ Car	150 Miles	80	Mario	Led 66 laps, set new race record
7/29/67	Mosport Park	2	1	Holman & Moody/Stroppe Ford #11	Road Course 2.459 miles	USAC Stock Car	125 Miles	50	Mario	
7/29/67	Mosport Park	1	4	Holman & Moody/Stroppe Ford #11	Road Course 2.459 miles	USAC Stock Car	125 Miles	50	Parnelli Jones	
7/30/67	Langhorne Speedway	2	1	Dean Van Lines Brawner/Hawk #1	Oval 1 mile	USAC Champ Car	150 Miles	150	Mario	Led all 150 laps
8/6/67	St. Jovite, Le Circuit Mt. Tremblant	3	1	Dean Van Lines Brawner/Hawk #1	Road Course 2.7 miles	USAC Champ Car	100 Miles	36	Mario	Led all 36 laps
8/6/67	St. Jovite, Le Circuit Mt. Tremblant	1	1	Dean Van Lines Brawner/Hawk #1	Road Course 2.7 miles	USAC Champ Car	100 Miles	36	Mario	Led all 36 laps
8/13/67	Wisconsin State Fair Park	1	34	Holman & Moody/Stroppe Ford #11	Oval 1 mile	USAC Stock Car	150 Miles		Jack Bowsher	Fast qualifier
8/17/67	Wisconsin State Fair Park	1	34	Holman & Moody/Stroppe Ford #11	Oval 1 mile	USAC Stock Car	200 Miles		Parnelli Jones	Fast qualifier
8/19/67	Illinois State Fairgrounds	3	2	Dean Kuzma Offy #1	Dirt oval 1 mile	USAC Champ Car	100 Miles	100	A. J. Foyt	Running
8/20/67	Wisconsin State Fair Park	2	1	Dean Van Lines Brawner/Hawk #1	Oval 1 mile	USAC Champ Car	200 Miles	200	Mario	Led 199 laps, new race record
8/27/67	Mid-America Raceways	2	14	Holman & Moody/Stroppe Ford #11	Road Course 2.75 miles	USAC Stock Car	200 Miles		Don White	
9/4/67	DuQuoin State Fairgrounds	11	2	Dean Kuzma Offy #1	Dirt oval 1 mile	USAC Champ Car	100 Miles	100	A. J. Foyt	
9/9/67	Indiana State Fairgrounds	2	1	Dean Kuzma Offy #1	Dirt oval 1 mile	USAC Champ Car	100 Miles	100	Mario	Led 86 laps
9/17/67	Bridgehampton	23	8	Paul Newman Holman & Moody Honker II Ford #17	Road Course 2.85 miles	CanAm	70 Laps	68	Denny Hulme	
9/23/67	Mosport Park	29		Paul Newman Holman & Moody Honker II Ford #17	Road Course 2.459 miles	CanAm	80 Laps	0	Denny Hulme	Did not start
9/24/67	Trenton Speedway	1	25	Dean Van Lines Brawner/Hawk #1	Oval 1 mile	USAC Champ Car	200 Miles	5	A. J. Foyt	Led 4 laps, broke suspension and spun
10/1/67	California State Fairgrounds	2	2	Dean Kuzma Offy #1	Dirt oval 1 mile	USAC Champ Car	100 Miles	100	A. J. Foyt	
10/22/67	Hanford Speedway	4	24	Dean Van Lines Brawner/Hawk #1	Oval 1.5 miles	USAC Champ Car	200 Miles	18	Gordon Johncock	Wreck
10/29/67	Riverside International Raceway	5	32	Paul Newman Holman & Moody Honker II Ford #17	Road Course 2.6 miles	CanAm	62 Laps	10	Bruce McLaren	Gearbox failure
11/19/67	Phoenix International Raceway	2	1	Dean Van Lines Brawner/Hawk #1	Oval 1 mile	USAC Champ Car	200 Miles	200	Mario	Led 20 laps
11/23/67	Ascot Park	3	4	Vel Meletich #98	Dirt oval .5 mile	USAC Sprint Car	30 laps			
11/26/67	Riverside International Raceway	6	3	Dean Van Lines Brawner/Hawk #1	Road course 2.6 miles	USAC Champ Car	300 Miles	116	Dan Gurney	Led 38 laps

In the Brawner Hawk, Mario won the 150-mile race at Indianapolis Raceway Park (IRP) in 1967. It was his second champ series victory of the year. *Ken Coles*

It is common among great racing drivers that they are tutored by exceptional mechanics early in their careers. In Mario's case, Clint Brawner and Jim McGee clearly helped hone his skills in the championship machinery. McGee (left) and Brawner (right) help Mario settle in at Trenton in 1967. Mario led all 150 laps to win the race from the pole. *John Mahoney*

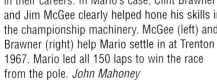

At the 1966 Los Angeles Times Grand Prix for Sports Cars, Mario drove this Lola, entered by John Mecom, as a teammate with Jackie Stewart. He dropped out of the race after 37 laps with engine failure. *Mike Smith*

1968

Colin Chapman didn't speak a word of Italian, so he said, "I have no idea what they're saying, but they're saying that they're not going to start." - Mario, on his first, unsuccessful attempt to race in Formula One.

Coming into 1968, Mario's racing world underwent a major change. When car owner Al Dean passed away in December of 1967, Mario elected to buy the racing team and keep it intact. Although he hadn't planned to become a car owner, he decided to make the most of it, having Clint Brawner and Jim McGee build a new monocoque Hawk based on Lotus' design.

The Andretti crew tried three different engines in 1968. Mario debuted the new Ford turbocharged powerplant at Indy, but the engine failed after two laps, while Bobby Unser won four of the first five races. Mario found himself in an early hole in the point chase.

He switched back and forth between the new chassis and the trusted original tube-frame Hawk. He reverted to the normally aspirated Ford and picked up a pair of victories. But with Bobby and Al Unser winning consistently with the Offy turbo, Brawner put one in the Hawk and Mario immediately won at Trenton.

In the second half of the season, Mario won four times and went into the final race at Riverside only needing a fifth place finish to earn his third crown in four seasons. When an engine failure put his car out early, he was able to replace Joe Leonard in the turbine. But Mario only completed one lap before making contact with another car. In an attempt to

claim the title, he arranged to quickly jump into Lloyd Ruby's car, which he steered to third. Receiving only a portion of the points for third, Bobby Unser edged him by just eleven points in the final count.

While managing his own championship racing team, Mario made his first foray into Formula 1. After very impressive testing sessions and qualifying at Monza, he was prohibited from starting the Grand Prix because he had raced the day before in the Hoosier Hundred. But a month later, Mario out-qualified Jackie Stewart for the pole for his first Grand Prix start before clutch problems sidelined his Lotus 49B.

USAC National Championship Points 1968

		Points	Wins
1.	Bobby Unser	4330	5
2.	**Mario**	**4319**	**4**
3.	Al Unser	2895	5
4.	Lloyd Ruby	2799	2
5.	Bill Vukovich Jr.	2410	
6.	A. J. Foyt	1860	4
7.	Dan Gurney	1800	3
8.	Gary Bettenhausen	1595	1
9.	Mel Kenyon	1355	
10.	Jim Malloy	1265	

At Indy Mario drove the Andretti Brawner Hawk with the new Ford turbo. Unfortunately, it burned a piston after only two laps. *Ken Coles*

Mario Andretti 1968 Record

Date	Event/Track	Qual	Finish	Entrant/Car/Number	Type Track	Sanction & Division	Distance	Laps Compl	Race Winner	Comments
2/4/68	24 Hours of Daytona Daytona International Speedway	11	6	Autodelta Alfa Romeo T33/2 #23	Road course 3.56 miles	WSCC	24 Hours	609	Vic Elford /Jochen Neerspasch	Co-drove with Lucien Bianchi, running
2/25/68	Daytona 500 Daytona International Speedway	20	29	Holman & Moody Mercury #11	Oval 2.5 mile	NASCAR Stock Car	500 Miles	105	Cale Yarborough	Blown engine, wreck
3/17/68	Hanford Speedway	3	23	Andretti Brawner/Ford #2	Oval 1.5 mile	USAC Champ Car	200 Miles	40	Gordon Johncock	Half shaft
3/31/68	Stardust International Raceway	3	2	Andretti Brawner/Ford #2	Road Course 3 miles	USAC Champ Car	150 Miles	50	Bobby Unser	Led 41 laps
4/7/68	Phoenix International Raceway	2	15	Andretti Brawner/Ford #2	Oval 1 mile	USAC Champ Car	150 Miles	80	Bobby Unser	led 24 laps, wrecked
4/21/68	Trenton Speedway	1	2	Andretti Overseas National Airways Brawner/Ford #2	Oval 1 mile	USAC Champ Car	150 Miles	150	Bobby Unser	Led 8 laps
5/30/68	Indianapolis 500 Indianapolis Motor Speedway	4	33	Andretti Overseas National Airways Brawner/Ford #2	Oval 2.5 miles	USAC Champ Car	500 Miles	2	Bobby Unser	First race with turbocharged Ford engine - burned piston, relieved Larry Dickson for 10 laps finished 28, piston
6/9/68	Wisconsin State Fair Park	9	2	Andretti Overseas National Airways Brawner/Ford #2	Oval 1 mile	USAC Champ Car	150 Miles	150	Lloyd Ruby	Led 23 laps
6/15/68	Mosport Park	2	2	Andretti Overseas National Airways Brawner/Ford #2	Road Course 2.459 miles	USAC Champ Car	100 Miles	40	Dan Gurney	Running
6/15/68	Mosport Park	2	2	Andretti Overseas National Airways Brawner/Ford #2	Road Course 2.459 miles	USAC Champ Car	100 Miles	40	Dan Gurney	Running
6/23/68	Langhorne Speedway	5	17	Andretti Overseas National Airways Brawner/Ford #2	Paved oval 1 mile	USAC Champ Car	150 Miles	44	Gordon Johncock	Valve
6/30/68	Pikes Peak Hill Climb	4	4	Overseas National Airways Brawner/Hawk #2	12.42 mile hill climb	USAC Champ Car	12.42 miles	1	Bobby Unser	
7/7/68	Continental Divide Raceway	5	15	Andretti Overseas National Airways Brawner/Ford #2	Road Course 2.66 miles	USAC Champ Car	150 miles	25	A. J. Foyt	Coil
7/13/68	Nazareth National Speedway	4	2	Andretti Overseas National Airways Kuzma #2	Dirt oval 1.125 miles	USAC Champ Car	100 Miles	89	Al Unser	First USAC championship race run at night under lights
7/21/68	Indianapolis Raceway Park	1	2	Andretti Overseas National Airways Brawner/Ford #2	Road Course 2.5 miles	USAC Champ Car	100 Miles	40	Al Unser	Led 16 laps
7/21/68	Indianapolis Raceway Park	2	2	Andretti Overseas National Airways Brawner/Ford #2	Road Course 2.5 miles	USAC Champ Car	100 Miles	40	Al Unser	
7/28/68	Langhorne Speedway	14	23	Leader Cards Zecol-Lubaid Watson #90	Oval 1 mile	USAC Champ Car	100 Miles	-	Al Unser	Blown engine in practice, switched to Leader Cards entry, did not compete in second heat race
8/4/68	St. Jovite, Le Circuit Mt. Tremblant	1	1	Andretti Overseas National Airways Brawner/Ford #2	Road Course 2.7 miles	USAC Champ Car	100 Miles	38	Mario	Led 26 laps
8/4/68	St. Jovite, Le Circuit Mt. Tremblant	1	1	Andretti Overseas National Airways Brawner/Ford #2	Road Course 2.7 miles	USAC Champ Car	100 Miles	38	Mario	Led all 38 laps
8/17/68	Illinois State Fairgrounds	6	18	Andretti Overseas National Airways Kuzma #2	Dirt 1 mile	USAC Champ Car	100 Miles	12	Roger McCluskey	Engine
8/18/68	Wisconsin State Fair Park	6	2	Andretti Overseas National Airways Brawner/Ford #2	Oval 1 mile	USAC Champ Car	200 Miles	200	Lloyd Ruby	Running
8/25/68	Mid-America Raceways	4	3	Holman & Moody Mercury #11	Road Course 2.75 miles	USAC Stock Car	200 Miles		Roger McCluskey	
9/1/68	Road America	8	DNF	Bignotti Lola T70 Ford #21	Road Course 4 miles	CanAm	200 Miles	48	Denny Hulme	Lost engine
9/2/68	DuQuoin State Fairgrounds	6	1	Andretti Overseas National Airways Kuzma #2	Dirt oval 1 mile	USAC Champ Car	100 Miles	100	Mario	Led 94 laps
9/7/68	Indiana State Fairgrounds	1	2	Andretti Overseas National Airways Kuzma #2	Dirt oval 1 mile	USAC Champ Car	100 Miles	100	A. J. Foyt	Set new qualifying track record
9/8/68	Italian Grand Prix, Monza	7	-	Lotus Cosworth 49B #18	Road Course 3.6 miles	F-1	190 Miles	0	Denny Hulme	Not permitted to start because of racing in Indianapolis the previous day
9/15/68	Bridgehampton	8	DNF	Bignotti Lola T70 Ford #21	Road Course 2.85 miles	CanAm	200 Miles	4	Mark Donohue	Lost oil pressure
9/22/68	Trenton Speedway	2	1	Andretti Overseas National Airways Brawner/Offy #2	Oval 1 mile	USAC Champ Car	200 Miles	200	Mario	Led 172 laps, first race with turbo Offy
9/29/68	California State Fairgrounds	1	4	Andretti Overseas National Airways Kuzma #2	Dirt oval 1 mile	USAC Champ Car	100 Miles	100	A. J. Foyt	
10/6/68	United States Grand Prix, Watkins Glen	1	DNF	Lotus Cosworth 49B #12	Road Course 2.3 mile	F-1	248 Miles	32	Jackie Stewart	Clutch failure
10/13/68	Michigan International Speedway	1	2	Andretti Overseas National Airways Brawner/Offy #2	Oval 2 mile	USAC Champ Car	250 Miles	124	Ronnie Bucknam	Led 1 lap – First race on track
10/27/68	Riverside International Raceway	-	-	Bignotti Lola T160 Ford	Road Course 2.6 miles	Can-Am	62 Laps	0	Bruce McLaren	Did not start the race
11/3/68	Hanford Speedway	2	3	Andretti Overseas National Airways Brawner/Offy #2	Oval 1.5 miles	USAC Champ Car	250 Miles	167	A. J. Foyt	Led 11 laps
11/10/68	Stardust International Raceway	6	12	Bignotti Lola T160 Ford #3	Road Course 3 miles	Can-Am	210 Miles	63	Denny Hulme	Running
11/17/68	Phoenix International Raceway	1	24	Andretti Overseas National Airways Brawner/Offy #2	Oval 1 mile	USAC Champ Car	200 Miles	6	Gary Bettenhausen	Led 4 laps, wreck, relieved Snider for 190 laps-finished 3rd
12/1/68	Riverside International Raceway	2	18	Andretti Overseas National Airways Brawner/Ford #2	Road Course 2.6 miles	USAC Champ Car	300 Miles	59	Dan Gurney	Engine, relieved Leonard for 1 lap, relieved Ruby for 44 laps-finished 3rd

This was in 1968 and it was to be my debut in Formula One in Italy, the Grand Prix of Italy. The same weekend, the Hoosier Hundred was running. The Hoosier Hundred always ran on a Saturday. Obviously I was committed to compete in the Hoosier Hundred, so I went to Italy ahead of time to test because that was my very first taste of Formula One. I was driving for Lotus and we tested very successfully. In fact, I came away with a brand new track record.

At Monza, in order to be able to qualify quickly you needed to have a pretty good drafting partner. So I talked Bobby Unser into coming to do the Grand Prix as well and I got him a ride with BRM. So, we went to Italy and the understanding with the organizer there was that they would waive what was then in effect, the 24-hour international rule. That said you could not compete in two international events, and believe it or not the Hoosier Hundred was considered at that level, within 24 hours. There was a two-hour discrepancy between the end of the Hoosier Hundred and the beginning of the Grand Prix. And they promised me that they were going to waive that.

We went there and I could only qualify, you can imagine, in the first session on Friday. Then we had to leave in the afternoon. So we went out there, balls to the board, and I was on the pole by a ton. Bobby gave me a hell of a pull, really a good tow. And I tried to pull him, but the BRM was so damn slow he couldn't even keep up with me on the straightaway by following me. So I couldn't help him a hell of a lot. And of course they had a second session and they had two sessions on Saturday and leaving that early, my time was still good enough for seventh on the grid.

So we came back to the states, we helicoptered from the track and got everything organized. We did the Hoosier Hundred. I finished second that day, behind Foyt. And right after the Hoosier Hundred, we had leased a Lear and we got dropped off in Boston. We had double seats reserved so we could sleep in first class and we arrived in Milan on time. We hustled over to the track and all of a sudden, nobody's talking to us. There's a big meeting. We were there about an hour before the start of the race. The meeting was all of the Italian race committee. I can never prove it, but I think Ferrari protested the ruling.

They had my car on the grid and they made it look like we never arrived, which actually pissed me off. I tried to get a press thing going, which in those days was a little tougher. Anyway, they would not allow us to start. So that was the debacle of the weekend. It was tremendously frustrating. But that's the way it is. Politics played then as well. *Mario*

Although he had won the Indianapolis Raceway Park 150 mile race for the three previous years, Mario finished second to Al Unser in 1968. With sponsorship from the Overseas National Airways, Mario was the racing team owner. *Ken Coles*

Mario set a new record qualifying for the 1968 Hoosier Hundred, but chased A. J. Foyt to the finish. *Ken Coles*

At the Riverside Can-Am race, Mario only completed five practice laps in this Lola T-160 entered by George Bignotti. Mechanical problems sidelined the machine. Mario had more success with Bignotti on the Vel's Parnelli Jones racing team beginning in 1972. *Mike Smith*

1969

I'm not at all sure the Lotus I crashed would have finished the race. In all honesty, a Lotus has the most ultimate potential as a race car, but it is not a proven race car. Although I have a singed-up face, I'm almost happy the crash happened.

Mario, Indianapolis News, May 31, 1969

While most remember 1969 as the year Mario scored his only Indy victory, overall it was a very full and satisfying racing season. His victory at Indianapolis was immensely popular. Mario qualified the Brawner Hawk in the middle of the front row with only two days of practice. It was also the first Indy 500 victory for car owner Andy Granatelli and mechanics Clint Brawner and Jim McGee. The photos of Granatelli bussing Mario's cheek in victory lane immortalized the emotional moment.

Mario continued to race the Hawk, which was the monocoque chassis that they had built and raced the year before. Over the winter, Brawner and McGee added fuel tanks on the sides and made several aerodynamic modifications. With the teething problems of the turbocharged Ford engine a thing of the past, Mario won at Hanford, Indianapolis, and Trenton, before clinching the USAC championship point title when he won his second race at Trenton. Mario also proved he hadn't lost his touch on the dirt. When the series returned to his hometown of Nazareth, he won. Another win on the dirt came at Springfield. He claimed victory in the Pikes Peak Hill Climb, which was counted as part of the championship schedule at the time. As the season concluded, Mario continued to win, claiming victories at Seattle and Riverside. He exceeded 5,000 points, which established a new benchmark in the national championship series.

Mario also continued to build on his efforts away from the championship series. Teamed with Chris Amon in a Ferrari 312P, he finished second in the 12 Hour classic at Sebring. Mario drove in three Grand Prix for Colin Chapman's Lotus team, working a four-wheel-drive Lotus at the Nurburgring and Watkins Glen. He also drove the Holman-Moody McLaren with a big-block Ford in three Can-Am events, picking up his best finish in that series to that point, a third at Riverside.

USAC National Championship Points 1969

		Points	Wins
1.	**Mario**	**5025**	**9**
2.	Al Unser	2630	5
3.	Bobby Unser	2585	1
4.	Dan Gurney	2280	2
5.	Gordon Johncock	2070	2
6.	Wally Dallenbach	1795	
7.	A. J. Foyt	1570	1
8.	Bill Vukovich Jr.	1280	
9.	Mike Mosley	1220	
10.	Lloyd Ruby	1190	

Mario Andretti 1969 Record

Date	Event/Track	Qual	Finish	Entrant/Car/Number	Type Track	Sanction & Division	Distance	Laps Compl	Race Winner	Comments
2/1/69	Riverside International Raceway	7	18	Holman Moody Ford #97	Road Course 2.3 miles	NASCAR Stock Car	500 Miles	132	Richard Petty	Motor Trend 500, blown engine
3/1/69	South African Grand Prix, Kyalami	6	DNF	Lotus-Cosworth 49B #3	Road Course 2.55 miles	F-1	204 Miles	31	Jackie Stewart	Gearbox failure while running third
3/8/69	Astrodome	38	7	Kenyon Brothers #61	Dirt oval 1/6 indoor	USAC Midget	100 Laps		Gary Bettenhausen	
3/9/69	Astrodome	17	8	Kenyon Brothers #61	Dirt oval 1/6 indoor	USAC Midget	100 Laps		Lee Kunzman	
3/22/69	12 Hours of Sebring Sebring International Raceway	1	2	Ferrari 312P #25	Road Course 5.2 miles	WSCC	12 Hours	238	Jacky Ickx/ Jackie Oliver	Co-drove with Chris Amon
3/30/69	Phoenix International Raceway	4	16	Granatelli STP Oil Treatment Hawk III #2	Oval 1 mile	USAC Champ Car	150 Miles	38	George Follmer	Led 27 laps, half shaft
4/13/69	Hanford Speedway	1	1	Granatelli STP Oil Treatment Hawk III #2	Oval 1.5 mile	USAC Champ Car	200 Miles	134	Mario	Led all 134 laps
4/25/69	Monza	1	DNF	Ferrari 312P #1	Road course 3.6 miles	WSCC	360 Miles	39	Jo Siffert/ Brian Redman	Engine failure
5/30/69	Indianapolis 500 Indianapolis Motor Speedway	2	1	Granatelli STP Oil Treatment Hawk III #2	Oval 2.5 miles	USAC Champ Car	500 Miles	200	Mario	Wrecked Lotus in practice, led 116 laps
6/8/69	Wisconsin State Fair Park	1	7	Granatelli STP Oil Treatment Hawk III #2	Oval 1 mile	USAC Champ Car	150 Miles	141	Art Pollard	Led 89 laps, ran out of fuel and wouldn't restart in pits
6/15/69	Langhorne Speedway	1	5	Granatelli STP Oil Treatment Hawk III #2	Oval 1 mile	USAC Champ Car	150 Miles	147	Bobby Unser	Running, led 41 laps
6/29/69	Pikes Peak Hill Climb	-	1	Granatelli STP Oil Treatment Special King #2	12.42 mile hill climb	USAC Champ Car	12.42 miles	1	Mario	Margin of victory was 21 seconds
7/6/69	Continental Divide Raceway	2	10	Granatelli STP Oil Treatment Hawk III #2	Road Course 2.66 miles	USAC Champ Car	150 miles	33	Gordon Johncock	Oil leak
7/12/69	Nazareth National Speedway	2	1	Granatelli STP Oil Treatment Kuzma #2	Dirt oval 1.125 miles	USAC Champ Car	100 Miles	89	Mario	Led 78 laps
7/19/69	Trenton Speedway	1	1	Granatelli STP Oil Treatment Hawk III #2	Oval 1.5 mile	USAC Champ Car	200 Miles	134	Mario	Led 58 laps
7/27/69	Indianapolis Raceway Park	2	9	Granatelli STP Oil Treatment Hawk III #2	Road Course 2.5 miles	USAC Champ Car	100 Miles	39	Dan Gurney	Running
7/27/69	Indianapolis Raceway Park	9	2	Granatelli STP Oil Treatment Hawk III #2	Road Course 2.5 miles	USAC Champ Car	100 Miles	40	Peter Revson	Running
8/3/69	German Grand Prix Nurburgring	12	DNF	Gold Leaf Lotus 63 Ford Cosworth #3	Road Course 14.2 miles	F-1	199 Miles	0	Jacky Ickx	Accident on lap 1
8/17/69	Wisconsin State Fair Park	2	4	Granatelli STP Oil Treatment Hawk III #2	Oval 1 mile	USAC Champ Car	200 Miles	196	Al Unser	Running
8/18/69	Illinois State Fairgrounds	2	1	Granatelli STP Oil Treatment Kuzma #2	Dirt oval 1 mile	USAC Champ Car	100 Miles	100	Mario	Sidelined by mechanical problem on original race date. When the race was delayed two days by rain, able to repair the car and lead 80 laps.
8/24/69	Dover Downs	3	11	Granatelli STP Oil Treatment Hawk III #2	Oval 1 mile	USAC Champ Car	200 Miles	137	Art Pollard	Led 19 laps, wreck
8/31/69	Road America	3	DNF	Holman & Moody McLaren M6B Ford #1	Road Course 4 miles	CanAm	200 Miles	0	Bruce McLaren	Broken U-joint
9/1/69	DuQuoin State Fairgrounds	2	2	Granatelli STP Oil Treatment Kuzma #2	Dirt oval 1 mile	USAC Champ Car	100 Miles	100	Al Unser	
9/6/69	Indiana State Fairgrounds	2	6	Granatelli STP Oil Treatment Kuzma #2	Dirt oval 1 mile	USAC Champ Car	100 Miles	100	A. J. Foyt	Led 54 laps, running
9/14/69	Donnybrooke Raceway	3	4	Granatelli STP Oil Treatment Hawk III #2	Road Course 2.833 miles	USAC Champ Car	100 Miles	34	Gordon Johncock	Running
9/14/69	Donnybrooke Raceway	4	3	Granatelli STP Oil Treatment Hawk III #2	Road Course 2.833 miles	USAC Champ Car	100 Miles	34	Dan Gurney	Running
9/21/69	Trenton Speedway	6	1	Granatelli STP Oil Treatment Hawk III #2	Oval 1.5 mile	USAC Champ Car	300 Miles	200	Mario	Led 59 laps
9/28/69	California State Fairgrounds	3	15	Granatelli STP Oil Treatment Kuzma #2	Dirt oval 1 mile	USAC Champ Car	100 Miles	83	Al Unser	Oil pressure
10/5/69	United States Grand Prix Watkins Glen	13	DNF	Gold Leaf Lotus 63 Ford Cosworth #9	Road Course 2.3 miles	F-1	248 Miles	3	Jochen Rindt	Suspension
10/12/69	Laguna Seca	8	4	Holman & Moody McLaren M6B Ford #1	Road Course 1.92 miles	CanAm	153.6 Miles	80	Bruce McLaren	Running
10/19/69	Seattle International Raceway	2	1	Granatelli STP Oil Treatment Hawk III #2	Road Course 2.25 miles	USAC Champ Car	100 Miles	45	Mario	Led all 45 laps
10/19/69	Seattle International Raceway	1	2	Granatelli STP Oil Treatment Hawk III #2	Road Course 2.25 miles	USAC Champ Car	100 Miles	45	Al Unser	Raced in rain, first time in history of USAC
10/26/69	Riverside International Raceway	6	3	Holman & Moody McLaren M6B Ford #1	Road Course 3.3 miles	Can-Am	201 Miles	60	Denny Hulme	Running
11/9/69	Texas International Speedway	2	22	Holman & Moody McLaren M6B Ford #1	Road Course 2.75 miles	Can-Am	192 Miles	10	Bruce McLaren	Engine failure
11/15-16/69	Phoenix International Raceway	2	21	Granatelli STP Oil Treatment Hawk III #2	Oval 1 mile	USAC Champ Car	200 Miles	73	Al Unser	Tangled with Bobby Unser, accident. Race halted after 83 laps because of rain, completed next day (11/16)
12/7/69	Riverside International Raceway	3	1	Granatelli STP Oil Treatment Hawk III #2	Road Course 2.6 miles	USAC Champ Car	300 Miles	120	Mario	Led 5 laps

After Mario wrecked the Lotus, Clint Brawner and Jim McGee quickly brought out the Hawk. With only two days of practice, Mario qualified on the front row. *Ken Coles*

Mario is on the gas so hard that he has both front wheels off the ground as he comes off turn four at the Indiana State Fairgrounds. He would lead 54 laps before falling back to sixth in the Hoosier Hundred. *Ken Coles*

Mario had his best effort to date in Can-Am driving the Holman-Moody McLaren M6B big block Ford V-8 in 1969. He finished third here at Riverside, after a fourth at Laguna Seca. *Mike Smith*

Surrounded by ardent reporters, Mario enjoys victory lane at Indianapolis. Andy Granatelli is to his right, making sure the STP logo on the jacket on Mario's shoulder is showing. *Photo courtesy of Indianapolis Motor Speedway*

CHAPTER 2 The 1970s

Entering a new decade, Mario Andretti was an established star in America. His services were in demand by the best teams in racing, and he was clearly a threat to win every race he entered. Some complained that he was hard on equipment. But everyone agreed that when he had a competitive car, Mario could put it into victory lane. This was never more evident than in the 1970s. He found himself in racing machines that were experimental in design, and he often struggled with designs that didn't work. And as engineers tested the boundaries of physics in search of speed, the cars were frequently too fragile to survive on the demanding tracks.

A disappointing stint with the Vel's Parnelli Jones Indy car superteam helped push Mario into Formula One. With success in endurance racing and F-5000, Mario became anxious to compete in road racing's center ring. Following seasons with Ferrari and Parnelli Jones' Grand Prix teams, Mario and Colin Chapman combined to take the Lotus to 16 victories and the Formula One championship.

Having spent his childhood in Italy, it would be misleading to pretend that Mario's aspirations hadn't been to race in Formula One. Everything up until 1976 had been preparation and positioning for that opportunity. Once he joined with Colin Chapman, every other form of racing became secondary.

Mario drives on the front straight at Hockenheim on his way to the Formula One championship in 1978. *Ken Coles*

Mario in the Parnelli F-5000 car at Ontario in 1974. He fought back to 2nd after starting 17th. The busy Labor Day weekend, Mario won the 100-mile USAC Silver Crown race at DuQuoin, Illinois, the next day. *Howard Koby*

Below: The 1976 IROC was Mario's first appearance in the series. The first rounds of the 1976 series were held in 1975 at Michigan and Riverside. Mario finished second to A. J. Foyt in the final points. *Mike Smith*

1970

No question that the skill that you develop on the dirt will always follow you and be put to good use. Quite honestly, I felt that what I've learned on the dirt as far as adapting to changing conditions is probably what has helped me the most driving in the wet, driving in the rain on the road courses. You would think that that's the furthest way to parallel the two as far as application. But I felt that a lot of the skills that I developed from the dirt, especially when it would get hard and slick, helped to be able to really play the throttle properly, to really be able to hook up every bit of power that you had at your disposal without wheel spin. I was pretty good, I won some pretty interesting road races in the wet, in fact in some of the worst conditions, one being in Japan in 1976. *Mario*

Mario's fifth-place finish in the 1970 national point championship was his worst result after joining the circuit full-time. George Bignotti and Jim McGee were no longer with the team, and a single victory at Continental Divide Raceway reflected Mario's lack of confidence in the new McNamara chassis. He was runner-up at Sears Point and Trenton, and also second on the dirt at Sedalia, Missouri.

He continued to strengthen his relationship with Enzo Ferrari and the Ferrari team through the World Sports Car Championship (WSCC) series. He scored a second win in the Sebring 12-Hour, even though his Ferrari broke while leading by 13 laps with just an hour to go. Mario was asked to climb into the third-running Ferrari, and just after he passed the Peter Revson/Steve McQueen car for sec-

ond, Pedro Rodriguez's Porsche broke. In three other WSCC races with Ferrari, Mario didn't finish worse than fifth.

He competed in five Grand Prix for the STP-sponsored March Ford team. When Mario earned his first podium finish, third at Jarama, Spain, it was the only Formula One race he would finish in his first three seasons.

USAC National Championship Points 1970

		Points	Wins
1.	Al Unser	5130	10
2.	Bobby Unser	2260	1
3.	Jim McElreath	2060	1
4.	Mike Mosley	1900	
5.	**Mario**	**1890**	**1**
6.	Roger McCluskey	1380	
7.	Gordon Johncock	1160	
8.	Art Pollard	1110	
9.	A. J. Foyt	1105	
10.	Wally Dallenbach	1220	

At Indy, Mario raced from eighth to sixth, finishing a lap off the pace in the STP McNamara. *Ken Coles*

Mario Andretti 1970 Record

Date	Event/Track	Qual	Finish	Entrant/Car/Number	Type Track	Sanction & Division	Distance	Laps Compl	Race Winner	Comments
2/1/70	24 Hours of Daytona Daytona International Speedway	1	3	Ferrari 512S Coupe #28	Road course 3.56 miles	WSCC	24 Hours	676	Pedro Rodriguez/ Leo Kinnunen/ Brian Redman	Running, co-drove with Arturo Merzario
3/7/70	South African Grand Prix, Kyalami	11	DNF	STP March Ford #8	Road course 2.55 miles	F-1	204 Miles	26	Jack Brabham	Overheating
3/21/70	12 Hours of Sebring Sebring International Raceway	7	1	Ferrari 512S Coupe #28	Road course 5.2 miles	WSCC	12 Hours	248	Ignazio Giunti/ Nino Vaccarella/ Mario	After the gearbox failed on his original 512S Ferrari, Mario was reassigned to the coupe for the final stint
3/28/70	Phoenix International Raceway	1	13	Granatelli STP Oil Treatment Hawk/Ford #1	Oval 1 mile	USAC Champ Car	150 Miles	78	Al Unser	Led 14 laps, valve
4/4/70	Sears Point	2	2	Granatelli STP Oil Treatment Hawk/Ford #1	Road Course 2.523 miles	USAC Champ Car	150 Miles	60	Dan Gurney	Led 3 laps, running
4/19/70	Spanish Grand Prix, Jarama	16	3	STP March Ford #18	Road Course 2.115 miles	F-1	190 Miles	89	Jackie Stewart	Running
4/26/70	Trenton Speedway	3	2	Granatelli STP Oil Treatment Hawk/Ford #1	Oval 1.5 mile	USAC Champ Car	200 Miles	134	Lloyd Ruby	Led 23 laps, running
5/30/70	Indianapolis 500 Indianapolis Motor Speedway	8	6	Granatelli STP Oil Treatment McNamara #1	Oval 2.5 miles	USAC Champ Car	500 Miles	199	Al Unser	Running
6/7/70	Wisconsin State Fair Park	1	5	Granatelli STP Oil Treatment McNamara #1	Oval 1 mile	USAC Champ Car	150 Miles	149	Joe Leonard	Running
6/14/70	Langhorne Speedway	4	8	Granatelli STP Oil Treatment Hawk/Ford #1	Oval 1 mile	USAC Champ Car	150 Miles	147	Bobby Unser	Running
6/28/70	Continental Divide Raceway	2	1	Granatelli STP Oil Treatment McNamara #1	Road Course 2.66 miles	USAC Champ Car	150 miles	57	Mario	Led 41 laps, first victory for McNamara chassis
7/4/70	Michigan International Speedway	2	21	Granatelli STP Oil Treatment Hawk/Ford #1	Oval 2 miles	USAC Champ Car	200 miles	9	Gary Bettenhausen	Blew RR tire
7/11/70	Watkins Glen	2	3	Ferrari 512S #92	Road Course 2.3 miles	WSCC	6 Hours	305	Pedro Rodriguez/ Leo Kinnunen	Running, co-drove with Ignazio Giunti
7/12/70	Watkins Glen	5	5	Ferrari 512S #92	Road Course 2.3 miles	CanAm	200 Miles	85	Denny Hulme	Running
7/18/70	British Grand Prix Brands Hatch	9	DNF	STP March Ford #26	Road Course 2.65 miles	F-1	212 Miles	29	Jochen Rindt	Suspension
7/26/70	Indianapolis Raceway Park	1	18	Granatelli STP Oil Treatment McNamara #1	Road Course 2.5 miles	USAC Champ Car	150 Miles	14	Al Unser	Wrecked
8/2/70	German Grand Prix Hockenheim	9	DNF	STP March Ford #26	Road Course 4.22 miles	F-1	211 Miles	15	Jochen Rindt	Gearbox failure
8/16/70	Austrian Grand Prix Österreichring	18	DNF	STP March Ford #5	Road Course 3.673 miles	F-1	220 Miles	13	Jacky Ickx	Accident
8/22/70	Illinois State Fairgrounds	5	24	Granatelli STP Oil Treatment King #1	Dirt oval 1 mile	USAC Champ Car	100 Miles	5	Al Unser	Broken suspension
8/23/70	Wisconsin State Fair Park	4	24	Granatelli STP Oil Treatment McNamara #1	Oval 1 mile	USAC Champ Car	200 Miles	4	Al Unser	Dropped valve
9/6/70	California 500 Ontario Motor Speedway	8	10	Granatelli STP Oil Treatment McNamara #1	Oval 2.5 miles	USAC Champ Car	500 miles	182	Jim McElreath	Engine
9/7/70	DuQuoin State Fairgrounds	2	17	Granatelli STP Oil Treatment King #1	Dirt oval 1 mile	USAC Champ Car	100 Miles	0	Al Unser	Engine
9/12/70	Indiana State Fairgrounds	14	11	Granatelli STP Oil Treatment King #1	Dirt oval 1 mile	USAC Champ Car	100 Miles	96	Al Unser	Running
9/19/70	Missouri State Fairgrounds	2	2	Granatelli STP Oil Treatment King #1	Dirt oval 1 mile	USAC Champ Car	100 Miles	99	Al Unser	Led 4 laps, ran out of fuel on backstretch on last lap
10/3/70	Trenton Speedway	2	21	Granatelli STP Oil Treatment McNamara #1	Oval 1.5 miles	USAC Champ Car	300 Miles	69	Al Unser	Broken suspension
10/4/70	California State Fairgrounds	1	14	Granatelli STP Oil Treatment King #1	Dirt oval 1 mile	USAC Champ Car	100 Miles	69	Al Unser	Led 1 lap, wrecked
11/21/70	Phoenix International Raceway	24	8	Granatelli STP Oil Treatment Hawk/Ford #20	Oval 1 mile	USAC Champ Car	150 Miles	146	Swede Savage	Running, wrecked McNamara in practice, took over car qualified by Steve Krisiloff

1971

As you can see, we qualified fourth, and I was right up there in the race. I don't think I would have beat Denny Hulme. I was chasing him down hard, but I'm not sure that I would have passed him. But then he had a suspension problem. Once he went out I was gone. Jackie Stewart was nowhere near to me. Mario on his victory at South Africa, reported by Pete Lyons

In 1971, Mario scored two victories, but neither was in the USAC National Championship series that had been his bread and butter since 1964. Following a gratifying winter of testing with Ferrari, Mario was hired as the team's third Formula One driver and opened the season with his first win, in the South African Grand Prix in Kyalami.

In late March, Mario divided his time between the Phoenix USAC event and the Questor Grand Prix at Ontario Motor Speedway in California. Questor, the corporation that built the Ontario oval, sponsored the non-point event held the year before being granted an Formula One Grand Prix date. Promoters scheduled a Formula One versus U.S. F-5000 showdown on the Ontario road course. Following an uneventful run at Phoenix, Andretti flew to California and the next day won both heats at Ontario to claim the only Questor Grand Prix ever held.

The McNamara chassis continued to frustrate Andretti, as a second and two fourths were his best finishes. Finishing ninth in the point standings spotlighted his freefall since the departure of old friends Clint Brawner and Jim McGee. He and Andy Granatelli split as the season concluded, and Mario soon announced a new home with the Vel Miletich Parnelli Jones team.

Mario drove five Formula One races for Ferrari in 1971. Here he started and finished 13th in the Canadian Grand Prix at Mosport Park. *Ken Coles*

USAC National Championship Points 1971

		Points	Wins
1.	Joe Leonard	3016	1
2.	A. J. Foyt	2320	1
3.	Bill Vukovich Jr.	2250	
4.	Al Unser	2200	5
5.	Lloyd Ruby	1830	
6.	Bobby Unser	1805	2
7.	Gary Bettenhausen	1800	
8.	Mark Donohue	1760	2
9.	**Mario**	**1370**	
10.	Wally Dallenbach	1220	

Formula One Points 1971

		Points	Wins
1.	Jackie Stewart	62	6
2.	Ronnie Peterson	33	
3.	Francois Cevert	26	1
4.	Jacky Ickx	19	1
	Jo Siffert	19	1
6.	Emerson Fittipaldi	16	
7.	Clay Regazzoni	13	
8.	**Mario**	**12**	**1**
9.	Peter Gethin	9	1
	Pedro Rodriguez	9	
	Chris Amon	9	
	Denny Hulme	9	
	Reine Wisell	9	

Mario Andretti 1971 Record

Date	Event/Track	Qual	Finish	Entrant/Car/Number	Type Track	Sanction & Division	Distance	Laps Compl	Race Winner	Comments
3/6/71	South African Grand Prix Kyalami	4	1	Ferrari 312B/2 #6	Road course 2.55 miles	F-1	178.5 Miles	70	Mario	Led final four laps
3/20/71	12 Hours of Sebring Sebring International Raceway	2	36	Ferrari 312PB #25	Road course 5.2 miles	WSCC	12 Hours	117	Vic Elford/ Gérard Larrousse	Codrove with Jacky Ickx
3/27/71	Phoenix International Raceway	8	9	Granatelli STP Oil Treatment McNamara #5	Oval 1 mile	USAC Champ Car	150 Miles	147	Al Unser	Running
3/28/71	Questor Grand Prix Ontario Motor Speedway	12	1	Ferrari 312B/2 #5	Road course 3.21 miles	F-1 and F-5000	102.7 Miles	32	Mario	Questor Grand Prix
3/28/71	Questor Grand Prix Ontario Motor Speedway	1	1	Ferrari 312B/2 #5	Road course 3.21 miles	F-1 and F-5000	102.7 Miles	32	Mario	Questor Grand Prix, Mario was the overall winner
4/18/71	Spanish Grand Prix Montjuich Park	8	DNF	Ferrari 312B/2 #6	Road course 2.356 miles	F-1	176.7 Miles	50	Jackie Stewart	Fuel pump failed
4/25/71	Trenton Speedway	3	18	Granatelli STP Oil Treatment McNamara #5	Oval 1.5 miles	USAC Champ Car	200 Miles	35	Mike Mosley	Led 26 laps, turbocharger bearing failed while leading
5/23/71	Monaco Grand Prix Monaco	-	-	Ferrari 312B/2 #6	Road Course 1.954 miles	F-1	156.3 Miles	0	Jackie Stewart	Did not qualify
5/29/71	Indianapolis 500 Indianapolis Motor Speedway	9	30	Granatelli STP Oil Treatment McNamara #5	Oval 2.5 miles	USAC Champ Car	500 Miles	11	Al Unser	Accident
6/6/71	Wisconsin State Fair Park	5	11	Granatelli STP Oil Treatment McNamara #5	Oval 1 mile	USAC Champ Car	150 Miles	142	Al Unser	Running
6/20/71	Dutch Grand Prix Zandvoort	18	DNF	Ferrari 312B/2 #4	Road Course 2.636 miles	F-1	184.5 Miles	5	Jacky Ickx	Fuel pump failed
7/3/71	Pocono 500 Pocono International Raceway	5	4	Granatelli STP Oil Treatment McNamara #5	Oval 2.5 miles	USAC Champ Car	500 Miles	198	Mark Donohue	Running
7/18/71	Michigan International Speedway	3	12	Granatelli STP Oil Treatment McNamara #5	Oval 2 miles	USAC Champ Car	200 miles	74	Mark Donohue	Turbocharger failure
7/24/71	Watkins Glen	3	DNF	Ferrari 312PB #40	Road Course 3.4 miles	WSCC	6 Hours	55	Andrea de Adamich/ Ronnie Peterson	Codrove with Jacky Ickx, starter motor failed during pit stop
7/25/71	Watkins Glen	5	4	Ferrari 712M #50	Road Course 3.4 miles	CanAm	279 Miles	80	Peter Revson	Running
8/1/71	German Grand Prix Nurburgring	11	4	Ferrari 312B/2 #5	Road Course 14.2 miles	F-1	170.4 Miles	12	Jackie Stewart	Running
8/15/71	Wisconsin State Fair Park	5	19	Granatelli STP Oil Treatment McNamara #5	Oval 1 mile	USAC Champ Car	200 Miles	92	Bobby Unser	Fuel leak
8/22/71	Illinois State Fairgrounds	5	13	STP Oil Treatment #5	Dirt oval 1 mile	USAC Silver Crown	100 Miles		A. J. Foyt	
9/5/71	California 500 Ontario Motor Speedway	8	33	Granatelli STP Oil Treatment McNamara #5	Oval 2.5 miles	USAC Champ Car	500 miles	0	Joe Leonard	Electrical
9/6/71	DuQuoin State Fairgrounds	3	17	STP Oil Treatment #5	Dirt oval 1 mile	USAC Silver Crown	100 Miles		George Snider	
9/11/71	Indiana State Fairgrounds	2	17	STP Oil Treatment #5	Dirt oval 1 mile	USAC Silver Crown	100 Miles		Al Unser	
9/19/71	Canadian Grand Prix Mosport Park	13	13	Ferrari 312B/2 #6	Road course 2.459 miles	F-1	157 miles	60	Jackie Stewart	Running
10/3/71	Trenton Speedway	13	2	Granatelli STP Oil Treatment McNamara #5	Oval 1.5 miles	USAC Champ Car	300 Miles	198	Bobby Unser	Running
10/23/71	Phoenix International Raceway	9	4	Granatelli STP Oil Treatment McNamara #5	Oval 1 mile	USAC Champ Car	150 Miles	149	A. J. Foyt	Led 8 laps, running
11/6/71	Kyalami	2	2	Ferrari 312PB #5	Road course 2.55 miles	Springbok	9 Hours	340	Clay Regazzoni/ Brian Redman	Running, codrove with Jacky Ickx

Mario finished fourth in the powerful Ferrari 712M at the Watkins Glen Can-Am in July, 1971. *Ken Coles*

Mario wheels the big champ dirt car through turn three at the Indiana State Fairgrounds in 1971. *John Mahoney*

Driving the McNamara at Indy in 1971, Mario was involved in an accident when he hit oil from a blown engine on lap 12. *Ken Coles*

1972

The cars that we ran at Parnelli's were designed by Maurice Phillippe, who was the designer for Colin Chapman, but Chapman, I think, had a lot of input into how the cars were designed and the concepts. Maurice was a good designer, but as far as being a concept guy and the overall idea of the car, he wasn't as good as Chapman. And that's the part that was missing in the puzzle. He could design anything, but it takes more than that when you're designing a race car because you have to have somebody there who really has the concept and the idea of what it should be. And then he has certain people who design areas of it. Where Maurice was a designer, he wasn't a concept guy who could give you the whole concept from the front of the car to the back of the car. And that was the case in a lot of instances where the car was overengineered in some areas and underengineered in other areas. The concept wasn't there. It was like building the whole house. You had a nice roof and the foundation was good, but everything in the middle was not up to par. So therefore you just really didn't have a good, consistent package. *Jim McGee*

In a year of struggle, Mario endured both the new Maurice Phillippe-designed Parnelli and an evil-handling Ferrari 312B2-72. With the guidance of George Bignotti, the Parnelli was made more raceable as the season progressed. And although Mario suffered a series of failures while running up front, teammate Joe Leonard won three times as he claimed the USAC national championship in a similar machine.

Mario's season-ending point standing slipped to 11th, with a second and third in the two races at Phoenix constituting his highlights.

Mario didn't earn a single podium finish in Grand Prix competition. A fourth at Kyalami was the best he could muster in the unpredictable Ferrari. Yet the most satisfying aspect of the 1972 season was the World Sports Car Championship, where he and codriver Jacky

Ickx captured four wins for Ferrari. It was his third victory at Sebring and first wins at Daytona [which had been shortened to six hours by the Fédération Internationale de l'Automobile (FIA)], Brands Hatch, and Watkins Glen.

When the season ended, Mario decided that Ferrari's Formula One program would get worse before it got better, and he elected not to re-sign for 1973.

Mario works in the Parnelli in its raceday configuration at Indianapolis. He would finish eighth when he ran out of fuel with five laps to go. *Ken Coles*

USAC National Championship Points 1972

		Points	Wins
1.	Joe Leonard	3460	3
2.	Bill Vukovich Jr.	2200	
3.	Roger McCluskey	1970	1
4.	Al Unser	1800	
5.	Mark Donohue	1720	1
6.	Mike Hiss	1665	
7.	Johnny Rutherford	1620	
8.	Bobby Unser	1600	4
9.	Sam Sessions	1440	
10.	Mike Mosley	1250	
11.	**Mario**	**1135**	

Mario Andretti 1972 Record

Date	Event/Track	Qual	Finish	Entrant/Car/Number	Type Track	Sanction & Division	Distance	Laps Compl	Race Winner	Comments
1/9/72	Buenos Aires	3	10	Ferrari 312PB #28	Road course 3.7 miles	WSCC	1000 Kilometers	152	Ronnie Peterson/ Tim Schenken	Co-drove with Jacky Ickx, running
1/23/72	Argentine Grand Prix Buenos Aires	9	DNF	Ferrari 312B2-72 #10	Road course 2.8 miles	F-1	266 Miles	20	Jackie Stewart	Engine misfire
2/6/72	**24 Hours of Daytona Daytona International Speedway**	**1**	**1**	**Ferrari 312PB #2**	**Road course 3.56 miles**	**WSCC**	**6 Hours**	**194**	**Mario/Jacky Ickx**	**24 Hours of Daytona shortened to 6 hours by FIA**
3/4/72	South African Grand Prix Kyalami	6	4	Ferrari 312B2-72 #7	Road course 2.55 miles	F-1	201 Miles	79	Denny Hulme	Running
3/18/72	Phoenix International Raceway	4	2	Vel's Parnelli Jones Viceroy VPJ Colt #9	Oval 1 mile	USAC Champ Car	150 Miles	150	Bobby Unser	Led 3 laps, running
3/25/72	12 Hours of Sebring Sebring International Raceway	1	1	Ferrari 312PB #2	Road course 5.2 miles	WSCC	12 Hours	259	Mario/Jacky Ickx	
4/16/72	**Brands Hatch**	**2**	**1**	**Ferrari 312PB #11**	**Road course 2.65 miles**	**WSCC**	**1000 Kilometers**	**235**	**Mario/Jacky Ickx**	**Fourth consecutive win of the season for Ferrari**
4/23/72	Trenton Speedway	4	22	Vel's Parnelli Jones Viceroy Parnelli #9	Oval 1.5 miles	USAC Champ Car	200 Miles	1	Gary Bettenhausen	Broken piston
5/1/72	Spanish Grand Prix Jarama	5	DNF	Ferrari 312B2-72 #7	Road course 2.115 miles	F-1	190 Miles	23	Emerson Fittipaldi	Engine
5/27/72	Indianapolis 500 Indianapolis Motor Speedway	5	8	Vel's Parnelli Jones Viceroy Parnelli #9	Oval 2.5 miles	USAC Champ Car	500 Miles	194	Mark Donohue	Ran out of fuel with five laps remaining
6/4/72	Wisconsin State Fair Park	8	8	Vel's Parnelli Jones Viceroy Parnelli #9	Oval 1 mile	USAC Champ Car	150 Miles	148	Bobby Unser	Led 14 laps, running
7/16/72	Michigan International Speedway	6	12	Vel's Parnelli Jones Viceroy Parnelli #9	Oval 2 mile	USAC Champ Car	200 miles	80	Joe Leonard	Led 12 laps, broke ring and pinion while leading
7/22/72	**Watkins Glen**	**2**	**1**	**Ferrari 312PB #85**	**Road course 3.4 miles**	**WSCC**	**6 Hours**	**195**	**Mario/Jacky Ickx**	
7/29/72	Pocono 500 Pocono International Raceway	3	7	Vel's Parnelli Jones Viceroy Parnelli #9	Oval 2.5 miles	USAC Champ Car	500 Miles	188	Joe Leonard	Led 105 laps, running
8/13/72	Wisconsin State Fair Park	1	11	Vel's Parnelli Jones Viceroy Parnelli #9	Oval 1 mile	USAC Champ Car	200 Miles	108	Joe Leonard	Led 107 laps, locked wheel in pits while leading
9/3/72	California 500 Ontario Motor Speedway	5	27	Vel's Parnelli Jones Viceroy Parnelli #9	Oval 2.5 miles	USAC Champ Car	500 Miles	52	Roger McCluskey	Blown engine
9/10/72	Italian Grand Prix Monza	7	7	Ferrari 312B2-72 #3	Road course 3.6 miles	F-1	198 Miles	54	Emerson Fittipaldi	Running
9/24/72	Trenton Speedway	2	28	Vel's Parnelli Jones Viceroy Parnelli #9	Oval 1.5 miles	USAC Champ Car	300 Miles	0	Bobby Unser	Broken half shaft
10/8/72	United States Grand Prix Watkins Glen	10	6	Ferrari 312B2-72 #9	Road course 3.4 miles	F-1	200 Miles	58	Jackie Stewart	Running
11/4/72	Phoenix International Raceway	2	3	Vel's Parnelli Jones Viceroy Parnelli #9	Oval 1 mile	USAC Champ Car	150 Miles	149	Bobby Unser	Led 53 laps, running

In the pits at Indy in 1972, Mario waits to go out in the Parnelli with the innovative dihedral wings. This design didn't work very well and was quickly removed. *Ken Coles*

1973

When I drop out early, I could just scream for a half-hour straight, to get it off my chest. You could just cry a thousand times. I've told my wife that I feel my heart is breaking and the cracks are as big as some of the ones in the pavement. It's a tremendous disappointment. Mario, Speed! Indy Car Racing, Chet Jezierski

The new Parnelli, again designed by Maurice Phillippe, was slightly more traditional in its thinking. The Vel's Parnelli Jones team had turbocharged Offys comparable to those of Unser and Foyt, but with their greater boost and horsepower, they lacked reliability. Yet at Trenton, Mario won his first USAC championship race since the Colorado 150 at Castle Rock in June of 1970.

Mario proved that he hadn't lost his touch on the dirt, as he won the first two of three USAC Silver Crown races held that year. When USAC took the dirt miles off the national championship schedule in 1971, a separate series was started. The Indy cars were called the Gold Crown, and the dirt cars were identified as the Silver Crown. For Mario it was his second victory at both DuQuoin and Springfield, and he finished his first Silver Crown season tied with Tom Bigelow for second in the point standings.

USAC National Championship Points 1973

		Points	Wins
1.	Roger McCluskey	3705	1
2.	Wally Dallenbach	2620	3
3.	Johnny Rutherford	2595	2
4.	Bill Vukovich Jr.	2440	1
5.	**Mario**	**2400**	**1**
6.	Mike Mosley	2345	
7.	Gordon Johncock	2240	3
8.	Gary Bettenhausen	2093	1
9.	Lloyd Ruby	1610	
10.	A. J. Foyt	1580	2

Mario led 28 laps but finished second to Wally Dallenbach at the 1973 California 500. *Howard Koby*

Mario hustles the Vel's Parnelli Jones Ford-powered Grant King dirt car during the Hoosier Hundred in 1973. When he ran into engine problems, the win and the championship went to his teammate, Al Unser. *Ken Coles*

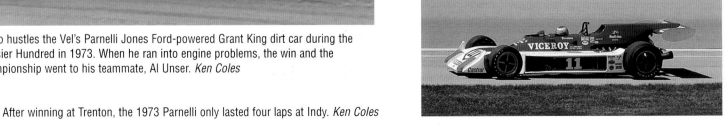

After winning at Trenton, the 1973 Parnelli only lasted four laps at Indy. *Ken Coles*

Mario Andretti 1973 Record

Date	Event/Track	Qual	Finish	Entrant/Car/Number	Type Track	Sanction & Division	Distance	Laps Compl	Race Winner	Comments
4/7/73	Texas World Speedway	3	25	Vel's Parnelli Jones Viceroy Parnelli #11	Oval 2 miles	USAC Champ Car	200 Miles	10	Al Unser	Broken piston
4/15/73	Trenton Speedway	8	4	Vel's Parnelli Jones Viceroy Parnelli #11	Oval 1.5 miles	USAC Champ Car	150 Miles	100	A. J. Foyt	Led 2 laps, running; event run in two 100 lap heats, starting order of second heat based on finish of first heat
4/15/73	**Trenton Speedway**	**4**	**1**	**Vel's Parnelli Jones Viceroy Parnelli #11**	**Oval 1.5 miles**	**USAC Champ Car**	**150 Miles**	**100**	**Mario**	**Led 52 laps, received a $1000 bonus for leading overall points**
5/30/73	Indianapolis 500 Indianapolis Motor Speedway	6	30	Vel's Parnelli Jones Viceroy Parnelli #11	Oval 2.5 miles	USAC Champ Car	500 Miles	4	Gordon Johncock	Burned piston
6/10/73	Wisconsin State Fair Park	11	8	Vel's Parnelli Jones Viceroy Parnelli #11	Oval 1 mile	USAC Champ Car	150 Miles	145	Bobby Unser	Running
7/1/73	Pocono 500 Pocono International Raceway	3	7	Vel's Parnelli Jones Viceroy Parnelli #11	Oval 2.5 miles	USAC Champ Car	500 Miles	184	A. J. Foyt	Led 10 laps, dropped valve
7/15/73	Michigan International Speedway	7	5	Vel's Parnelli Jones Viceroy Parnelli #11	Oval 2 miles	USAC Champ Car	200 miles	99	Roger McCluskey	Running
8/12/73	Wisconsin State Fair Park	9	19	Vel's Parnelli Jones Viceroy Parnelli #11	Oval 1 mile	USAC Champ Car	200 Miles	93	Wally Dallenbach	Broken suspension
8/19/73	**Illinois State Fairgrounds**	**3**	**1**	**Vel's Parnelli Jones King Ford #15**	**Dirt oval 1 mile**	**USAC Silver Crown**	**100 Miles**	**100**	**Mario**	
8/26/73	Ontario Motor Speedway	2	12	Vel's Parnelli Jones Viceroy Parnelli #11	Oval 2.5 miles	USAC Champ Car	100 Miles	28	Johnny Rutherford	Broken shift link, qualification heat for 500 mile race
9/2/73	**California 500** Ontario Motor Speedway	**15**	**2**	**Vel's Parnelli Jones Viceroy Parnelli #11**	Oval 2.5 miles	USAC Champ Car	500 Miles	200	Wally Dallenbach	Led 28 laps, running
9/3/73	**DuQuoin State Fairgrounds**	**2**	**1**	**Vel's Parnelli Jones King Ford #15**	**Dirt oval 1 mile**	**USAC Silver Crown**	**100 Miles**	**100**	**Mario**	
9/15/73	Indiana State Fairgrounds	7	21	Vel's Parnelli Jones King Ford #15	Dirt oval 1 mile	USAC Silver Crown	100 Miles	32	Al Unser	Engine, rained out on Sept. 8
9/16/73	Michigan International Speedway	8	5	Vel's Parnelli Jones Viceroy Parnelli #11	Oval 2 miles	USAC Champ Car	126 Miles	63	Billy Vukovich	Running
9/16/73	Michigan International Speedway	3	2	Vel's Parnelli Jones Viceroy Parnelli #11	Oval 2 miles	USAC Champ Car	126 Miles	62	Johnny Rutherford	Led 4 laps, running
9/23/73	Trenton Speedway	5	7	Vel's Parnelli Jones Viceroy Parnelli #11	Oval 1.5 miles	USAC Champ Car	200 Miles	131	Gordon Johncock	Running
10/6/73	Texas World Speedway	1	17	Vel's Parnelli Jones Viceroy Parnelli #11	Oval 2 miles	USAC Champ Car	200 Miles	39	Gary Bettenhausen	Led 19 laps, broken valve
10/14/73	Laguna Seca	13	17	MRE/Commander Homes McLaren M20 Chevy Turbo #96	Road course 1.92 miles	CanAm	125.5 Miles	3	Mark Donohue	Accident, codriver John Cannon
10/29/73	Riverside International Raceway	-	-	MRE/Commander Homes McLaren M20 Chevy Turbo #96	Road course 3.3 miles	CanAm	162 Miles		Mark Donohue	Practiced but did not race. John Cannon made 12 laps before oil pressure problems
11/3/73	Phoenix International Raceway	17	7	Vel's Parnelli Jones Viceroy Parnelli #11	Oval 1 mile	USAC Champ Car	150 Miles	148	Gordon Johncock	Running

1974

When they decided to take the dirt tracks out of the Championship schedule, I had some real objections to that. I thought it would take away tremendously from the dirt. Maybe it was a sign of the times; the prize money just wasn't there at those fairgrounds tracks. Mario, Open Wheel Magazine, June 1993

Mario found a lot of success in 1974, as he continued to search for results with the Vel's Parnelli Jones "Super Team" in USAC's national series. The Indy car team switched from the home-grown Parnellis to Eagle chassis, but Mario's best finish didn't come until the final race of the year when he ran third behind Gordon Johncock and Bobby Unser at Phoenix.

With victories at Sedalia and Springfield on consecutive days, and a third win at DuQuoin, Mario earned the USAC Silver Crown championship in what would be his final season in dirt cars. He battled his teammate and the defending champion, Al Unser, through the final race at the traditional Hoosier Hundred. When he took third to Unser's second, he locked up the title.

USAC joined with the Sports Car Club of America (SCCA) to present the F-5000 series, and Mario brought the Vel's Parnelli Jones team into the picture. Driving a Lola T-332, Mario earned victories in three of the seven races, losing the title to Brian Redman. Mario has said that he could have won that championship as well, if more attention had been paid to little things in preparing the Lola.

The VPJ F-5000 effort was in preparation for their entry in Formula One in 1975. Using a new Maurice Phillippe design, the Parnelli Jones' Formula One effort debuted at the Canadian Grand Prix with a satisfying seventh-place finish. However, at Watkins Glen a week later, an electrical problem on the grid led to Mario's car being pushed out of the way to be worked on by his crew, and he was disqualified after completing four laps.

Mario led 30 laps before running out of fuel while in the lead in the USAC championship season opener at Ontario. *Howard Koby*

USAC/SCCA Formula 5000 Points 1974

		Points	Wins
1.	Brian Redman	105	3
2.	**Mario**	**97**	**3**
3.	David Hobbs	55	1
4.	Eppie Wietzes	49	
5.	Brett Lunger	33	
6.	John Gunn	27	
7.	Warwick Brown	20	
8.	Graham McRae	19	
9.	Evan Noyes	18	
10.	Tuck Thomas	16	

After starting fifth at Indy in 1974, Mario fell out when his Parnelli dropped a valve with only two laps completed. *Ken Coles*

Mario Andretti 1974 Record

Date	Event/Track	Qual	Finish	Entrant/Car/Number	Type Track	Sanction & Division	Distance	Laps Compl	Race Winner	Comments
3/3/74	Ontario Motor Speedway	3	9	Vel's Parnelli Jones Viceroy Parnelli #5	Oval 2.5 miles	USAC Champ Car	100 Miles	37	Johnny Rutherford	Led 30 laps, ran out of fuel while leading
3/10/74	California 500 Ontario Motor Speedway	14	25	Vel's Parnelli Jones Viceroy Parnelli #5	Oval 2.5 miles	USAC Champ Car	500 Miles	91	Bobby Unser	Blown engine
3/17/74	Phoenix International Raceway	7	5	Vel's Parnelli Jones Viceroy Eagle #5	Oval 1 mile	USAC Champ Car	150 Miles	150	Mike Mosley	Running
4/7/74	Trenton Speedway	1	9	Vel's Parnelli Jones Viceroy Parnelli #5	Oval 1.5 miles	USAC Champ Car	150 Miles	73	Bobby Unser	Led 33 laps, burned piston
4/25/74	**Monza**	**1**	**1**	**Autodelta Alfa Romeo 33TT12 #3**	**Road Course 3.6 miles**	**WSCC**	**1000 Kilometers**	**174**	**Mario/Arturo Merzario**	
5/26/74	Indianapolis 500 Indianapolis Motor Speedway	5	31	Vel's Parnelli Jones Viceroy Eagle #5	Oval 2.5 miles	USAC Champ Car	500 Miles	2	Bobby Unser	Engine valve
6/2/74	Mid-Ohio Raceway	1	13	Parnelli Jones Viceroy Lola #5	Road Course 2.4 miles	USAC F-5000	100.8 Miles	34	Brian Redman	Led 23 laps, broken steering linkage
6/9/74	Wisconsin State Fair Park	11	17	Vel's Parnelli Jones Viceroy Parnelli #5	Oval 1 mile	USAC Champ Car	150 Miles	65	Johnny Rutherford	Turbocharger failed
6/15/74	Mosport Park	1	4	Parnelli Jones Viceroy Lola #5	Road Course 2.459 miles	USAC F-5000	98 Miles	40	David Hobbs	Running
6/30/74	Pocono 500 Pocono International Raceway	8	17	Vel's Parnelli Jones Viceroy Eagle #5	Oval 2.5 miles	USAC Champ Car	500 Miles	132	Johnny Rutherford	Wrecked
7/4/74	New York State Fairgrounds	1	2	Vel's Parnelli Jones Viceroy King Ford #2	Dirt oval 1 mile	USAC Silver Crown	100 Miles	100	Al Unser	Led 87 laps, running
7/13/74	Watkins Glen	3	DQ	Autodelta Alfa Romeo 33TT12 #60	Road Course 3.4 miles	WSCC	6 Hours	171	Jean-Pierre Jarier/ Jean-Pierre Beltoise	Disqualified for receiving assistance, co-driver Arturo Merzario
7/14/74	**Watkins Glen**	**1**	**1**	**Parnelli Jones Viceroy Lola #5**	**Road Course 3.4 miles**	**USAC F-5000**	**102 Miles**	**30**	**Mario**	**Led 30 laps**
7/21/74	Michigan International Speedway	3	18	Vel's Parnelli Jones Viceroy Eagle #5	Oval 2 miles	USAC Champ Car	200 miles	48	Bobby Unser	Led 1 lap, broken piston
7/28/74	**Road America**	**1**	**1**	**Parnelli Jones Viceroy Lola #5**	**Road Course 4 miles**	**USAC F-5000**	**100 Miles**	**25**	**Mario**	**Led all 25 laps**
8/11/74	Wisconsin State Fair Park	12	8	Vel's Parnelli Jones Viceroy Eagle #5	Oval 1 mile	USAC Champ Car	200 Miles	197	Gordon Johncock	Running
8/17/74	**Missouri State Fairgrounds**	**1**	**1**	**Vel's Parnelli Jones Viceroy King Ford #2**	**Dirt oval 1 mile**	**USAC Silver Crown**	**100 Miles**	**100**	**Mario**	**Led all 100 laps**
8/18/73	**Illinois State Fairgrounds**	**2**	**1**	**Vel's Parnelli Jones Viceroy King Ford #2**	**Dirt oval 1 mile**	**USAC Silver Crown**	**100 Miles**	**100**	**Mario**	**Led 100 laps, two wins in consecutive days**
9/1/74	Ontario Motor Speedway	17	2	Parnelli Jones Viceroy Lola #5	Road Course 3.19 miles	USAC F-5000	108.5 miles	34	Brian Redman	Running
9/2/74	**DuQuoin State Fairgrounds**	**1**	**1**	**Vel's Parnelli Jones Viceroy King Ford #2**	**Dirt oval 1 mile**	**USAC Silver Crown**	**100 Miles**	**100**	**Mario**	**Led 52 laps**
9/7/74	Indiana State Fairgrounds	3	3	Vel's Parnelli Jones Viceroy King Ford #2	Dirt oval 1 mile	USAC Silver Crown	100 Miles	100	Jackie Howerton	Won championship
9/15/74	Michigan International Speedway	5	10	Vel's Parnelli Jones Viceroy Eagle #5	Oval 2 miles	USAC Champ Car	250 Miles	82	Al Unser	Broken piston
9/22/74	Canadian Grand Prix Mosport Park	16	7	Vel's Parnelli Jones Viceroy Parnelli VPJ4 Cosworth #55	Road Course 2.459 miles	F-1	197 Miles	79	Emerson Fittipaldi	Running
10/6/74	United States Grand Prix Watkins Glen	3	DQ	Vel's Parnelli Jones Viceroy Parnelli VPJ4 Cosworth #55	Road Course 3.4 miles	F-1	200 Miles	4	Carlos Reutemann	Electrical problems on the grid, disqualified when he was push started
10/13/74	Laguna Seca	1	3	Parnelli Jones Viceroy Lola #5	Road course 1.92 miles	USAC F-5000	96 Miles	50	Brian Redman	Led 38 laps, running
10/27/74	**Riverside International Raceway**	**1**	**1**	**Parnelli Jones Viceroy Lola #5**	**Road course 2.54 miles**	**USAC F-5000**	**101.6 Miles**	**40**	**Mario**	**Mario won his qualifying heat by 16.6 seconds, led 31 laps**
11/2/74	Phoenix International Raceway	5	3	Vel's Parnelli Jones Viceroy Eagle #5	Oval 1 mile	USAC Champ Car	150 Miles	148	Gordon Johncock	Running

After practicing in this McLaren for the Can-Am race at Riverside, Mario stepped out to let teammate John Cannon drive the car in the race. *Mike Smith*

Watkins Glen was the second Formula One race for the Parnelli team. After qualifying third, everything went sour. Mario was disqualified when an electrical problem on the grid kept the car from starting and it was illegally pushed to the side. *Ken Coles*

Mario finished a close second to Brian Redman in the F-5000 series in 1974. He also finished second to Redman in the VPJ F-5000 Lola on the Ontario road course. *Howard Koby*

Below: Mario was on the pole for the 1974 Riverside Grand Prix. Next to him, Bobby Unser starts an Eagle with a turbocharged Offy. After Unser's engine broke, Andretti led the rest of the way to the checkers. *Howard Koby*

1975

It may be his last race in Formula One, but it won't be mine! *Mario after retiring from the U.S. Grand Prix and being advised by Chris Economaki that Vel Miletich had announced that the VPJ team was through with Grand Prix racing.*

By 1975, Mario's focus had shifted almost completely to road racing. For the first time, Mario and the Vel's Parnelli Jones team competed the full Grand Prix season. With the suspension revamped by John Bernard, the Parnelli was more competitive. Mario turned the fastest race lap in the Swedish Grand Prix at Monjuich Park, and finished in the points at South Africa, Spain, and Watkins Glen.

For the second consecutive season, Brian Redman out-pointed Mario in F-5000. By taking the final two races of the series, Mario matched the Brit's four victories. But Redman finished in the first three in eight of the nine races, and while Redman's worst finish was 8th at Elkhart Lake, Mario had 3 finishes outside the top 10.

This left little time for the USAC championship series races. Mario ran only four races, with little success. At Indy something failed on the rear of his Viceroy Eagle as he came off turn two and he spun into the inside wall. His best result came at Phoenix in Jerry O'Connell's Sugaripe Prune Eagle, where he finished third.

Mario made his first appearance in the 1976 International Race of Champions (IROC) series at Michigan, which ran the three, of it's first four races at Michigan and Riverside in late 1975. He finished fourth and third on consecutive days at Riverside.

A mechanical failure put Mario into the turn three wall after completing 49 laps at Indy. He was scored 28th.
Ken Coles

Formula One Points 1975

		Points	Wins
1.	Niki Lauda	64.5	5
2.	Emerson Fittipaldi	45	2
3.	Carlos Reutemann	37	1
4.	James Hunt	33	1
5.	Clay Regazzoni	25	1
6.	Carlos Pace	24	1
7.	Jody Scheckter	20	1
	Jochen Mass	20	
9.	Patrick Depailler	12	
10.	Tom Pryce	8	
14.	**Mario**	**5**	

Mario meets the press following the 1975 Ontario 500.
Howard Koby

Mario Andretti 1975 Record

Date	Event/Track	Qual	Finish	Entrant/Car/Number	Type Track	Sanction & Division	Distance	Laps Compl	Race Winner	Comments
1/12/75	Argentine Grand Prix Buenos Aires	10	DNF	Vel's Parnelli Jones Viceroy VPJ4 Cosworth #27	Road Course 3.7 miles	F-1	196 Miles	27	Emerson Fittipaldi	Transmission failure
1/26/75	Brazilian Grand Prix Interlagos	18	7	Vel's Parnelli Jones Viceroy VPJ4 Cosworth #27	Road Course 4.94 miles	F-1	197.6 Miles	40	Carlos Pace	
3/1/75	South African Grand Prix Kyalami	6	17	Vel's Parnelli Jones Viceroy VPJ4 Cosworth #27	Road Course 2.55 miles	F-1	199 Miles	70	Jody Scheckter	CV joint broke
3/9/75	California Grand Prix Ontario Motor Speedway	18	28	Vel's Parnelli Jones Viceroy Eagle #21	Oval 2.5 miles	USAC Champ Car	500 Miles	15	A. J. Foyt	Broken connecting rod
4/13/75	Silverstone		3	Vel's Parnelli Jones Viceroy VPJ4 Cosworth #27	Road Course 2.9 miles	BRDC	116 Miles	40	Niki Lauda	BRDC Daily Express International Trophy Race (non-points)
4/27/75	Spanish Grand Prix Montjuich Park	4	DNF	Vel's Parnelli Jones Viceroy VPJ4 Cosworth #27	Road Course 2.35 miles	F-1	68 Miles	16	Jochen Mass	Ran fastest lap of the race on lap 14, suspension/accident
5/11/75	Monaco Grand Prix Monaco	13	DNF	Vel's Parnelli Jones Viceroy VPJ4 Cosworth #27	Road Course 2.04 miles	F-1	153 Miles	9	Niki Lauda	Oil leak
5/25/75	Indianapolis 500 Indianapolis Motor Speedway	27	28	Vel's Parnelli Jones Viceroy Eagle #21	Oval 2.5 miles	USAC Champ Car	500 Miles	49	Bobby Unser	Mechanical failure, wreck.
6/1/75	Pocono International Raceway	2	18	Parnelli Jones Viceroy Lola #5	Road Course 2.8 miles	USAC F-5000	98 Miles	24	Brian Redman	Led 18 laps, engine failure
6/8/75	Swedish Grand Prix, Anderstorp	15	4	Vel's Parnelli Jones Viceroy VPJ4 Cosworth #27	Road Course 2.5 miles	F-1	200 Miles	80	Niki Lauda	
6/15/75	Mosport Park	1	1	Parnelli Jones Viceroy Lola #5	Road Course 2.459 miles	USAC F-5000	98 Miles	40	Mario	
6/29/75	Pocono International Raceway	10	25	Vel's Parnelli Jones Viceroy Eagle #21	Oval 2.5 mile	USAC Champ Car	500 Miles	79	A. J. Foyt	Engine, 425 miles – rain
7/6/75	French Grand Prix Paul Ricard	15	5	Vel's Parnelli Jones Viceroy VPJ4 Cosworth #27	Road Course 3.6 miles	F-1	195 Miles	54	Niki Lauda	Running
7/13/75	Watkins Glen	1	6	Parnelli Jones Viceroy Lola #5	Road Course 3.4 miles	USAC F-5000	102 Miles	29	Brian Redman	Running
7/19/75	British Grand Prix Silverstone	12	12	Vel's Parnelli Jones Viceroy VPJ4 Cosworth #27	Road Course 2.9 miles	F-1	164 Miles	54	Emerson Fittipaldi	Race stopped by rain, finishers 2 through 5 involved in an accident on lap 56, order reverted to start of lap 56
7/27/75	Road America	1	1	Parnelli Jones Viceroy Lola #5	Road Course 4 miles	USAC F-5000	100 Miles	25	Mario	Led 25 laps
8/3/75	German Grand Prix Nurburgring	13	10	Vel's Parnelli Jones Viceroy VPJ4 Cosworth #27	Road Course 14.2 miles	F-1	199 Miles	12	Carlos Reutemann	Out of fuel
8/10/75	Mid-Ohio Raceway	1	18	Parnelli Jones Viceroy Lola #5	Road Course 2.4 miles	USAC F-5000	100.8 Miles	32	Brian Redman	Led 31 laps
8/13/75	Watkins Glen	4	2	Kauhsen Alfa Romeo 33TT12 #3	Road Course 3.4 miles	WSCC	6 Hours	152	Henri Pescarolo/ Derek Bell	Co-driver Arturo Merzario
8/17/75	Austrian Grand Prix Österreichring	19	DNF	Vel's Parnelli Jones Viceroy VPJ4 Cosworth #27	Road Course 3.673 miles	F-1	106.5 Miles	1	Vittorio Brambilla	Accident in rain, race halted after 29 laps
8/31/75	Road Atlanta	16	3	Parnelli Jones Viceroy Lola #5	Road Course 2.52 miles	USAC F-5000	100.8 Miles	26	Al Unser	Led 10 laps, running
9/13/75	Michigan International Speedway	1	9	Chevrolet Camaro	Oval 2 mile	IROC	100 Miles	40	David Pearson	First race of 1976 IROC
9/7/75	Italian Grand Prix Monza	15	DNF	Vel's Parnelli Jones Viceroy VPJ4 Cosworth #27	3.6	F-1	187 Miles	1	Clay Regazzoni	Multi-car accident
9/28/75	Long Beach Grand Prix Long Beach	3	13	Parnelli Jones Viceroy Lola #5	Road Course 2.02 miles	USAC F-5000	101 Miles	33	Brian Redman	Led 12 laps, transmission failure
10/5/75	United States Grand Prix Watkins Glen	5	DNF	Vel's Parnelli Jones Viceroy VPJ4 Cosworth #27	Road Course 3.4 miles	F-1	200.6 Miles	9	Niki Lauda	Suspension
10/12/75	Laguna Seca	1	1	Parnelli Jones Viceroy Lola #5	Road course 1.92 miles	USAC F-5000	96 Miles	50	Mario	Led all 50 laps
10/25/75	Riverside International Raceway	4	3	Chevrolet Camaro	Road course 2.54 miles	IROC	76.2 Miles	30	Bobby Unser	Second race of 1976 IROC
10/26/75	Riverside International Raceway	1	1	Parnelli Jones Viceroy Lola #5	Road course 2.54 miles	USAC F-5000	101.6 Miles	40	Mario	Led all 40 laps
10/26/75	Riverside International Raceway	10	4	Chevrolet Camaro	Road course 2.54 miles	IROC	76.2 Miles	30	Bobby Allison	Third race of 1976 IROC
11/9/75	Phoenix International Raceway	3	3	O'Connell Sugaripe Prune Eagle #12	Oval 1 mile	USAC Champ Car	150 Miles	149	A. J. Foyt	Led 40 laps, running

Mario buckles into his IROC Camaro at Michigan. It was the first race of the 1976 series and although Mario came home ninth, he had better luck in the other three events and finished second to Foyt in the points. *Ken Coles*

Mario at speed in the F-5000 Parnelli in front of more than 56,000 fans at Riverside in 1975. This would be his second consecutive victory in the First National City Traveler's Checks California Grand Prix. *Howard Koby*

Mario ran four championship races for Roger Penske in 1976. At Indy, Mario was eighth when it began to rain. *Ken Coles*

1976

My favorite track on the Formula One circuit was the Nurburgring in Germany— the old Nurburgring. That was definitely the most challenging course, and because of that, I would have to consider it the best. Mario

With the intense battling between James Hunt and Niki Lauda, the 1976 grand prix season was turbulent. It was fueled by Ferrari's protests and Hunt's eventual disqualification from the British Grand Prix, which he had won. Lauda suffered critical injuries at Germany and made a miraculous return weeks later to resume the battle for the championship. The final event, which would conclude the title battle, was the first Grand Prix held in Japan. The race was reluctantly begun by the drivers who felt the rain too heavy for racing. Lauda pulled in at the end of the first lap. Mario scored his second Grand Prix victory, while Hunt won the title.

After losing the Viceroy sponsorship, Vel Miletich and Parnelli Jones didn't decide to close their Formula One team until March, three races into the season. When Colin Chapman offered Mario a chance to be the number one driver at Lotus, which had struggled in recent years, Mario quickly accepted and quit VPJ. With Chapman's increased effort, the Lotus 77 began to improve quickly. For the first time, Mario competed the full Formula One schedule with the exception of Monaco, resulting in a sixth-place finish in points and his second career win.

Mario agreed to drive selected national championship events for Roger Penske, beginning with Indianapolis. He missed the first weekend of qualifying because of the Belgian Grand Prix, and had to start in the seventh row. After working his way into eighth position, it began to rain and the race was stopped, giving Mario his first top 10 since 1972. In the other three races he ran with Penske, Mario finished fifth, fourth, and third.

With his third-place finish in the highly competitive round at Daytona, Mario secured second position in the 1976 IROC series, behind A. J. Foyt. It was Mario's first IROC competition in the Camaros.

Mario moved back to Lotus for the 1976 Formula One season, but he ran two races for Parnelli Jones. Here he's at the Long Beach Grand Prix before dropping out after 15 laps. *Howard Koby*

Formula One Points 1976

		Points	Wins
1.	James Hunt	69	6
2.	Niki Lauda	68	5
3.	Jody Scheckter	49	1
4.	Patrick Depailler	39	
5.	Clay Regazzoni	31	1
6.	**Mario**	**22**	**1**
7.	John Watson	20	1
	Jacques Laffite	20	
9.	Jochen Mass	19	
10.	Gunnar Nilsson	11	

USAC National Championship Points 1976

		Points	Wins
1.	Gordon Johncock	4240	2
2.	Johnny Rutherford	4220	3
3.	Wally Dallenbach	3105	
4.	Al Unser	3020	3
5.	Mike Mosley	2120	1
6.	Bobby Unser	2080	2
7.	A. J. Foyt	1720	2
8.	Tom Sneva	1570	
9.	**Mario**	**1200**	
10.	Johnny Parsons Jr.	980	

Mario Andretti 1976 Record

Date	Event/Track	Qual	Finish	Entrant/Car/Number	Type Track	Sanction & Division	Distance	Laps Compl	Race Winner	Comments
1/25/76	Brazilian Grand Prix, Interlagos	16	DNF	John Player Lotus 77 Cosworth #6	Road Course 4.94 miles	F-1	197.6 Miles	6	Niki Lauda	Accident
2/13/76	Daytona International Speedway	6	3	Chevrolet Camaro	Oval 2.5 miles	IROC	100 Miles	40	Benny Parsons	Running
3/6/76	South African Grand Prix, Kyalami	13	6	VPJ American Racing Wheels VPJ4B Cosworth #27	Road Course 2.55 miles	F-1	199 Miles	77	Niki Lauda	Running
3/28/76	United States Grand Prix West Long Beach	15	DNF	VPJ American Racing Wheels VPJ4B Cosworth #27	Road Course 2.02 miles	F-1	161.6 Miles	15	Clay Regazzoni	Water leak
5/2/76	Spanish Grand Prix Jarama	9	DNF	John Player Lotus 77 Cosworth #5	Road Course 2.115 miles	F-1	158.6 Miles	34	James Hunt	Gearbox failure
5/16/76	Belgian Grand Prix Zolder	11	DNF	John Player Lotus 77 Cosworth #5	Road Course 2.65 miles	F-1	185.5 Miles	28	Niki Lauda	CV joint
5/30/76	Indianapolis 500 Indianapolis Motor Speedway	19	8	Penske CAM-2 McLaren #6	Oval 2.5 miles	USAC Champ Car	500 Miles	101	Johnny Rutherford	Running, stopped by rain
6/13/76	Swedish Grand Prix, Anderstorp	2	DNF	John Player Lotus 77 Cosworth #5	Road Course 2.5 miles	F-1	180 Miles	45	Jody Scheckter	Led 45 laps, was to be penalized one minute for jumping the start, engine failure
6/27/76	Pocono 500 Pocono International Raceway	3	5	Penske CAM-2 McLaren #6	Oval 2.5 mile	USAC Champ Car	500 Miles	198	Al Unser	Led 45 laps, running
7/4/76	French Grand Prix Paul Ricard	7	5	John Player Lotus 77 Cosworth #5	Road Course 3.6 miles	F-1	205 Miles	54	James Hunt	Running
7/18/76	British Grand Prix Brands Hatch	3	DNF	John Player Lotus 77 Cosworth #5	Road Course 2.61 miles	F-1	198 Miles	4	Niki Lauda	Engine problems. James Hunt took the checkers but was later disqualified
8/1/76	German Grand Prix Nurburgring	12	12	John Player Lotus 77 Cosworth #5	Road Course 14.2 miles	F-1	199 Miles	14	James Hunt	Running
8/15/76	Austrian Grand Prix Österreichring	9	5	John Player Lotus 77 Cosworth #5	Road Course 3.67 miles	F-1	198 Miles	54	John Watson	Running
8/29/76	Dutch Grand Prix Zandvoort	6	3	John Player Lotus 77 Cosworth #5	Road Course 2.63 miles	F-1	197 Miles	75	James Hunt	Running
9/12/76	Italian Grand Prix, Monza	14	DNF	John Player Lotus 77 Cosworth #5	Road Course 3.6 miles	F-1	187 Miles	23	Ronnie Peterson	Accident
10/3/76	Canadian Grand Prix Mosport Park	5	3	John Player Lotus 77 Cosworth #5	Road Course 2.459 miles	F-1	197 Miles	80	James Hunt	Running
10/10/76	United States Grand Prix East Watkins Glen	11	DNF	John Player Lotus 77 Cosworth #5	Road Course 3.4 miles	F-1	200.6 Miles	23	James Hunt	Suspension
10/24/76	**Japanese Grand Prix Mt. Fuji**	**1**	**1**	**John Player Lotus 77 Cosworth #5**	**Road course 2.7 miles**	**F-1**	**197 Miles**	**73**	**Mario**	**Led 10 laps, first Japanese Grand Prix**
10/31/76	Texas World Speedway	4	4	Penske Norton Spirit McLaren #68	Oval 2 miles	USAC Champ Car	200 Miles	99	Johnny Rutherford	Led 1 lap, running
11/7/76	Phoenix International Raceway	3	3	Penske Norton Spirit McLaren #68	Oval 1 mile	USAC Champ Car	150 Miles	150	Al Unser	Led 1 lap, running

In his Grand Prix career, Mario earned 19 podium (top-three) finishes. His fourth podium came when he finished third in this John Player Lotus 77 at Mosport in 1976. *Ken Coles*

1977

It was not that I was given a break, I out-braked (Jody Scheckter) clean. To me, it was just as satisfying a win. Jody tried to say that the only reason I passed him was because the tire was going down; but if that was the case, he would have had a lot of smoke and a lot of locking up, and there was none of that. So, it was a good, satisfying win. Mario after his victory in the US Grand Prix at Long Beach, FORIX.com

The new Lotus 78 showed great improvement with its innovative ground effects design. The concept was proven conclusively when Mario swept past Scheckter on the outside of the Parabolica at Monza to win the Italian Grand Prix. There were three other Formula One victories, at Long Beach, Spain, and France. Mario finished third in points.

But the disturbing side of the season was that in the remaining 13 events, his Lotus Cosworth DFV suffered six engine failures (including four in a row and two while leading). This prevented him from challenging Niki Lauda and Jody Scheckter for the championship.

Indy ended after only 47 laps as Mario's McLaren suffered a broken header in 1977. *Ken Coles*

Formula One Points 1977

		Points	Wins
1.	Niki Lauda	72	3
2.	Jody Scheckter	55	3
3.	**Mario**	**47**	**4**
4.	Carlos Reutemann	42	1
5.	James Hunt	40	3
6.	Jochen Mass	25	
7.	Alan Jones	22	1
8.	Gunnar Nilsson	20	1
	Patrick Depailler	20	
10.	Jacques Laffite	18	1

USAC National Championship Points 1977

		Points	Wins
1.	Tom Sneva	3965	2
2.	Al Unser	3030	1
3.	A. J. Foyt	2840	3
	Johnny Rutherford	2840	4
5.	Gordon Johncock	2830	2
6.	Wally Dallenbach	2635	1
7.	**Mario**	**1580**	
8.	Pancho Carter	1420	
9.	Tom Bigelow	1370	
10.	Mike Mosley	1030	

Mario Andretti 1977 Record

Date	Event/Track	Qual	Finish	Entrant/Car/Number	Type Track	Sanction & Division	Distance	Laps Compl	Race Winner	Comments
1/9/77	Argentine Grand Prix Buenos Aires	8	5	John Player Lotus 78 #5	Road Course 3.7 miles	F-1	196 Miles	51	Jody Scheckter	Wheel bearing failure while running second
1/23/77	Brazilian Grand Prix, Interlagos	3	DNF	John Player Lotus 78 #5	Road Course 4.94 miles	F-1	197.6 Miles	19	Carlos Reutemann	Ignition
3/5/77	South African Grand Prix, Kyalami	6	DNF	John Player Lotus 78 #5	Road Course 2.55 miles	F-1	199 Miles	43	Niki Lauda	Accident, front suspension damage
3/20/77	Race of Champions Brands Hatch	2	DNF	John Player Lotus 78 #5	Road Course 2.614 miles	BRDC	104.5 Miles		James Hunt	
3/27/77	Phoenix International Raceway	-	-	Penske CAM-2 McLaren #9	Oval 1 mile	USAC Champ Car	150 Miles	0	Johnny Rutherford	Blew engine in practice
4/3/77	**United States Grand Prix West Long Beach**	**2**	**1**	**John Player Lotus 78 #5**	**Road Course 2.02 miles**	**F-1**	**161.6 Miles**	**80**	**Mario**	**Led 4 laps**
4/30/77	Trenton Speedway	2	16	Penske CAM-2 McLaren #9	Oval 1.5 miles	USAC Champ Car	200 Miles	37	Wally Dallenbach	Led 29 laps, engine
5/8/77	**Spanish Grand Prix Jarama**	**1**	**1**	**John Player Lotus 78 #5**	**Road Course 2.115 miles**	**F-1**	**158.6 Miles**	**75**	**Mario**	**Dominating performance – led all 75 laps from the pole**
5/22/77	Monaco Grand Prix Monaco	10	5	John Player Lotus 78 #5	Road Course 2.06 miles	F-1	156.5 Miles	76	Jody Scheckter	Running
5/29/77	Indianapolis 500 Indianapolis Motor Speedway	6	26	Penske CAM-2 McLaren #9	Oval 2.5 miles	USAC Champ Car	500 Miles	47	A. J. Foyt	Broken header
6/5/77	Belgian Grand Prix Zolder	1	DNF	John Player Lotus 78 #5	Road Course 2.65 miles	F-1	185.5 Miles	1	Gunnar Nilsson	Tangled with John Watson in the rain
6/19/77	Swedish Grand Prix, Anderstorp	1	6	John Player Lotus 78 #5	Road Course 2.5 miles	F-1	180 Miles	72	Jacques Laffite	Led 68 laps, fuel metering problem while leading with three laps to go, fastest lap
6/26/77	Pocono 500 Pocono International Raceway	3	2	Penske CAM-2 McLaren #9	Oval 2.5 mile	USAC Champ Car	500 Miles	200	Tom Sneva	Led 30 laps, Penske 1 – 2 finish
7/3/77	**French Grand Prix Dijon-Prenois**	**1**	**1**	**John Player Lotus 78 #5**	**Road Course 2.36 miles**	**F-1**	**189 Miles**	**80**	**Mario**	**Passed John Watson on last lap for victory, led one lap**
7/16/77	British Grand Prix Silverstone	6	14	John Player Lotus 78 #5	Road Course 2.9 miles	F-1	197 Miles	62	James Hunt	Engine failure
7/31/77	German Grand Prix Hockenheim	7	DNF	John Player Lotus 78 #5	Road Course 4.22 miles	F-1	198 Miles	34	Niki Lauda	Engine failure
8/14/77	Austrian Grand Prix Österreichring	3	DNF	John Player Lotus 78 #5	Road Course 3.69 miles	F-1	199 Miles	11	Alan Jones	Led 11 laps, engine failure while leading
8/28/77	Dutch Grand Prix Zandvoort	1	DNF	John Player Lotus 78 #5	Road Course 2.63 miles	F-1	197 Miles	75	Niki Lauda	Engine failure
9/4/77	Ontario Motor Speedway	2	4	Penske CAM-2 McLaren #9	Oval 2.5 miles	USAC Champ Car	500 Miles	197	Al Unser	Led 12 laps, running
9/11/77	**Italian Grand Prix, Monza**	**4**	**1**	**John Player Lotus 78 #5**	**Road Course 3.6 miles**	**F-1**	**187 Miles**	**52**	**Mario**	**Led 43 laps, set fastest lap**
9/17/77	Michigan International Speedway	6	7	Chevrolet Camaro	Oval 2 miles	IROC	50 Laps	50	Al Unser	Running, rain delay after lap 1 wreck
9/17/77	Michigan International Speedway	2	20	Penske CAM-2 McLaren #9	Oval 2 miles	USAC Champ Car	150 Miles	21	Gordon Johncock	Clutch failure
10/2/77	United States Grand Prix East Watkins Glen	4	2	John Player Lotus 78 #5	Road Course 3.4 miles	F-1	200.6 Miles	59	James Hunt	Running
10/9/77	Canadian Grand Prix Mosport Park	1	9	John Player Lotus 78 #5	Road Course 2.459 miles	F-1	197 Miles	80	Jody Scheckter	Led 76 laps, engine failure while leading
10/23/77	Japanese Grand Prix Mt. Fuji	1	DNF	John Player Lotus 78 #5	Road course 2.7 miles	F-1	197 Miles	1	James Hunt	Accident with Laffite
10/15/77	Riverside International Raceway	4	4	Chevrolet Camaro	Road Course 2.54 miles	IROC	30 Laps	30	Al Unser	Running
10/16/77	Riverside International Raceway	9	2	Chevrolet Camaro	Road Course 2.54 miles	IROC	30 Laps	30	Cale Yarborough	Running
10/29/77	Phoenix International Raceway	5	4	Penske CAM-2 McLaren #9	Oval 1 mile	USAC Champ Car	150 Miles	149	Gordon Johncock	Running

For five years (1976 – 1980) there were two U.S. races on the Grand Prix calendar. While the United States Grand Prix West (Long Beach) was held in the spring, the Watkins Glen race was always in early October. In 1977, Mario finished second to James Hunt in a race that started in the wet at Watkins Glen. *Ken Coles*

Mario talks with a Lotus crewman while teammate Gunnar Nilsson looks on. Nilsson, a Swede who lost a battle with cancer in 1978, scored his only Grand Prix win at Belgium and finished eighth in points. *Howard Koby*

Mario led the first 12 laps and finished fourth in Roger Penske's CAM-2 McLaren in the 1977 Ontario 500. *Howard Koby*

Ronnie Peterson was nearly a match for Mario in the Lotus 79. He had nine top-five finishes including two victories, and finished second to Mario in 1978 points. *Howard Koby*

While Mario was racing in the Belgian Grand Prix, Mike Hiss qualified the Gould Charge Penske. Mario had to start at the rear of the field and was 15 laps behind, and in 12th at the finish. *Ken Coles*

1978

The concept was refined further. Chapman put all of the fuel in a central tank behind the driver, which enabled him to narrow the chassis and incorporate uncompromised venturis. He also added skirts that slid up and down over surface irregularities to enhance the ground-effect seal. All of these developments to the 78 gave the 79 a vast performance edge over its rivals.... The Concise Encyclopedia of Formula One

In 1978, Mario achieved a lifelong dream when he won the Formula One World Championship. His road had been different from many others, focused on the purely American mix of ovals, road courses, and dirt tracks, rather than a progression of increasingly powerful formula cars. Perhaps this background gave him an edge as he helped develop the new Lotus 79 that took greater advantage of ground effects than any previous chassis.

Mario earned eight pole positions, and among his six victories, he and teammate Ronnie Peterson scored 1-2 finishes in Belgium, Spain, France, and the Netherlands. Following the French Grand Prix, Mario admitted that there were team orders and, given his commanding lead in the points, Peterson was to let him past if necessary to win. He contends that these orders didn't come into play in any of the races.

When Mario led all 75 laps to win the Dutch event, everyone had been eliminated from championship contention except his teammate. Then a vicious wreck on the first lap at Monza put Peterson in the hospital with severe leg injuries. When another bad accident just before the restart caused yet another delay, the race was shortened to 40 laps. Mario led the final 6 laps and took the checkers, but he and Gilles Villeneuve were penalized one minute for jumping the restart. Even though he was relegated to sixth, Mario was the Formula One champion. Tragically, Peterson died the next morning as the result of complications from leg surgery.

Despite problems in the final two races, Andretti and Peterson had earned enough points to finish the season first and second in points. This gave Colin Chapman and Lotus their final driver and constructor championship honors.

Mario competed in seven national championship races, again for Roger Penske. His last victory in USAC competition came in September, at Trenton.

On his way to a second-place finish, Mario leads Jacques Laffite during the 1978 Long Beach Grand Prix. Laffite finished fourth in his Ligier. *Howard Koby*

Championship Summary

		Rank
Races	16	
Victories	**6**	**1**
Pole Positions	**8**	**1**
Fastest Laps	3	2 (tie)
Podiums	**7**	**1 (tie)**
Front Row	**12**	**1**
Laps Completed	870	3
Miles Completed	2433.3	3
Races Led	**11**	**1**
Laps Led	**451**	**1**
Miles Led	**1326**	**1**

Formula One Points 1978

		Points	Wins
1.	**Mario**	**64**	**6**
2.	Ronnie Peterson	51	2
3.	Carlos Reutemann	48	4
4.	Niki Lauda	44	2
5.	Patrick Depailler	34	1
6.	John Watson	25	
7.	Jody Scheckter	24	
8.	Jacques Laffite	19	
9.	Gilles Villeneuve	17	1
	Emerson Fittipaldi	17	

Mario Andretti 1978 Record

Date	Event/Track	Qual	Finish	Entrant/Car/Number	Type Track	Sanction & Division	Distance	Laps Compl	Race Winner	Comments
1/15/78	Argentine Grand Prix Buenos Aires	1	1	John Player Lotus 78 #5	Road Course 3.7 miles	F-1	193 Miles	52	Mario	Led every lap from the pole
1/29/78	Brazilian Grand Prix Jacarepagua	3	4	John Player Lotus 78 #5	Road Course 3.12 miles	F-1	196.5 Miles	63	Carlos Reutemann	Running, jammed in fourth gear for last 6 laps
2/17/78	Daytona International Speedway	5	1	Chevrolet Camaro	Oval 2.5 miles	IROC	100 Miles	40	Mario	Final race of 1978 IROC series
3/4/78	South African Grand Prix, Kyalami	2	7	John Player Lotus 78 #5	Road Course 2.55 miles	F-1	199 Miles	77	Ronnie Peterson	Led 20 laps, had fastest race lap, lost 1 lap because of a late race fuel stop
3/19/78	International Trophy Silverstone	3	DNF	John Player Lotus 78 Cosworth	Road Course 2.93 miles	BRDC	117 Miles	2	Keke Rosberg	Accident
3/26/78	Ontario Motor Speedway	2	15	Penske Gould Charge Penske #7	Oval 2.5 miles	USAC Champ Car	200 Miles	35	Danny Ongais	Led 18 laps, engine
4/2/78	United States Grand Prix West Long Beach	4	2	John Player Lotus 78 #5	Road Course 2.02 miles	F-1	161.6 Miles	80	Carlos Reutemann	Running
4/15/78	Texas World Speedway	2	5	Penske Gould Charge Penske #7	Oval 2 miles	USAC Champ Car	200 Miles	98	Danny Ongais	Led 23 laps, running
4/23/78	Trenton Speedway	3	13	Penske Gould Charge Penske #7	Oval 1.5 miles	USAC Champ Car	200 Miles	92	Gordon Johncock	Engine
5/7/78	Monaco Grand Prix Monaco	4	11	John Player Lotus 78 #5	Road Course 2.06 miles	F-1	154.5 Miles	69	Patrick Depailler	Fixed fuel leak, running, 6 laps behind
5/21/78	Belgian Grand Prix Zolder	1	1	John Player Lotus 79 Cosworth #5	Road Course 2.65 miles	F-1	185.5 Miles	70	Mario	Led all 70 laps, first race for new Lotus 79
5/28/78	Indianapolis 500 Indianapolis Motor Speedway	33	12	Penske Gould Charge Penske #7	Oval 2.5 miles	USAC Champ Car	500 Miles	185	Al Unser	Qualified 8th by Mike Hiss, running
6/4/78	Spanish Grand Prix Jarama	1	1	John Player Lotus 79 Cosworth #5	Road Course 2.115 miles	F-1	158.6 Miles	75	Mario	Led 70 laps, fastest lap
6/17/78	Swedish Grand Prix, Anderstorp	1	DNF	John Player Lotus 79 Cosworth #5	Road Course 2.5 miles	F-1	175 Miles	46	Niki Lauda	Led 38 laps, engine failure
6/25/78	Pocono 500 Pocono International Raceway	6	23	Penske Gould Charge Penske #7	Oval 2.5 miles	USAC Champ Car	500 Miles	73	Al Unser	Led 1 lap, gearbox
7/2/78	French Grand Prix Paul Ricard	2	1	John Player Lotus 79 Cosworth #5	Road Course 3.61 miles	F-1	195 Miles	54	Mario	Passed John Watson on first lap, led all 54 laps
7/16/78	British Grand Prix Brands Hatch	2	DNF	John Player Lotus 79 #5	Road Course 2.6 miles	F-1	197 Miles	28	Carlos Reutemann	Led 23 laps, flat tire, engine failure
7/30/78	German Grand Prix Hockenheim-Ring	1	1	John Player Lotus 79 #5	Road Course 4.22 miles	F-1	190 Miles	45	Mario	Led 41 laps
8/13/78	Austrian Grand Prix Österreichring	2	DNF	John Player Lotus 79 #5	Road Course 3.69 miles	F-1	199 Miles	0	Ronnie Peterson	Accident with Reutemann on first lap
8/27/78	Dutch Grand Prix Zandvoort	1	1	John Player Lotus 79 #5	Road Course 2.63 miles	F-1	197 Miles	75	Mario	Led all 75 laps from pole
9/10/78	Italian Grand Prix, Monza	1	6	John Player Lotus 79 #5	Road Course 3.6 miles	F-1	144 Miles	40	Niki Lauda	Led last 6 laps, penalized 1 minute for jumping restart
9/16/78	Michigan International Speedway	4	20	Penske Gould Charge Penske #7	Oval 2.5 miles	USAC Champ Car	500 Miles	0	Danny Ongais	Engine problem
9/23/78	Trenton Speedway	3	1	Penske Gould Charge Penske #7	Oval 1.5 miles	USAC Champ Car	150 Miles	100	Mario	Led 33 laps
10/1/78	United States Grand Prix East Watkins Glen	1	DNF	John Player Lotus 79 #5	Road Course 3.4 miles	F-1	200.6 Miles	59	Carlos Reutemann	Led 2 laps, engine failure
10/8/78	Canadian Grand Prix Montreal	9	10	John Player Lotus 79 #5	Road Course 2.8 miles	F-1	196 Miles	69	Gilles Villeneuve	Spun on lap 6, running
10/14/78	Riverside International Raceway	6	3	Chevrolet Camaro	Road Course 2.54 miles	IROC	30 Laps	30	Peter Gregg	Road racing qualifying events of 1979 IROC
10/15/78	Riverside International Raceway	7	1	Chevrolet Camaro	Road Course 2.54 miles	IROC	30 Laps	30	Mario	Road racing qualifying events of 1979 IROC
10/28/78	Phoenix International Raceway	5	7	Penske Gould Charge Penske #7	Oval 1 mile	USAC Champ Car	150 Miles	148	Johnny Rutherford	Running

1979

Chapman failed to keep pace with the imitators his design had spawned, and Andretti was not given competitive equipment in his remaining two seasons with Lotus. *The Concise Encyclopedia of Formula One*

As fulfilling as the 1978 season had been, 1979 was its equal in frustration. The season was marked by nine DNFs. While Colin Chapman had made the initial breakthroughs in the implementation of ground effect and downforce, other teams, notably Ligier and Williams, took the technology to the next level and the Lotus was left behind. And even though Mario's best Grand Prix finish, third at Spain, was in the newly designed Lotus 80, the machine was only raced again at Monaco and France before it was abandoned.

In the first of the two oval races he competed that in season, Mario finished second in the concluding IROC event of the 1979 series at Atlanta in March. With a victory and second places in the two races at Riverside at the end of 1978, Mario won the $75,000 IROC championship. This was the only time Mario would win the IROC title in six attempts. In October, he began the 1980 IROC with a victory in one of the two road racing qualification races at Riverside.

Many of the national championship car owners had started a new series they named Championship Auto Racing Teams (CART),

breaking off from USAC's leadership. They showed up to compete at Indianapolis, which was still the biggest race of the year, but otherwise fielded their own schedule. The Monte Carlo Grand Prix conflicted with Indianapolis and for the first time since 1965, Mario wasn't in Indianapolis for the Memorial Day event. In September, Mario finished third at Ontario, trailing Penske teammates Bobby Unser and Rick Mears. But two weeks later, a practice crash at Michigan kept him from taking the green flag in that 150-mile event.

Formula One Points 1979

		Points	Wins
1.	Jody Scheckter	51	3
2.	Gilles Villeneuve	47	3
3.	Alan Jones	40	4
4.	Jacques Laffite	36	2
5.	Clay Regazzoni	29	1
6.	Patrick Depailler	20	1
	Carlos Reutemann	20	
8.	Rene Arnoux	17	
9.	John Watson	15	
10.	**Mario**	**14**	
	Jean Pierre Jarier	14	
	Didier Pironi	14	

Watkins Glen was the final race of the disastrous 1979 Formula One season. Mario qualified 17th in the Lotus 79 and retired with gearbox failure after only 16 laps, his eighth retirement in the last 10 events. *Ken Coles*

Mario Andretti 1979 Record

Date	Event/Track	Qual	Finish	Entrant/Car/Number	Type Track	Sanction & Division	Distance	Laps Compl	Race Winner	Comments
1/21/79	Argentine Grand Prix Buenos Aires	7	5	Martini Racing Team Essex Lotus 79 Cosworth #1	Road Course 3.7 miles	F-1	196 Miles	52	Jacques Laffite	Running
2/4/79	Brazilian Grand Prix Interlagos	4	DNF	Martini Racing Team Essex Lotus 79 Cosworth #1	Road Course 4.89 miles	F-1	195.6 Miles	2	Jacques Laffite	Fuel leak, fire
3/3/79	South African Grand Prix, Kyalami	8	4	Martini Racing Team Essex Lotus 79 Cosworth #1	Road Course 2.55 miles	F-1	199 Miles	78	Gilles Villeneuve	Running
3/6/79	Donington Park	-	12	BMW M1	Road Course 1.96 miles	Special event	59 Miles	30	Nelson Piquet	Running, Gunnar Nilsson Memorial Trophy Race
3/17/79	Atlanta Motor Speedway	1	2	Chevrolet Camaro	Oval 1.522 miles	IROC	100 Miles	66	Neil Bonnett	Won 1979 IROC series
4/8/79	United States Grand Prix West Long Beach	6	4	Martini Racing Team Essex Lotus 79 Cosworth #1	Road Course 2.02 miles	F-1	161.6 Miles	80	Gilles Villeneuve	Running
4/15/79	Race of Champions Brands Hatch	1	3	Martini Racing Team Essex Lotus 79 Cosworth #1	Road Course 2.61 miles	BRDC	104 Miles	40	Gilles Villeneuve	Running, non-points race
4/29/79	Spanish Grand Prix Jarama	4	3	Martini Racing Team Essex Lotus 80 Cosworth #1	Road Course 2.115 miles	F-1	158.6 Miles	75	Patrick Depailler	Running
5/12/79	Zolder	-	9	BMW M1#1	Road Course 2.65 miles	Procar BMW	53 Miles	15	Elio de Angelis	Running
5/13/79	Belgian Grand Prix Zolder	5	DNF	Martini Racing Team Essex Lotus 79 Cosworth #1	Road Course 2.65 miles	F-1	185.5 Miles	27	Jody Scheckter	Brakes
5/27/79	Monaco Grand Prix Monaco	13	DNF	Martini Racing Team Essex Lotus 80 Cosworth #1	Road Course 2.06 miles	F-1	156.6 Miles	21	Jody Scheckter	Rear suspension
7/1/79	French Grand Prix Dijon-Prenois	12	DNF	Martini Racing Team Essex Lotus 80 Cosworth #1	Road Course 2.36 miles	F-1	189 Miles	51	Jean-Pierre Jabouille	Brakes, suspension
7/14/79	British Grand Prix Silverstone	9	DNF	Martini Racing Team Essex Lotus 79 Cosworth #1	Road Course 2.9 miles	F-1	197 Miles	3	Clay Regazzoni	Wheel bearing failure
7/29/79	German Grand Prix Hockenheim	11	DNF	Martini Racing Team Essex Lotus 79 Cosworth #1	Road Course 4.22 miles	F-1	190 Miles	16	Alan Jones	Transmission
8/12/79	Austrian Grand Prix Österreichring	15	DNF	Martini Racing Team Essex Lotus 79 Cosworth #1	Road Course 3.69 miles	F-1	199 Miles	0	Alan Jones	Clutch
8/26/79	Dutch Grand Prix Zandvoort	17	DNF	Martini Racing Team Essex Lotus 79 Cosworth #1	Road Course 2.64 miles	F-1	198 Miles	9	Alan Jones	Rear suspension
9/2/79	California 500 Ontario Motor Speedway	4	3	Penske Gould Charge PC6/78 #99	Oval 2.5 miles	CART/SCCA	500 Miles	200	Bobby Unser	Running
9/9/79	Monza	-	DNF	BMW M1	Road Course 3.6 miles	Procar BMW	64.8 Miles		Hans-Joachim Stuck	Engine
9/9/79	Italian Grand Prix, Monza	10	5	Martini Racing Team Essex Lotus 79 Cosworth #1	Road Course 3.6 miles	F-1	180 Miles	50	Jody Scheckter	Running
9/15/79	Michigan International Speedway	0	0	Penske Gould Charge PC6/78 #99	Oval 2 miles	CART/SCCA	150 Miles	0	Bobby Unser	Wrecked in practice
9/30/79	Canadian Grand Prix Montreal	10	10	Martini Racing Team Essex Lotus 79 Cosworth #1	Road Course 2.74 miles	F-1	197 Miles	66	Alan Jones	Ran out of fuel
10/17/79	United States Grand Prix East Watkins Glen	17	DNF	Martini Racing Team Essex Lotus 79 Cosworth #1	Road Course 3.4 miles	F-1	200.6 Miles	16	Gilles Villeneuve	Gearbox
10/27/79	Riverside International Raceway	1	1	Chevrolet Camaro	Road Course 2.54 miles	IROC	30 Laps	30	Mario	Road racing qualifying events of 1980 IROC
10/28/79	Riverside International Raceway	3	3	Chevrolet Camaro	Road Course 2.54 miles	IROC	30 Laps	30	Darrell Waltrip	Road racing qualifying events of 1979 IROC

The 1980s

Mario had achieved a lifelong dream when he won the Formula One championship. But the tumble from the pinnacle of Formula One to "also ran" can take but a matter of months. Coming into the 1980s the Lotus team was out-gunned in the rapid implementation of new engine and chassis technology. It was Mario's third decade in racing, and by 1980 his interest in Formula One was beginning to wane. The number of really competitive rides on the Grand Prix circuit was more limited than ever before. Plus, modern car designs had greatly reduced the driver's skill in the man-machine equation.

Mario was at the peak of his abilities and had a storehouse of experience that most racing drivers only dream of attaining. The still-developing CART organization appeared to be taking the national championship series in new directions that offered Mario fresh challenges. The machinery was evolving quickly, but the window of opportunity was open wider than in Formula One and more teams and cars were capable of winning any race. The fields still included the usual suspects: Foyt, Rutherford, Johncock, Mears, and the Unser brothers. But exciting new drivers including Tom Sneva, Bobby Rahal, and Danny Sullivan, were emerging.

Mario was still under contract with Lotus, but as 1980 began, could he guess that within three years he would be out of Formula One and back with a new team as a regular on the national circuit? And would he envision that among the challenges he would soon face was to look across the grid and into the eyes of his son, Michael?

In 1980, Mario had his best F-1 finish (sixth) and scored his only point in the Lotus 81 at Watkins Glen. It was his last appearance in a Lotus. *Ken Coles*

Mario is on his way to victory in the 150-mile Gould Grand Prix at Michigan. Mario outran teammates Bobby Unser and Rick Mears, and Rutherford's "Yellow Submarine." It was his first of many CART wins. *Ken Coles*

Mario, Michael, and John Andretti drove this Porsche 962 for more than 3,100 miles to finish sixth at LeMans in 1988. *Aysedasi*

Starting in the middle of the front row at Indianapolis in 1980, Mario raced with the leaders until the Essex Penske rolled to a stop on the track with an engine problem short of the halfway mark. *Ken Coles*

1980

The competitor in Formula One is faceless. In the event of an accident or something, I am very cold about those things and I couldn't care less. It's just another one out of the way. Awful, awful way to think, but I just don't have that feeling for them…they're too distant. Here at home, I can get to know the guys more intimately to a degree that I'm not sure which one I like best at different times. *Mario, Speed! Indy Car Racing, Chet Jezierski*

Mario with the spoils of victory after the Gould Grand Prix at Michigan.
Ken Coles

Lotus' newest effort, the 81, had only two flaws. It wasn't particularly fast and it was too fragile. Only once did Mario qualify better than ninth the whole season. The transmission and engine counted for six of the eight DNFs. At the end of the day, Mario was running at the checkered flag in only five Grand Prix. His lone point was collected in the final event of the season, at Watkins Glen.

Mario thought he had his best chance to win Indy in years. He battled with eventual winner Johnny Rutherford, and teammates Bobby Unser and Rick Mears, before being sidelined with an engine problem. Running three additional events, Mario found his first victory under the CART banner, the 150-mile race at Michigan, particularly satisfying. It was his first win in the champ cars in two years. He led 53 of the 75 laps.

Formula One Points 1980

		Points	Wins
1.	Alan Jones	67	5
2.	Nelson Piquet	54	3
3.	Carlos Reutemann	42	1
4.	Jacques Laffite	34	1
5.	Didier Pironi	32	1
6.	Rene Arnoux	29	2
7.	Elio de Angelis	13	
8.	Jean Pierre Jabouille	9	1
9.	Ricardo Patrese	7	
10.	Keke Rosberg	6	
	Derek Daly	6	
	John Watson	6	
	Jean Pierre Jarier	6	
	Gilles Villeneuve	6	
20.	**Mario**	**1**	
	Hector Rebaque	1	

Mario Andretti 1980 Record

Date	Event/Track	Qual	Finish	Entrant/Car/Number	Type Track	Sanction & Division	Distance	Laps Compl	Race Winner	Comments
1/13/80	Argentine Grand Prix Buenos Aires	6	DNF	Team Essex Lotus 81 Cosworth #11	Road Course 3.7 miles	F-1	196 Miles	20	Alan Jones	Fuel system metering
1/27/80	Brazilian Grand Prix Interlagos	11	DNF	Team Essex Lotus 81 Cosworth #11	Road Course 4.89 miles	F-1	195.6 Miles	1	Rene Arnoux	Spin
3/1/80	South African Grand Prix, Kyalami	15	12	Team Essex Lotus 81 Cosworth #11	Road Course 2.55 miles	F-1	199 Miles	76	Rene Arnoux	Running
3/15/80	Atlanta Motor Speedway	3	8	Chevrolet Camaro	Oval 1.522 miles	IROC	100 Miles	2	Bobby Allison	Lap 2 accident, fifth in final 1980 IROC points
4/30/80	United States Grand Prix West Long Beach	15	DNF	Team Essex Lotus 81 Cosworth #11	Road Course 2.02 miles	F-1	161.6 Miles	0	Nelson Piquet	Accident with Jarier
5/4/80	Belgian Grand Prix Zolder	17	DNF	Team Essex Lotus 81 Cosworth #11	Road Course 2.65 miles	F-1	191 Miles	41	Didier Pironi	Gear linkage
5/18/80	Monaco Grand Prix Monaco	19	7	Team Essex Lotus 81 Cosworth #11	Road Course 2.06 miles	F-1	156.6 Miles	73	Carlos Reutemann	Running
5/25/80	Indianapolis 500 Indianapolis Motor Speedway	2	20	Penske Essex PC9/80 #12	Oval 2.5 miles	USAC	500 Miles	70	Johnny Rutherford	Engine seized
6/1/80	Spanish Grand Prix Jarama	8	DNF	Team Essex Lotus 81 Cosworth #11	Road Course 2.115 miles	F-1	169 Miles	28	Alan Jones	Engine failure, ruled to be a nonpoint race
6/22/80	Pocono 500 Pocono International Raceway	3	17	Penske Essex PC9/80 #12	Oval 2.5 miles	CART	500 Miles	105	Bobby Unser	Led 4 laps, transmission failure
6/29/80	French Grand Prix Paul Ricard	12	DNF	Team Essex Lotus 81 Cosworth #11	Road Course 3.61 miles	F-1	195 Miles	18	Alan Jones	Gearbox failed
7/13/80	British Grand Prix Brands Hatch	9	DNF	Team Essex Lotus 81 Cosworth #11	Road Course 2.9 miles	F-1	220 Miles	57	Alan Jones	Gearbox failed
7/20/80	Road America	3	25	Haas Lola T530	Road Course 4 miles	CanAm	160 Miles	18	Al Holbert	Broken throttle spring
8/10/80	German Grand Prix Hockenheim	9	7	Team Essex Lotus 81 Cosworth #11	Road Course 4.22 miles	F-1	190 Miles	45	Jacques Laffite	Running
8/17/80	Austrian Grand Prix Österreichring	17	DNF	Team Essex Lotus 81 Cosworth #11	Road Course 3.69 miles	F-1	199 Miles	6	Jean-Pierre Jabouille	Engine failure
8/31/80	Zandvoort	-	DNF	BMW M1	Road Course 2.64 miles	Procar BMW	53 Miles		Nelson Piquet	
8/31/80	Dutch Grand Prix Zandvoort	10	8	Team Essex Lotus 81 Cosworth #11	Road Course 2.64 miles	F-1	190 Miles	70	Nelson Piquet	Ran out of fuel
9/14/80	Italian Grand Prix, Imola	10	DNF	Team Essex Lotus 81 Cosworth #11	Road Course 3.1 miles	F-1	186 Miles	40	Nelson Piquet	Engine failure
9/20/80	**Michigan International Speedway**	**1**	**1**	**Penske AB Dick Pacemaker PC9/80 #12**	**Oval 2 miles**	**CART**	**150 Miles**	**75**	**Mario**	**Led 53 laps**
9/28/80	Canadian Grand Prix Montreal	18	DNF	Team Essex Lotus 81 Cosworth #11	Road Course 2.74 miles	F-1	192 Miles	11	Alan Jones	Involved in multicar accident on start, restarted backup car, engine failure
10/5/80	United States Grand Prix East Watkins Glen	11	6	Team Essex Lotus 81 Cosworth #11	Road Course 3.4 miles	F-1	200.6 Miles	58	Alan Jones	Running, only point scored during season
11/8/80	Phoenix international Raceway	1	2	Penske AB Dick Pacemaker PC9/80 #12	Oval 1 mile	CART	150 Miles	150	Tom Sneva	Led 1 lap, running

1981

The part that actually bothered me was the fact that after all the motions of appeals and everything else, they assembled a panel outside the jurisdiction of USAC and they decided the penalty was too severe. So they fined Bobby, they said yes he did pass, but they fined him $40,000, which is kind of a ridiculous thing. *Mario, Gamenight, ESPN*

Coming all the way from 16th, Mario finished 7th in the Marlboro Alfa Romeo at Montreal. *Ken Coles*

After being courted by McLaren, Mario signed with Alfa Romeo for the 1981 Grand Prix season. When he finished fourth in the opening race at Long Beach, he didn't realize that it was to be his best result of the year. The team was hampered with failures in the Alfa's 3.0 V-12 engine. With the results of both Mario and teammate Bruno Giacomelli combined, Alfa finished tied for eighth in constructors' points.

Mario joined Pat Patrick's CART team for the races that did not conflict with his Formula One commitments. This combination appeared to hit paydirt quickly. At Indianapolis Wally Dallenbach qualified Mario's Wildcat and Mario had to start in the last row. But running at a steady pace without incidents, Mario worked his way to the front. Coming out of the pits under a late race caution behind leader Bobby Unser, Mario saw Unser pass nine cars before pulling into line. Taking the checkers behind Unser, Mario was surprised the next morning to learn that Chief Steward Tom Binford had penalized Unser a lap for the illegal passes. While Mario spent the next several days enjoying the victors' spoils, Unser and Penske filed a formal protest. After hearings, a USAC board reinstated Unser as the race winner, but imposed a $40,000 fine. Mario had a string of top-four finishes that included Milwaukee, Atlanta, Michigan and Phoenix.

Formula One Points 1981

		Points	Wins
1.	Nelson Piquet	50	3
2.	Carlos Reutemann	49	2
3.	Alan Jones	46	2
4.	Jacques Laffite	44	2
5.	Alain Prost	43	3
6.	John Watson	27	1
7.	Gilles Villeneuve	25	2
8.	Elio de Angelis	14	
9.	Rene Arnoux	11	
	Hector Rebaque	11	
17.	**Mario**	**3**	

Mario passes teammate Gordon Johncock at Indy. He was named the winner in an overnight ruling when Bobby Unser was penalized for passing cars while coming out of the pits. *John Mahoney*

Mario Andretti 1981 Record

Date	Event/Track	Qual	Finish	Entrant/Car/Number	Type Track	Sanction & Division	Distance	Laps Compl	Race Winner	Comments
3/15/81	United States Grand Prix West Long Beach	6	4	Marlboro Team Alfa Romeo 179C #22	Road Course 2.02 miles	F-1	161.6 Miles	80	Alan Jones	Running
3/22/81	Phoenix International Raceway	4	11	Patrick Petroleum Wildcat #40	Oval 1 mile	CART	150 Miles	139	Johnny Rutherford	Led 30 laps, fuel pump failure
3/29/81	Brazilian Grand Prix Interlagos	9	DNF	Marlboro Team Alfa Romeo 179C #22	Road Course 3.12 miles	F-1	193.4 Miles	0	Carlos Reutemann	Involved in first lap wreck
4/12/81	Argentine Grand Prix Buenos Aires	17	8	Marlboro Team Alfa Romeo 179C #22	Road Course 3.7 miles	F-1	196 Miles	52	Nelson Piquet	Running
5/3/81	San Marino Grand Prix, Imola	12	DNF	Marlboro Team Alfa Romeo 179C #22	Road Course 3.1 miles	F-1	186 Miles	26	Nelson Piquet	Gearbox
5/17/81	Belgian Grand Prix Zolder	18	10	Marlboro Team Alfa Romeo 179C #22	Road Course 2.65 miles	F-1	143 Miles	53	Carlos Reutemann	Running
5/24/81	Indianapolis 500 Indianapolis Motor Speedway	32	2	STP Oil Treatment Wildcat #40	Oval 2.5 miles	USAC	500 Miles	200	Bobby Unser	Mario ruled winner when Unser was penalized 1 lap, decision reversed by appeal panel
5/31/81	Monaco Grand Prix Monaco	12	DNF	Marlboro Team Alfa Romeo 179C #22	Road Course 2.06 miles	F-1	156.6 Miles	0	Gilles Villeneuve	Accident at start with Elio de Angelis
6/7/81	Wisconsin State Fair Park	6	3	STP Oil Treatment Wildcat #40	Oval 1 mile	CART	150 Miles	148	Mike Mosley	Led 6 laps, running
6/21/81	Spanish Grand Prix Jarama	8	8	Marlboro Team Alfa Romeo 179C #22	Road Course 2.06 miles	F-1	165 Miles	80	Gilles Villeneuve	Running
6/28/81	Atlanta Motor Speedway	3	3	STP Oil Treatment Wildcat #40	Oval 1.522 miles	CART	126.3 Miles	83	Rick Mears	First race of twin 125's, running
6/28/81	Atlanta Motor Speedway	3	2	STP Oil Treatment Wildcat #40	Oval 1.522 miles	CART	126.3 Miles	83	Rick Mears	Second race of twin 125's, running
7/5/81	French Grand Prix Dijon-Prenois	10	8	Marlboro Team Alfa Romeo 179C #22	Road Course 2.36 miles	F-1	189 Miles	79	Alain Prost	Running
7/18/81	British Grand Prix Silverstone	11	DNF	Marlboro Team Alfa Romeo 179C #22	Road Course 2.9 miles	F-1	197 Miles	59	John Watson	Throttle cable broke
8/2/81	German Grand Prix Hockenheim	12	9	Marlboro Team Alfa Romeo 179C #22	Road Course 4.22 miles	F-1	190 Miles	44	Nelson Piquet	Running
8/16/81	Austrian Grand Prix Österreichring	13	DNF	Marlboro Team Alfa Romeo 179C #22	Road Course 3.69 miles	F-1	196 Miles	46	Jacques Laffite	Running
8/30/81	Dutch Grand Prix Zandvoort	7	DNF	Marlboro Team Alfa Romeo 179C #22	Road Course 2.64 miles	F-1	190 Miles	62	Alain Prost	Blown tire, accident
9/13/81	Italian Grand Prix, Monza	13	DNF	Marlboro Team Alfa Romeo 179C #22	Road Course 3.6 miles	F-1	187 Miles	41	Alain Prost	Engine failure
9/20/81	Michigan International Speedway	3	2	STP Oil Treatment Wildcat #40	Oval 2 miles	CART	148 Miles	74	Rick Mears	Led 24 laps, running
9/27/81	Canadian Grand Prix Montreal	16	7	Marlboro Team Alfa Romeo 179C #22	Road Course 2.74 miles	F-1	172.6 Miles	62	Jacques Laffite	Running
10/4/81	Watkins Glen	1	16	STP Oil Treatment Wildcat #40	Road Course 3.37 miles	CART	202.6 Miles	25	Rick Mears	Led 23 laps, gearbox failure
10/17/81	USA Las Vegas Grand Prix Las Vegas	10	DNF	Marlboro Team Alfa Romeo 179C #22	Road Course 2.27 miles	F-1	170 Miles	29	Alan Jones	Suspension failure
10/31/81	Phoenix International Raceway	4	4	STP Oil Treatment Wildcat #40	Oval 1 mile	CART	150 Miles	150	Tom Sneva	Led 4 laps, running

After taking the lead with nine laps to go, Mario lost out to Rick Mears on the last circuit of the Detroit News Grand Prix at Michigan. *Ken Coles*

Overall, he had a hell of a career and he got out of racing with all of his bones in one piece. And for a guy that ran as many races in as many different formulas as he did over the years, he's a miracle man for sure. Not many people would have survived in either champ cars or Formula One. In stock cars he was able to survive, sprint cars, he ran all of the different series that were probably the most dangerous to run in motorsports and he was able to survive. Jim McGee

After three frustrating seasons in Formula One, Mario decided it was time to leave the series, but opportunities were offered to drive in three events. Carlos Reutemann retired from racing after the second race and Williams asked Mario to drive as a teammate to Keke Rosberg at Long Beach. Fighting the stiff suspension, Mario bounced off a wall when the suspension failed. Then in September, Ferrari asked him to replace the injured Didier Pironi in the Italian Grand Prix at Monza. When Mario put the Ferrari on the pole, the Italian fans went wild. But a sticking throttle and balky turbocharger slowed him during the race and he finished third. In his final Grand Prix at Las Vegas, the suspension failed on the Ferrari after 26 laps.

Mario stayed with Patrick's team, sponsored by STP, to compete the full CART schedule. Patrick's Wildcats were maintained by his old friend Jim McGee, and Mario only qualified outside the top five once all season. He earned a strong second in the opening race at Phoenix, the first of four runner-up finishes.

The others came at Cleveland's new Burke Lakefront Airport track, in the Michigan 500, and again when the series returned to Michigan for the 150-miler in September. He finished third in points, behind Rick Mears and Bobby Rahal.

Attacking Indy with renewed energy, Mario had the luxury of being able to devote his time to preparing for the race instead of intercontinental travel. But he was eliminated before the race began. In a freak accident, front row starter Kevin Cogan lost control as the field came off turn four, swerved into A. J. Foyt, then skidded into the side of Mario's fourth place car, pinning him against the wall.

In June, Mario was presented an opportunity to race at Le Mans, with son Michael as codriver, in a Mirage M12 entered by Grand Touring Cars. But a questionable last-second ruling by officials, literally as the cars were on the grid waiting to start, disallowed the car in a squabble involving the oil cooler.

At Indy, Mario's Lola was taken out when Kevin Cogan lost control as the field came down the front straight for the start. He was scored 31st. *Ken Coles*

CART Points 1982

		Points	Wins
1.	Rick Mears	294	4
2.	Bobby Rahal	242	2
3.	**Mario**	**188**	
4.	Gordon Johncock	186	3
5.	Tom Sneva	144	2
6.	Kevin Cogan	136	
7.	Al Unser	125	
8.	Geoff Brabham	110	
9.	Roger Mears	103	
10.	Tony Bettenhausen	80	

Mario Andretti 1982 Record

Date	Event/Track	Qual	Finish	Entrant/Car/Number	Type Track	Sanction & Division	Distance	Laps Compl	Race Winner	Comments
3/28/82	Phoenix International Raceway	5	2	STP Oil Treatment Wildcat 8B #40	Oval 1 mile	CART	150 Miles	150	Rick Mears	Led 8 laps, running
4/4/82	United States Grand Prix West Long Beach	14	DNF	TAG Saudia Williams FW07D #5	Road Course 2.13 miles	F-1	160 Miles	19	Niki Lauda	Accident
5/1/82	Atlanta Motor Speedway	2	11	STP Oil Treatment Wildcat 8B #40	Oval 1.522 miles	CART	201 Miles	88	Rick Mears	Led 9 miles, engine failure
5/29/82	Indianapolis 500 Indianapolis Motor Speedway	4	31	STP Intermedics Wildcat 8B #40	Oval 2.5 miles	USAC	500 Miles	0	Gordon Johncock	Wreck at start
6/13/82	Wisconsin State Fair Park	3	9	STP Intermedics Wildcat 8B #40	Oval 1 mile	CART	150 Miles	143	Gordon Johncock	Brakes
6/19/82	24 Hours of Le Mans	9	DQ	Mirage M12 Ford Cosworth DFL #27	Road course 8.47 miles	ACO WSCC	24 Hours	0	Jacky Ickx/Derek Bell	Co-driver Michael Andretti Disqualified before start, oil cooler
7/4/82	Burke Lakefront Airport	3	2	STP Intermedics Wildcat 8B #40	Road course 2.48 miles	CART	310 Miles	125	Bobby Rahal	Led 9 laps, running
7/18/82	Michigan 500 Michigan International Speedway	3	2	STP Intermedics Wildcat 8B #40	Oval 2 miles	CART	500 Miles	250	Gordon Johncock	Led 35 laps, running
8/1/82	Wisconsin State Fair Park	5	3	STP Intermedics Wildcat 8B #40	Oval 1 mile	CART	200 Miles	199	Tom Sneva	Running
8/15/82	Pocono 500 Pocono International Raceway	4	14	STP Intermedics Wildcat 8B #40	Oval 2.5 miles	CART	500 Miles	114	Rick Mears	Gearbox
8/29/82	Riverside International Raceway	2	23	STP Intermedics Wildcat 8B #40	Road Course 3.3 miles	CART	313.5 Miles	11	Rick Mears	Led first 10 laps until transmission failed
9/19/82	Road America	4	14	STP Intermedics Wildcat 8B #40	Road Course 4 miles	CART	196 Miles	29	Hector Rebaque	Led 20 laps, transmission
9/12/82	Italian Grand Prix, Monza	1	3	Ferrari 126C2 #28	Road Course 3.6 miles	F-1	187 Miles	52	Rene Arnoux	Running
9/25/82	USA Las Vegas Grand Prix Las Vegas	7	DNF	Ferrari 126C2 #28	Road Course 2.27 miles	F-1	170 Miles	26	Michele Alboreto	Suspension failure
9/26/82	Michigan International Speedway	25	2	STP Intermedics Wildcat 8B #40	Oval 2 miles	CART	150 Miles	75	Bobby Rahal	Led 17 laps, running
11/6/82	Phoenix International Raceway	2	3	STP Intermedics Wildcat 8B #40	Oval 1 mile	CART	150 Miles	150	Tom Sneva	Running

Mario pits during the September 150-miler at Michigan; he started 25th but took the lead after 56 miles. He finished second in both races at Michigan International Speedway in 1982. *Ken Coles*

1983

I've won fifty-some Indy car races. If I'd stayed in the midgets, racing against those guys, I'm not sure if I'd have won that many midget races. Mario, Open Wheel Magazine, June 1993

The list of racing cars Mario helped develop is long. It began with the Brawner Hawk and included the McNamara, several Parnellis, and a variety of Lotuses. For 1983, Mario joined Carl Haas and Paul Newman in a new CART team. Haas enlisted Lola's Eric Broadley to design the machine, the first Indy car effort for Lola. Working with engineer Tony Cicale, the car was ready to race by opening day. In its first outing Mario finished fifth. They kept working on the car, and in July, Mario scored the Lola's first Indy car win, at Road America. In the last five races of the season, Mario had a win, three seconds, and a fourth.

Mario returned to Le Mans with Michael and Frenchman Philipe Alliot as codrivers in a Kremer Porsche 956. They covered 3,083.4 miles in 364 laps, finishing third behind the Roth-mans-sponsored factory Porsches.

CART Points 1983

		Points	Wins
1.	Al Unser	151	1
2.	Teo Fabi	146	4
3.	**Mario**	**133**	**2**
4.	Tom Sneva	96	2
5.	Bobby Rahal	94	1
6.	Rick Mears	92	1
7.	Al Unser Jr.	89	
8.	John Paul Jr.	84	1
9.	Chip Ganassi	56	
10.	Pancho Carter	53	

When Mario finished third in the Budweiser colors at Michigan, it was the Lola's best finish to that point. But a win would come in their next race, at Elkhart Lake.
Ken Coles

Mario Andretti 1983 Record

Date	Event/Track	Qual	Finish	Entrant/Car/Number	Type Track	Sanction & Division	Distance	Laps Compl	Race Winner	Comments
4/17/83	Atlanta Motor Speedway	6	5	Newman-Haas Budweiser Lola T700 #3	Oval 1.522 miles	CART	201 Miles	128	Gordon Johncock	Running
5/29/83	Indianapolis 500 Indianapolis Motor Speedway	11	23	Newman-Haas Budweiser Lola T700 #3	Oval 2.5 miles	USAC	500 Miles	79	Tom Sneva	Wreck with Johnny Parsons Jr.
6/12/83	Wisconsin State Fair Park	12	18	Newman-Haas Budweiser Lola T700 #3	Oval 1 mile	CART	150 Miles	58	Tom Sneva	Overheated
6/18-19/83	24 Hours of Le Mans	8	3	Kremer Racing Porsche 956	Road course 8.46 miles	ACO WSCC	24 Hours	364	Vern Schuppan/ Al Holbert/ Hurley Haywood	Co-drivers Michael Andretti, Philippe Alliot, running
7/3/83	Burke Lakefront Airport	1	14	Newman-Haas Budweiser Lola T700 #3	Road course 2.48 miles	CART	310 Miles	56	Al Unser	Led 34 laps, overheating
7/17/83	Michigan 500 Michigan International Speedway	18	3	Newman-Haas Budweiser Lola T700 #3	Oval 2 miles	CART	500 Miles	250	John Paul Jr.	Led 21 laps, running
7/31/83	**Road America**	**1**	**1**	**Newman-Haas Budweiser Lola T700 #3**	**Road Course 4 miles**	**CART**	**200 Miles**	**50**	**Mario**	**Led 6 laps, first win for Lola in CART**
8/14/83	Pocono 500 Pocono International Raceway	9	7	Newman-Haas Budweiser Lola T700 #3	Oval 2.5 miles	CART	500 Miles	197	Teo Fabi	Running
8/28/83	Riverside International Raceway	3	16	Newman-Haas Budweiser Lola T700 #3	Road Course 3.3 miles	CART	313.5 Miles	57	Bobby Rahal	Led 18 laps, transmission failure while leading
9/11/83	Mid-Ohio	4	2	Newman-Haas Budweiser Lola T700 #3	Road Course 2.4 miles	CART	201.6 Miles	84	Teo Fabi	Led 4 laps, running
9/18/83	Michigan International Speedway	6	4	Newman-Haas Budweiser Lola T700 #3	Oval 2 miles	CART	200 Miles	99	Rick Mears	Led 4 laps, running
10/8/83	**Las Vegas**	**3**	**1**	**Newman-Haas Budweiser Lola T700 #3**	**Road Course 1.125 miles**	**CART**	**200.25 Miles**	**178**	**Mario**	**Led 112 laps**
10/23/83	Laguna Seca	6	2	Newman-Haas Budweiser Lola T700 #3	Road Course 1.9 miles	CART	186.2 Miles	98	Teo Fabi	Led 3 laps, running
10/29/83	Phoenix International Raceway	2	2	Newman-Haas Budweiser Lola T700 #3	Oval 1 mile	CART	150 Miles	150	Teo Fabi	Led 12 laps, trailed Fabi by .09 second at finish

It's great when your relatives come to watch you race, especially when your uncle is an Indy 500 winner. Mario joined his brother Aldo at an Indianapolis Speedrome midget race to check nephew John's progress in 1983. Following the Andretti tradition, John won the series championship and rookie of year honors. The future Indy car and Winston Cup star is flanked by Mario (left), his father, and car owner Sherman Armstrong. *John Mahoney*

1984

Mario led the 1984 Michigan 500 twice for 51 laps. But the finish was climactic as Pancho Carter wrecked spectacularly on the backstretch and Mario edged Tom Sneva at the finish by 0.14 of a secon—a couple of feet. It was Mario's third victory of the season. *Ken Coles*

When Mario opened the 1984 CART campaign with his second victory in the Long Beach Grand Prix, he became the only driver who would ever win Long Beach under both Formula One and CART sanctioning. More importantly, by leading flag-to-flag and finishing more than a minute ahead of runner-up Geoff Brabham, it signaled that Mario's Budweiser Lola T800 was going to be the car to beat.

Mario came as close to sweeping the CART series as anyone else has. He won on a street course (Long Beach), a temporary track constructed in a parking lot (Meadowlands), bona fide road courses (Road America and Mid-Ohio), and twice on a superspeedway (Michigan). Then he wrapped up the season with back-to-back seconds at Laguna Seca and Las Vegas. It was his fourth national championship in twenty years.

In February, Mario and Michael gave a Porsche 962 a strong run at Daytona until retiring after 127 laps with a transmission failure. Michael had been a rookie on the CART circuit, and ended the season seventh in points. Michael had finished with 3,363 miles completed, ranking fourth in that category and only 27 miles behind his father.

CART Points 1984

		Points	Wins
1.	**Mario**	176	6
2.	Tom Sneva	163	3
3.	Bobby Rahal	137	2
4.	Danny Sullivan	110	3
	Rick Mears	110	1
6.	Al Unser Jr.	103	
7.	Michael Andretti	102	
8.	Geoff Brabham	87	
9.	Al Unser	76	
10.	Danny Ongais	53	

Mario Andretti 1984 Record

Date	Event/Track	Qual	Finish	Entrant/Car/Number	Type Track	Sanction & Division	Distance	Laps Compl	Race Winner	Comments
2/5/84	24 Hours of Daytona Daytona International Speedway	1	66	Porsche 962 #1	Road course 3.81 miles	IMSA	24 Hours	125	Sarel van der Merwe, Tony Martin, Graham Duxbury	Codriver, Michael Andretti, transmission failure
4/1/84	**Long Beach Grand Prix Long Beach**	1	1	Newman-Haas Budweiser Lola T800 #3	Road course 1.67 miles	CART	187.04 Miles	112	Mario	Led all 112 laps from the pole, won by more than a minute (63.2 sec.)
4/18/84	Phoenix International Raceway	3	20	Newman-Haas Budweiser Lola T800 #3	Oval 1 mile	CART	150 Miles	88	Tom Sneva	Led 7 laps, CV joint failure
5/27/84	Indianapolis 500 Indianapolis Motor Speedway	6	17	Newman-Haas Budweiser Lola T800 #3	Oval 2.5 miles	USAC	500 Miles	153	Rick Mears	Led 29 laps, broken nose cone
6/3/84	Wisconsin State Fair Park	3	8	Newman-Haas Budweiser Lola T800 #3	Oval 1 mile	CART	200 Miles	196	Tom Sneva	Running
6/17/84	Portland International Raceway	1	26	Newman-Haas Budweiser Lola T800 #3	Road course 1.915 miles	CART	199 Miles	13	Al Unser Jr.	Led 4 laps, overheating
7/1/84	**Meadowlands**	1	1	Newman-Haas Budweiser Lola T800 #3	Road course 1.8 miles	CART	180 Miles	100	Mario	Led all 100 laps, margin of victory 71.7 seconds
7/8/84	Burke Lakefront Airport	1	21	Newman-Haas Budweiser Lola T800 #3	Road course 2.48 miles	CART	218 Miles	49	Danny Sullivan	Led first 28 laps, ignition
7/22/84	**Michigan 500 Michigan International Speedway**	1	1	Newman-Haas Budweiser Lola T800 #3	Oval 2 miles	CART	500 Miles	250	Mario	Led 51 laps, victory by .14 seconds
8/5/84	**Road America**	1	1	Newman-Haas Budweiser Lola T800 #3	Road Course 4 miles	CART	200 Miles	50	Mario	Led 34 laps, victory by more than a minute
8/19/84	Pocono 500 Pocono International Raceway	3	19	Newman-Haas Budweiser Lola T800 #3	Oval 2.5 miles	CART	500 Miles	163	Danny Sullivan	Engine failure
9/2/84	**Mid-Ohio**	1	1	Newman-Haas Budweiser Lola T800 #3	Road Course 2.4 miles	CART	201.6 Miles	84	Mario	Led 78 laps
9/9/84	Sanair Super Speedway	4	7	Newman-Haas Budweiser Lola T800 #3	Oval .826 mile	CART	185.8 Miles	222	Danny Sullivan	Running
9/24/84	**Michigan International Speedway**	3	1	Newman-Haas Budweiser Lola T800 #3	Oval 2 miles	CART	200 Miles	100	Mario	Led 37 laps, halted by rain after 33 laps, completed next day
10/14/84	Phoenix International Raceway	7	12	Newman-Haas Budweiser Lola T800 #3	Oval 1 mile	CART	150 Miles	144	Bobby Rahal	Led 59 laps, tangled with Johncock on frontstretch, running
10/21/84	Laguna Seca	1	2	Newman-Haas Budweiser Lola T800 #3	Road Course 1.9 miles	CART	186.2 Miles	98	Bobby Rahal	Led 24 laps, running
11/11/84	Las Vegas	2	2	Newman-Haas Budweiser Lola T800 #3	Road Course 1.125 miles	CART	200.25 Miles	178	Tom Sneva	Led 10 laps, running

Nigel Bennett's design of the Lola T800 proved imminently more successful than the T700. Mario won six races and finished second twice more, winning the CART championship. But he didn't have his best luck at Indy. After leading three times, he developed a broken exhaust header. Then Josele Garza cut in front of Mario as they came down pit lane in a pack and in the impact the Budweiser car's nose cone was damaged beyond repair. *Ken Coles*

1985

If Indy was 400 miles, I would have had six on my mantle. I don't know how to explain that. The man upstairs has the last word. When it's your day, it's your day.
Mario, International Herald Tribune

When 1985 began, it seemed like a continuation of the previous year. Mario won Long Beach for the second year in a row. He was second at Indy, then a pair of victories at Milwaukee and Portland sandwiched a third at Mid-Ohio. In the first five races, he hadn't finished worse than third and was leading the points handily.

But Mario suffered a broken hip, collarbone, and four ribs when his car lost a wheel and slammed the wall during the Michigan 500. He missed the next race, at Elkhart Lake, where Alan Jones finished third as a substitute. Mario returned to the cockpit for the Pocono 500, where he finished seventh, two laps off the pace. Through the rest of the season, his best finish was third at Phoenix.

In the IROC series, Mario was sidelined early with mechanical failure at Daytona. Then he led at Mid-Ohio until he was nudged and spun by Bobby Rahal. The Talladega race was rained out in July, and Mario sat out the final race because of his injuries. He finished 11th out of 12 in the final standings.

CART Points 1985

		Points	Wins
1.	Al Unser	151	1
2.	Al Unser Jr.	150	2
3.	Bobby Rahal	134	3
4.	Danny Sullivan	126	2
5.	**Mario**	**114**	**3**
6.	Emerson Fittipaldi	104	1
7.	Tom Sneva	66	
8.	Jacques Villeneuve	54	1
9.	Michael Andretti	53	
10.	Rick Mears	51	1
	Johnny Rutherford	51	

After closing a four-second gap, Danny Sullivan dove inside of Mario in turn one on lap 120. Sullivan had to use the apron inside the white line to make the pass and as he accelerated through turn one, the back end of the Penske car broke loose and Sullivan spun directly in Mario's path. Mario, hard on the brakes on the right, expected Sullivan to collect the wall. Instead, the car made a complete 360 degree loop, and Sullivan drove away. After a pit stop for fresh tires, Sullivan again caught Mario and this time passed him cleanly for the win. *Photo courtesy of Indianapolis Motor Speedway*

Mario Andretti 1985 Record

Date	Event/Track	Qual	Finish	Entrant/Car/Number	Type Track	Sanction & Division	Distance	Laps Compl	Race Winner	Comments
2/15/85	Daytona International Speedway	2	12	Chevrolet Camaro	Oval 2.5 miles	IROC	100 Miles	5	Darrell Waltrip	Mechanical
4/14/85	Long Beach Grand Prix Long Beach	1	1	Newman-Haas Beatrice Lola T900 #1	Road course 1.67 miles	CART	150.3 Miles	90	Mario	Led 70 laps, margin of victory more than 1 second
5/26/85	Indianapolis 500 Indianapolis Motor Speedway	4	2	Newman-Haas Beatrice Lola T900 #3	Oval 2.5 miles	USAC	500 Miles	200	Danny Sullivan	Led 107 laps, trailed by 2.47 seconds
6/2/85	Wisconsin State Fair Park	1	1	Newman-Haas Beatrice Lola T900 #1	Oval 1 mile	CART	200 Miles	200	Mario	Led 196 laps
6/8/85	Mid-Ohio	1	3	Chevrolet Camaro	Road Course 2.4 miles	IROC	69.6 Miles	29	Bobby Rahal	Led 27 laps, spun after contact with Rahal
6/16/85	Portland International Raceway	4	1	Newman-Haas Beatrice Lola T900 #1	Road course 1.915 miles	CART	199 Miles	104	Mario	Led 29 laps
6/30/85	Meadowlands	1	26	Newman-Haas Beatrice Lola T900 #1	Road course 1.68 miles	CART	168 Miles	34	Al Unser Jr.	Led 19 laps, wreck while leading
7/7/85	Burke Lakefront Airport	3	14	Newman-Haas Beatrice Lola T900 #1	Road course 2.48 miles	CART	218 Miles	84	Al Unser Jr.	Led 75 laps, car caught fire on course while leading
7/28/85	Michigan 500 Michigan International Speedway	3	10	Newman-Haas Beatrice Lola T900 #1	Oval 2 miles	CART	500 Miles	241	Emerson Fittipaldi	Led 16 laps, wrecked, race delayed one week because of tire problems
8/18/85	Pocono 500 Pocono International Raceway	10	7	Newman-Haas Beatrice Lola T900 #1	Oval 2.5 miles	CART	500 Miles	198	Rick Mears	Led 1 lap, running
9/1/85	Mid-Ohio	4	7	Newman-Haas Beatrice Lola T900 #1	Road Course 2.4 miles	CART	201.6 Miles	82	Bobby Rahal	Led 1 lap, wrecked
9/8/85	Sanair Super Speedway	8	15	Newman-Haas Beatrice Lola T900 #1	Oval .826 mile	CART	185.8 Miles	154	Johnny Rutherford	Broken hose clamp
9/22/85	Michigan International Speedway	2	21	Newman-Haas Beatrice Lola T900 #1	Oval 2 miles	CART	200 Miles	71	Bobby Rahal	Transmission failure
10/6/85	Laguna Seca	8	11	Newman-Haas Beatrice Lola T900 #1	Road Course 1.9 miles	CART	186.2 Miles	94	Bobby Rahal	Engine fire
10/13/85	Phoenix International Raceway	7	3	Newman-Haas Beatrice Lola T900 #1	Oval 1 mile	CART	150 Miles	149	Al Unser	Running
11/9/85	Tamiami Park Raceway	9	27	Newman-Haas Beatrice Lola T900 #1	Road Course 1.74 miles	CART	195 Miles	0	Danny Sullivan	Multicar wreck at start

Starting fourth, Mario finished second at Indy in 1985. He had a strong machine and led more than half of the race as he set a record pace. He finished two seconds behind Danny Sullivan. *Ken Coles*

Mario was running third at Michigan when he lost a wheel and walloped the wall on lap 242. *Ken Coles*

1986

Equipment failures are something I quite honestly fear, because it's the only time we feel totally helpless.... The mandatory rules on forward construction of the tub definitely have done a better job than ever before. Mario a day after a suspension failure caused his already qualified machine to slam into the wall causing painful lacerations and abrasions. Indy 500 Yearbook

It was the middle of June before Mario won his first race of the season. The event was memorable because Mario caught Michael, who was low of fuel, as they exited the last turn at Portland, and just edged him at the checkers, winning by 0.07 of a second. It would have been Michael's third win in four races. Instead, he wished Mario a Happy Father's Day in Victory Lane.

Mario's only other victory came in the Pocono 500 where Mario led five times, for 199 laps. In his best performance of the season, Mario finished a lap plus four seconds ahead of Kevin Cogan on the 2.5 mile track. He also scored top five finishes at Long Beach, Milwaukee, Cleveland, Toronto, Laguna Seca, and Phoenix.

CART Points 1986

		Points	Wins
1.	Bobby Rahal	179	7
2.	Michael Andretti	171	2
3.	Danny Sullivan	147	2
4.	Al Unser Jr.	137	1
5.	**Mario**	**136**	**2**
6.	Kevin Cogan	115	1
7.	Emerson Fittipaldi	103	1
8.	Rick Mears	89	
9.	Roberto Guerrero	87	
	Tom Sneva	87	

After qualifying for the fifth starting spot at Indy, Mario's Lola broke loose and collected the wall during a practice run. He had to start a back-up car from 30th on raceday, which was delayed a week because of rain. By 10 laps, Mario had climbed to 21st, but after battling ignition problems was sidelined with what was reported as "poor handling." *Ken Coles*

Mario Andretti 1986 Record

Date	Event/Track	Qual	Finish	Entrant/Car/Number	Type Track	Sanction & Division	Distance	Laps Compl	Race Winner	Comments
4/6/86	Phoenix International Raceway	1	7	Newman-Haas Lola T86/00 #5	Oval 1 mile	CART	200 Miles	195	Kevin Cogan	Led 17 laps, ran out of fuel
4/13/86	Long Beach Grand Prix Long Beach	3	5	Newman-Haas Lola T86/00 #5	Road course 1.67 miles	CART	158.6 Miles	94	Michael Andretti	Running
6/1/86	Indianapolis 500 Indianapolis Motor Speedway	30	32	Newman-Haas Lola T86/00 #2	Oval 2.5 miles	USAC	500 Miles	19	Bobby Rahal	Ignition, race delayed one week by rain
6/8/86	Wisconsin State Fair Park	4	5	Newman-Haas Lola T86/00 #5	Oval 1 mile	CART	200 Miles	198	Michael Andretti	Running
6/15/86	**Portland International Raceway**	7	1	**Newman-Haas Hanna Car Wash Lola T86/00 #5**	**Road course 1.915 miles**	**CART**	**199 Miles**	104	**Mario**	Led 1 lap
6/29/86	Meadowlands	2	24	Newman-Haas Hanna Car Wash Lola T86/00 #5	Road course 1.68 miles	CART	168 Miles	8	Danny Sullivan	Led 4 laps, broken water pipe
7/6/86	Burke Lakefront Airport	5	3	Newman-Haas Hanna Car Wash Lola T86/00 #5	Road course 2.48 miles	CART	218 Miles	88	Danny Sullivan	Running
7/20/86	Molson Indy Toronto	3	3	Newman-Haas Hanna Car Wash Lola T86/00 #5	Road course 1.78 miles	CART	183.3 Miles	103	Bobby Rahal	Running
8/2/86	Michigan 500 Michigan International Speedway	10	21	Newman-Haas Hanna Car Wash Lola T86/00 #5	Oval 2 miles	CART	500 Miles	69	Johnny Rutherford	Wreck
8/17/86	**Pocono 500 Pocono International Raceway**	3	1	**Newman-Haas Hanna Car Wash Lola T86/00 #5**	**Oval 2.5 miles**	**CART**	**500 Miles**	200	**Mario**	Led 119 laps
8/31/86	Mid-Ohio	1	24	Newman-Haas Hanna Car Wash Lola T86/00 #5	Road Course 2.4 miles	CART	201.6 Miles	13	Bobby Rahal	Led 12 laps, exhaust
9/7/86	Sanair Super Speedway	5	8	Newman-Haas Hanna Car Wash Lola T86/00 #5	Oval .826 mile	CART	185.8 Miles	219	Bobby Rahal	Led 42 laps, incident with Tony Bettenhausen lap 136, running
9/28/86	Michigan International Speedway	10	10	Newman-Haas Hanna Car Wash Lola T86/00 #5	Oval 2 miles	CART	200 Miles	123	Bobby Rahal	Led 1 lap, engine failure
10/4/86	Road America	6	9	Newman-Haas Hanna Car Wash Lola T86/00 #5	Road Course 4 miles	CART	200 Miles	49	Emerson Fittipaldi	Race started on Sept. 21 but stopped after lap 4 because of rain. Completed Oct. 4, running
10/12/86	Laguna Seca	1	4	Newman-Haas Hanna Car Wash Lola T86/00 #5	Road Course 1.9 miles	CART	186.2 Miles	98	Bobby Rahal	Led 8 laps, running
10/19/86	Phoenix International Raceway	5	4	Newman-Haas Hanna Car Wash Lola T86/00 #5	Oval 1 mile	CART	200 Miles	199	Michael Andretti	Running
11/9/86	Tamiami Park Raceway	5	11	Newman-Haas Hanna Car Wash Lola T86/00 #5	Road Course 1.784 miles	CART	200 Miles	107	Al Unser Jr.	Running

Mario started on the pole at Mid-Ohio in 1986. He led the first 12 laps of the race until a broken exhaust header put him out. *Ken Coles*

1987

For the third time in four years, Mario opened the season with a win on the streets at Long Beach. A second win came at Road America, in August. Mario had Adrian Newey and Tyler Alexander preparing his racers and running the Newman-Haas team. They switched from Cosworth to the new Ilmor Chevrolet Indy V-8 powerplant. The car was fast, earning eight poles, but the engine proved to be fragile, as Mario led 150 more laps than anyone else, but only finished five races.

At Indianapolis, 20 years after he had last qualified for the pole, Mario did it again. On raceday, he was dominant, cruising toward victory. But a valve spring broke 20 laps from the finish. Testing by Ilmor's engineers later determined that Mario had actually created the situation that caused the failure by being too easy on the car and running lower rpms when he had a big lead.

The 1987 IROC was Mario's last of six appearances in the invitation-only series, and one of his least successful. He was involved in a four-car wreck at Daytona, but finished the race five laps behind winner Geoff Bodine. Then Mario had a pair of 8ths at Mid-Ohio and Michigan. At Watkins Glen, Mario raced from 10th to 6th, and finished the series ninth in points.

1987 was a mixed season for Mario and the Hanna Car Wash Rain-X Lola. With the Ilmor engine, the car's speed was not matched by the engine's reliability, or Mario's luck. Here the car is in road-course trim at Mid-Ohio. *Ken Coles*

CART Points 1987

		Points	Wins
1.	Bobby Rahal	188	3
2.	Michael Andretti	158	4
3.	Al Unser Jr.	107	
4.	Roberto Guerrero	106	2
5.	Rick Mears	102	1
6.	**Mario**	**100**	**2**
7.	Arie Luyendyk	98	
8.	Geoff Brabham	90	
9.	Danny Sullivan	87	
10.	Emerson Fittipaldi	78	2

Mario Andretti 1987 Record

Date	Event/Track	Qual	Finish	Entrant/Car/Number	Type Track	Sanction & Division	Distance	Laps Compl	Race Winner	Comments
2/13/87	Daytona International Speedway	6	7	Chevrolet Camaro	Oval 2.5 miles	IROC	100 Miles	35	Geoff Bodine	Running, involved in a multi-car accident on lap 16
4/5/87	**Long Beach Grand Prix** Long Beach	**1**	**1**	**Newman-Haas Hanna Car Wash Lola T87/00 #5**	**Road course 1.67 miles**	**CART**	**158.6 Miles**	**95**	**Mario**	**Led all 95 laps**
4/12/87	Phoenix International Raceway	1	5	Newman-Haas Hanna Car Wash Lola T87/00 #5	Oval 1 mile	CART	200 Miles	198	Roberto Guerrero	Led 30 laps, running
5/24/87	Indianapolis 500 Indianapolis Motor Speedway	1	9	Newman-Haas Hanna Car Wash Lola T87/00 #5	Oval 2.5 miles	USAC	500 Miles	180	Al Unser	Led 170 laps, broken valve spring
5/31/87	Wisconsin State Fair Park	3	17	Newman-Haas Hanna Car Wash Lola T87/00 #5	Oval 1 mile	CART	200 Miles	149	Michael Andretti	Led 46 laps, lost wing and wrecked while leading
6/6/87	Mid-Ohio	6	8	Chevrolet Camaro	Road Course 2.4 miles	IROC	69.6 Miles	29	Bobby Rahal	Running
6/14/87	Portland International Raceway	5	10	Newman-Haas Hanna Car Wash Lola T87/00 #5	Road course 1.915 miles	CART	199 Miles	65	Bobby Rahal	Fuel pickup
6/28/87	Meadowlands	1	2	Newman-Haas Hanna Car Wash Lola T87/00 #5	Road course 1.68 miles	CART	168 Miles	100	Bobby Rahal	Led 15 laps, running
7/5/87	Burke Lakefront Airport	3	10	Newman-Haas Hanna Car Wash Lola T87/00 #5	Road course 2.48 miles	CART	198 Miles	75	Emerson Fittipaldi	Engine failure
7/19/87	Molson Indy Toronto	5	15	Newman-Haas Hanna Car Wash Lola T87/00 #5	Road course 1.78 miles	CART	183.3 Miles	46	Emerson Fittipaldi	Off course
8/1/87	Michigan 500	3	8	Chevrolet Camaro	Oval 2 miles	IROC	100 Miles	50	Al Unser Jr.	Running
8/2/87	Michigan International Speedway	3	19	Newman-Haas Hanna Car Wash Lola T87/00 #5	Oval 2 miles	CART	500 Miles	156	Michael Andretti	Led 118 laps, engine failure while leading
8/8/87	Watkins Glen	10	6	Chevrolet Camaro	Road Course 2.428 miles	IROC	72.8 Miles	30	Geoff Bodine	Running
8/16/87	Pocono 500 Pocono International Raceway	1	19	Newman-Haas Hanna Car Wash Lola T87/00 #5	Oval 2.5 miles	CART	500 Miles	88	Rick Mears	Led 22 laps, wrecked
8/30/87	**Road America**	**1**	**1**	**Newman-Haas Hanna Car Wash Lola T87/00 #5**	**Road Course 4 miles**	**CART**	**200 Miles**	**50**	**Mario**	**Led all 50 laps**
9/6/87	Mid-Ohio	4	17	Newman-Haas Hanna Car Wash Lola T87/00 #5	Road Course 2.4 miles	CART	201.6 Miles	64	Bobby Rahal	Accident
9/20/87	Nazareth Speedway	7	19	Newman-Haas Hanna Car Wash Lola T87/00 #5	Oval 1 mile	CART	200 Miles	106	Michael Andretti	Contact with Rutherford, wrecked
10/11/87	Laguna Seca	1	17	Newman-Haas Hanna Car Wash Lola T87/00 #5	Road Course 1.9 miles	CART	186.2 Miles	68	Bobby Rahal	Led 61 laps, engine failure
11/1/87	Tamiami Park Raceway	1	4	Newman-Haas Hanna Car Wash Lola T87/00 #5	Road course 1.784 miles	CART	183.7 Miles	102	Michael Andretti	Led 3 laps, race ended at 103 laps because of heavy rain, running

For Mario's legion of fans, his bad luck at Indy was painful to watch. In 1987 Mario had everyone covered, leading 170 of the first 177 laps before the engine broke. *Ken Coles*

Mario (22) racing with Wally Dallenbach Jr. in the IROC at Michigan. A decade earlier, he had battled with Wally's father in the USAC championship series. *Ken Coles*

The sun is out but the track is still moist and slippery. Mario was capable in the wet, as he demonstrated racing from fourth to second at Mid-Ohio in 1988. *Ken Coles*

1988

We were trying to salvage what we could out of the day. I mean, you put forth such an effort, you're here for so long this month, and you don't really want to give up. But you really have to give up. Mario, after dropping out of the 1988 Indy 500, The Indianapolis Star, May 30, 1988

Wins in the first race, at Phoenix, and on Independence Day weekend in Cleveland highlighted the 1988 season. Tony Cicale returned to engineer the Newman-Haas car and his expertise paid dividends. Mario was competitive, qualifying in the top four a dozen times. He led 10 of the 15 races, and added a second and three thirds to his results. But mechanical gremlins, three when he was leading, and including one engine failure, dropped Mario to fifth in the points.

When he teamed with Michael and Aldo's son John, at LeMans, they demonstrated the challenge of endurance racing. Starting third, the Andrettis' Porsche encountered engine problems with eight hours still to go. Running on five cylinders, they soldiered on to finish sixth, only 160 miles behind Jan Lammers, Johnny Dumfries, and Andy Wallace, completing 3,153 miles.

Mario admired engineer Tony Cicale as much for his work ethic as for his abilities. Here Mario huddles with Cicale (left) and chief mechanic Tyler Alexander at Indianapolis. *Ken Coles*

CART Points 1988

		Points	Wins
1.	Danny Sullivan	182	4
2.	Al Unser Jr.	149	4
3.	Bobby Rahal	136	1
4.	Rick Mears	129	2
5.	**Mario**	**126**	**2**
6.	Michael Andretti	119	
7.	Emerson Fittipaldi	105	2
8.	Raul Boesel	89	
9.	Derek Daly	53	
10.	Teo Fabi	44	
	John Jones	44	

Mario Andretti 1988 Record

Date	Event/Track	Qual	Finish	Entrant/Car/Number	Type Track	Sanction & Division	Distance	Laps Compl	Race Winner	Comments
4/10/88	Phoenix International Raceway	3	1	Newman-Haas Amoco/Kmart Lola T88/00 #6	Oval 1 mile	CART	200 Miles	200	Mario	Led 135 laps
4/17/88	Long Beach Grand Prix Long Beach	2	15	Newman-Haas Amoco/Kmart Lola T88/00 #6	Road course 1.67 miles	CART	158.6 Miles	70	Al Unser Jr.	Led 1 lap, mechanical problem
5/29/88	Indianapolis 500 Indianapolis Motor Speedway	4	20	Newman-Haas Amoco/Kmart Lola T87/00 #6	Oval 2.5 miles	USAC	500 Miles	118	Rick Mears	Electrical failure
6/5/88	Wisconsin State Fair Park	2	17	Newman-Haas Amoco/Kmart Lola T88/00 #6	Oval 1 mile	CART	200 Miles	147	Rick Mears	Led 9 laps, broken rear axle
6/12/88	24 Hours of Le Mans	3	6	Shell Porsche 962C #19	Road Course 8.41 miles	ACO	24 Hours	375	Jan Lammers, Johnny Dumfries, Andy Wallace	Codrivers Michael and John Andretti
6/19/88	Portland International Raceway	5	5	Newman-Haas Amoco/Kmart Lola T88/00 #6	Road course 1.915 miles	CART	200 Miles	103	Danny Sullivan	Running
7/3/88	Burke Lakefront Airport	3	1	Newman-Haas Amoco/Kmart Lola T88/00 #6	Road course 2.48 miles	CART	198 Miles	80	Mario	Led 24 laps
7/17/88	Molson Indy Toronto	2	25	Newman-Haas Amoco/Kmart Lola T88/00 #6	Road course 1.78 miles	CART	183.3 Miles	11	Al Unser Jr.	Mechanical failure
7/24/88	Meadowlands	2	2	Newman-Haas Amoco/Kmart Lola T88/00 #6	Road course 1.2 miles	CART	182.5 Miles	149	Al Unser Jr.	Led 11 laps, broken ring gear while leading
8/7/88	Michigan 500 Michigan International Speedway	3	12	Newman-Haas Amoco/Kmart Lola T87/00 #6	Oval 2 miles	CART	500 Miles	180	Danny Sullivan	Led 10 laps, engine failure
8/21/88	Pocono 500 Pocono International Raceway	5	17	Newman-Haas Amoco/Kmart Lola T87/00 #6	Oval 2.5 miles	CART	500 Miles	116	Bobby Rahal	Led 25 laps, wreck with Simon while leading
9/4/88	Mid-Ohio	4	2	Newman-Haas Amoco/Kmart Lola T88/00 #6	Road Course 2.4 miles	CART	201.6 Miles	84	Emerson Fittipaldi	Led 18 laps, running
9/11/88	Road America	6	3	Newman-Haas Amoco/Kmart Lola T88/00 #6	Road Course 4 miles	CART	200 Miles	50	Emerson Fittipaldi	Running
9/25/88	Nazareth Speedway	3	3	Newman-Haas Amoco/Kmart Lola T88/00 #6	Oval 1 mile	CART	200 Miles	199	Danny Sullivan	Running
10/16/88	Laguna Seca	2	3	Newman-Haas Amoco/Kmart Lola T88/00 #6	Road course 2.2 miles	CART	186 Miles	84	Danny Sullivan	Led 2 laps, running
11/6/88	Tamiami Park Raceway	2	15	Newman-Haas Amoco/Kmart Lola T88/00 #6	Road Course 1.784 miles	CART	200 Miles	43	Al Unser Jr.	Led 5 laps, fuel system problem while leading

At LeMans in 1988, Mario teamed with Michael and John in this Porsche 962. They completed 375 laps and finished sixth in spite running nearly a third of the race on five cylinders. *Aysedasi*

1989

It looks that way. I hope not. Obviously I know how he feels. He was in good shape for the win. I feel we had two of the best cars in the field. Mario after finishing fourth in the Indy 500, responding to the question, "Do you think that Michael inherited your luck at the Speedway?"

When Mario convinced Carl Haas to add a second car for Michael, the Newman-Haas team became a strong 1 – 2 threat. But in 1989, the new Penske PC-18 chassis designed by Nigel Bennett, with the Chevy Indy V-8, was clearly the package to have. While Fittipaldi and Mears captured eight victories in their PC-18/89s, it seemed that Mario and Michael were frequently racing for best in class.

Mario was only eliminated twice by mechanical failures and twice by accidents on the track. He didn't win any races, but finished second both at Cleveland and in the finale at Laguna Seca. His best chance to win may have been at Long Beach, where he led until Al Unser Jr. poked his nose inside at a tight corner and the resulting collision took Mario out of the race, while Unser went on to win.

In February, Mario returned to the Rolex 24 Hour race at Daytona. Again, he teamed with Michael to drive a Porsche from the late Al Holbert's stable. But after more than 780 miles, the car was retired with an unrepairable brake problem.

CART Points 1989

		Points	Wins
1.	Emerson Fittipaldi	196	5
2.	Rick Mears	186	3
3.	Michael Andretti	150	2
4.	Teo Fabi	141	1
5.	Al Unser Jr.	136	1
6.	**Mario**	**110**	
7.	Danny Sullivan	107	2
8.	Scott Pruett	101	
9.	Bobby Rahal	88	1
10.	Arie Luyendyk	75	

In the 1980s Mario applied his experiences at Monaco and Long Beach to CART's temporary street circuits. Working through a turn at Detroit in 1989, Mario started fourth and finished third in a race that was won by another Monaco veteran, Emerson Fittipaldi. *Ken Coles*

Mario Andretti 1989 Record

Date	Event/Track	Qual	Finish	Entrant/Car/Number	Type Track	Sanction & Division	Distance	Laps Compl	Race Winner	Comments
2/5/89	24 Hours of Daytona Daytona International Raceway	9	47	Busby Racing Porsche 962 #68	Road course 3.3 miles	IMSA	24 Hours	237	John Andretti/ Derek Bell/ Bob Wollek	Co-driver Michael Andretti, brake failure
4/9/89	Phoenix International Raceway	4	8	Newman-Haas Kmart/ Havoline Lola T89/00 #5	Oval 1 mile	CART	200 Miles	195	Rick Mears	Running
4/16/89	Long Beach Grand Prix Long Beach	5	18	Newman-Haas Kmart/ Havoline Lola T89/00 #5	Road course 1.67 miles	CART	158.6 Miles	83	Al Unser Jr.	Led 8 laps, damage from contact with Unser Jr. while leading
5/28/89	Indianapolis 500 Indianapolis Motor Speedway	5	4	Newman-Haas Kmart/ Havoline Lola T89/00 #5	Oval 2.5 miles	USAC	500 Miles	193	Emerson Fittipaldi	Led 1 lap, running
6/4/89	Wisconsin State Fair Park	6	7	Newman-Haas Kmart/ Havoline Lola T89/00 #5	Oval 1 mile	CART	200 Miles	195	Rick Mears	Running
6/18/89	Detroit Grand Prix	4	3	Newman-Haas Kmart/ Havoline Lola T89/00 #5	Street course 2.49 miles	CART	155 Miles	62	Emerson Fittipaldi	Led 2 laps, running
6/25/89	Portland International Raceway	3	25	Newman-Haas Kmart/ Havoline Lola T89/00 #5	Road course 1.915 miles	CART	200 Miles	19	Emerson Fittipaldi	Electrical failure
7/2/89	Burke Lakefront Airport	3	2	Newman-Haas Kmart/ Havoline Lola T89/00 #5	Road course 2.48 miles	CART	198 Miles	80	Emerson Fittipaldi	Running
7/16/89	Meadowlands	2	20	Newman-Haas Kmart/ Havoline Lola T89/00 #5	Road course 1.2 miles	CART	173.7 Miles	75	Bobby Rahal	Led 1 lap, broken suspension, race halted 5 laps early because of heavy rain
7/23/89	Molson Indy Toronto	7	26	Newman-Haas Kmart/ Havoline Lola T89/00 #5	Road course 1.78 miles	CART	183.3 Miles	8	Michael Andretti	Hit Guerrero's disabled car parked on the course
8/6/89	Michigan 500 Michigan International Speedway	6	3	Newman-Haas Kmart/ Havoline Lola T89/00 #5	Oval 2 miles	CART	500 Miles	249	Michael Andretti	Led 45 laps, running
8/20/89	Pocono 500 Pocono International Raceway	5	5	Newman-Haas Kmart/ Havoline Lola T89/00 #5	Oval 2.5 miles	CART	500 Miles	199	Danny Sullivan	Running
9/3/89	Mid-Ohio	11	7	Newman-Haas Kmart/ Havoline Lola T89/00 #5	Road Course 2.4 miles	CART	201.6 Miles	83	Teo Fabi	Running
9/10/89	Road America	7	7	Newman-Haas Kmart/ Havoline Lola T89/00 #5	Road Course 4 miles	CART	200 Miles	49	Danny Sullivan	Ran out of fuel
9/24/89	Nazareth Speedway	9	8	Newman-Haas Kmart/ Havoline Lola T89/00 #5	Oval 1 mile	CART	200 Miles	194	Emerson Fittipaldi	Running
10/15/89	Laguna Seca	8	2	Newman-Haas Kmart/ Havoline Lola T89/00 #5	Road Course 2.2 miles	CART	186 Miles	84	Rick Mears	Led 20 laps, running

Mario's fourth-place finish at Indy was one of five top-4 runs in 1989. Here he races with Derek Daly. *John Mahoney*

The 1990s

Every time Mario climbed into a race car in the 1990s, he was entering into a battle against time that he knew he couldn't win. He was honored for his accomplishments and recognized as a legend, but that recognition didn't help him shave any seconds off lap times on the track. Coming into the 1990s, a new generation of drivers was grabbing the headlines. This wasn't anything new, but the annoying part of it was that a couple of Andrettis, Michael, nephew John, and Little Al, the offspring of his old rival Al Unser, led them.

While the younger drivers weren't cutting Mario any slack, he was still able to fight for wins. When matched against bravery, skill, and young eyes and reflexes, there is a point where experience and hard work begin delivering diminishing returns. The top finishes were getting harder to come by and sharing the podium with Michael brought great satisfaction. Mario knew that he was approaching the time to step aside. But first, there was a little more racing ahead.

Mario works amid scenic downtown Detroit landscape in 1991. *Ken Coles*

LeMans at night. The atmosphere after the sun sets is truly unique. *Aysedasi*

Below: In his 25th Indy 500, Mario started next to Michael in the second row, but his engine failed on lap 60. *Ken Coles*

1990

The modern driver is a little more courteous. I find him a little more correct. I can't say A. J. was never correct on the track. Parnelli was more of a "bumpsie"-type driver but those were accepted facts of the day. Today's drivers possess more finesse, and it's expected of you. Mario, Indianapolis 500 program, 1990

With 10 top-five finishes in 16 CART races, 1990 was a solid year for Mario. Yet it was his second straight season without a victory, and he finished seventh in points. His best results came at Portland and Mid-Ohio, where he was second to Michael in both races. At Portland, either he or Michael led each lap, but he was nearly four seconds behind at the checkers.

Mario was especially proud of their effort in the first test of the revamped layout at the Mid-Ohio course. The rain was so bad at one point that the field ran seven laps under full-course caution flags. Mario started in the fourth row and fought his way to the front, taking the lead on lap 46. As they had at Portland, he and Michael led the whole way.

CART Points 1990

		Points	Wins
1.	Al Unser Jr.	210	6
2.	Michael Andretti	181	5
3.	Rick Mears	168	1
4.	Bobby Rahal	153	
5.	Emerson Fittipaldi	144	1
6.	Danny Sullivan	139	2
7.	**Mario**	**136**	
8.	Arie Luyendyk	90	1
9.	Eddie Cheever	80	
	John Andretti	80	

Mario works with his youngest son, Jeff, during Rookie Orientation at the Indianapolis Motor Speedway in 1990. Although Jeff's car didn't have the speed to make the race, he returned in 1991 and added his name to the Rookie of the Year trophy. *Ken Coles*

Mario Andretti 1990 Record

Date	Event/Track	Qual	Finish	Entrant/Car/Number	Type Track	Sanction & Division	Distance	Laps Compl	Race Winner	Comments
4/8/90	Phoenix International Raceway	6	4	Newman-Haas Kmart/ Havoline Lola T90/00 #6	Oval 1 mile	CART	200 Miles	199	Rick Mears	Running
4/22/90	Long Beach Grand Prix Long Beach	6	5	Newman-Haas Kmart/ Havoline Lola T90/00 #6	Road course 1.67 miles	CART	158.6 Miles	95	Al Unser Jr.	Led 4 laps, running
5/27/90	Indianapolis 500 Indianapolis Motor Speedway	6	27	Newman-Haas Kmart/ Havoline Lola T90/00 #6	Oval 2.5 miles	USAC	500 Miles	60	Arie Luyendyk	Engine failure
6/3/90	Wisconsin State Fair Park	4	21	Newman-Haas Kmart/ Havoline Lola T90/00 #6	Oval 1 mile	CART	200 Miles	59	Al Unser Jr.	Led 7 laps, radiator
6/17/90	Detroit Grand Prix	3	25	Newman-Haas Kmart/ Havoline Lola T90/00 #6	Street course 2.49 miles	CART	155 Miles	14	Michael Andretti	Engine failure
6/24/90	Portland International Raceway	4	2	Newman-Haas Kmart/ Havoline Lola T90/00 #6	Road course 1.915 miles	CART	200 Miles	104	Michael Andretti	Led 3 laps, running
7/8/90	Burke Lakefront Airport	6	4	Newman-Haas Kmart/ Havoline Lola T90/00 #6	Road course 2.369 miles	CART	201.4 Miles	85	Danny Sullivan	Running
7/15/90	Meadowlands	2	24	Newman-Haas Kmart/ Havoline Lola T90/00 #6	Road course 1.2 miles	CART	182.5 Miles	41	Michael Andretti	Led 22 laps, wreck with Rahal
7/22/90	Molson Indy Toronto	3	6	Newman-Haas Kmart/ Havoline Lola T90/00 #6	Road course 1.78 miles	CART	167.3 Miles	93	Al Unser Jr.	Led 6 laps, running
8/5/90	Michigan 500 Michigan International Speedway	11	3	Newman-Haas Kmart/ Havoline Lola T90/00 #6	Oval 2 miles	CART	500 Miles	249	Al Unser Jr.	Running
8/26/90	Denver Grand Prix	4	4	Newman-Haas Kmart/ Havoline Lola T90/00 #6	Road Course 1.9 miles	CART	152 Miles	80	Al Unser Jr.	Led 2 laps, running
9/2/90	Vancouver	8	3	Newman-Haas Kmart/ Havoline Lola T90/00 #6	Road Course 1.7 miles	CART	165 Miles	97	Al Unser Jr.	Running
9/16/90	Mid-Ohio	8	2	Newman-Haas Kmart/ Havoline Lola T90/00 #6	Road Course 2.25 miles	CART	200 Miles	89	Michael Andretti	Led 25 laps, running
9/23/90	Road America	3	5	Newman-Haas Kmart/ Havoline Lola T90/00 #6	Road Course 4 miles	CART	200 Miles	50	Michael Andretti	Running, race halted for one hour because of Foyt accident
10/7/90	Nazareth Speedway	7	4	Newman-Haas Kmart/ Havoline Lola T90/00 #6	Oval 1 mile	CART	200 Miles	198	Emerson Fittipaldi	Running
10/21/90	Laguna Seca	2	26	Newman-Haas Kmart/ Havoline Lola T90/00 #6	Road Course 2.2 miles	CART	186 Miles	2	Danny Sullivan	Electrical failure

While Mario only lasted 35 miles at Detroit, he was heartened when Michael started on the pole and led every lap. *Ken Coles*

1991

A lot of people think it's something we've dreamed about all our lives. That's not true at all. I never thought I'd be driving with the kids in my arena. Time went on and "boom!" there it was. It seemed like I was just wiping spaghetti off their eyebrows and here I have to go out on the track and beat them. At best, it was like a shock. Mario, Indianapolis 500 program, 1991

Andretti fans had a lot to cheer about at Indianapolis in 1991. Mario's youngest son, Jeff, came to Indy through Barber Formula Fords, Super Vees, and the American Racing Series. When Jeff qualified for the 11th starting spot, it put an Andretti in each of the first four rows. Mario was on the outside of the front row, and took the green next to Rick Mears and A. J. Foyt. Michael and John, driving for Jim Hall, started fifth and seventh.

Mario took the lead from Mears on lap 12, and put two seconds between them in the next two circuits. At one point, Mario,

Michael, John, and Jeff were running first, second, sixth, and tenth, all on the lead lap. But at midrace, Mario was penalized a lap for "multiple infractions" of the new "not below the white line" rule, while Michael took the lead. Michael and Rick Mears waged a memorable battle in the final 30 laps, with Rick scoring his fourth Indy win. Unfortunately, an engine problem ended Mario's run at 187 circuits, enough to be paid for seventh place. While Jeff finished 15th, John's fifth-place run put three Andrettis in the top ten.

Demonstrating his versatility, Mario's best

finishes in 1991 came on a tight old mile oval, a challenging new breed of downtown street course and on a couple of road courses of the traditional style. At Milwaukee, after leading the first 31 laps he finished third, behind Michael and John. Mario was second on the streets of Toronto while Michael led every lap. And at Elkhart Lake and Laguna Seca he ran third, trailing Michael and Little Al in both races.

But the season belonged to Michael, as he won eight times and earned the title. Only Mario and John completed more laps than Michael, who dominated virtually every other category.

CART Points 1991

		Points	Wins
1.	Michael Andretti	234	8
2.	Bobby Rahal	200	1
3.	Al Unser Jr.	197	2
4.	Rick Mears	144	2
5.	Emerson Fittipaldi	140	1
6.	Arie Luyendyk	134	2
7.	**Mario**	**132**	
8.	John Andretti	105	1
9.	Eddie Cheever	91	
10.	Scott Pruett	67	

Teamed with Michael and Jeff in a Porsche 962, Mario finished fifth in the Rolex 24 Hours at Daytona after 2,188 miles. *Ken Coles*

Mario Andretti 1991 Record

Date	Event/Track	Qual	Finish	Entrant/Car/Number	Type Track	Sanction & Division	Distance	Laps Compl	Race Winner	Comments
2/3/91	24 Hours of Daytona Daytona International Speedway	6	5	Dauer Racing Porsche 962C #00	Road Course 3.3 miles	IMSA	24 Hours	663	John Winter/ Frank Jelinski/ Henri Pescarolo/ Hurley Haywood/ Bob Wollek	Codrivers Michael and Jeff Andretti, overheating
3/17/91	Surfers Paradise	5	17	Newman-Haas Kmart/ Havoline Lola T91/00 #6	Street course 2.8 miles	CART	181.5 Miles	41	John Andretti	Wreck with Unser Jr. and Cheever
4/14/91	Long Beach Grand Prix Long Beach	7	19	Newman-Haas Kmart/ Havoline Lola T91/00 #6	Road course 1.67 miles	CART	158.6 Miles	49	Al Unser Jr.	Electrical
4/21/91	Phoenix International Raceway	3	9	Newman-Haas Kmart/ Havoline Lola T91/00 #6	Oval 1 mile	CART	200 Miles	197	Arie Luyendyk	Led 33 laps, running
5/26/91	Indianapolis 500 Indianapolis Motor Speedway	3	7	Newman-Haas Kmart/ Havoline Lola T91/00 #6	Oval 2.5 miles	USAC	500 Miles	187	Rick Mears	Led 22 laps, engine failure, stalled at pit entrance
6/2/91	Wisconsin State Fair Park	2	3	Newman-Haas Kmart/ Havoline Lola T91/00 #6	Oval 1 mile	CART	200 Miles	199	Al Unser Jr.	Led 31 laps, running
6/16/91	Detroit Grand Prix	5	7	Newman-Haas Kmart/ Havoline Lola T91/00 #6	Street course 2.49 miles	CART	156 Miles	62	Emerson Fittipaldi	Running. Made contact with an emergency vehicle blocking track on lap 48, race was stopped for 55 minutes
6/23/91	Portland International Raceway	7	5	Newman-Haas Kmart/ Havoline Lola T91/00 #6	Road course 1.915 miles	CART	200 Miles	104	Michael Andretti	Running
7/7/91	Burke Lakefront Airport	5	6	Newman-Haas Kmart/ Havoline Lola T91/00 #6	Road course 2.369 miles	CART	201.4 Miles	85	Michael Andretti	Led 1 lap, running
7/14/91	Meadowlands	5	15	Newman-Haas Kmart/ Havoline Lola T91/00 #6	Road course 1.2 miles	CART	182.5 Miles	134	Bobby Rahal	Contact with Unser Jr. lap 20, running
7/21/91	Molson Indy Toronto	5	2	Newman-Haas Kmart/ Havoline Lola T91/00 #6	Road course 1.78 miles	CART	167.3 Miles	103	Michael Andretti	Running
8/4/91	Michigan 500 Michigan International Speedway	3	4	Newman-Haas Kmart/ Havoline Lola T91/00 #6	Oval 2 miles	CART	500 Miles	245	Rick Mears	Led 14 laps, engine failure
8/25/91	Denver Grand Prix	5	15	Newman-Haas Kmart/ Havoline Lola T91/00 #6	Road Course 1.9 miles	CART	133 Miles	50	Al Unser Jr.	Wreck with Scott Brayton
9/1/91	Vancouver	10	4	Newman-Haas Kmart/ Havoline Lola T91/00 #6	Road Course 1.7 miles	CART	167.7 Miles	99	Michael Andretti	Running
9/15/91	Mid-Ohio	6	7	Newman-Haas Kmart/ Havoline Lola T91/00 #6	Road Course 2.25 miles	CART	200 Miles	89	Michael Andretti	Led 1 lap, running
9/22/91	Road America	6	3	Newman-Haas Kmart/ Havoline Lola T91/00 #6	Road Course 4 miles	CART	200 Miles	50	Michael Andretti	Running
10/6/91	Nazareth Speedway	4	5	Newman-Haas Kmart/ Havoline Lola T91/00 #6	Oval 1 mile	CART	200 Miles	200	Arie Luyendyk	Running
10/20/91	Laguna Seca	6	3	Newman-Haas Kmart/ Havoline Lola T91/00 #6	Road Course 2.2 miles	CART	186 Miles	84	Michael Andretti	Running

Mario starts outside of Mears and Foyt at Indy. There was an Andretti in each of the first four rows. *David Nearpass*

Mario led 22 laps early at Indianapolis, but an engine failure let him down. *David Nearpass*

1992

The competition up front has always been fierce, no question. I think that what you have in Formula One, there never was, and because of the formula, there never will be depth in competition. You will always have two, sometimes three teams that dominate. And any driving talent that is involved in any of those top three teams are the only ones that are going to be winning in those particular seasons. Again that's the way it is, that's the way it was. In champ car racing it's different. And it's different because the depth in the field is better than ever before because engineering talent and equipment and everything else is so equal. So I think that in the '60s and '70s it was just as hard to finish in the top three as it is today. But today, it's harder to finish fifth than it was then. It was a lot easier to finish fifth. *Mario*

From June through October, even without a victory, Mario registered top-six finishes in 9 of 11 point races from Portland to Monterey. His best finish came in the season finale, running second to Michael, who led every lap at Laguna Seca.

In contrast to the milestone events of the previous year, Mario has called the 1992 Indy 500 his worst day in racing. On an unseasonably cold and blustery day, cold tires were troubling rookies and veterans alike. On a restart after putting on new tires, Mario spun in turn four, smashing into the wall and breaking toes on both feet. Then, as Mario was being attended to in the infield hospital, Jeff slammed into the turn two concrete and received severe leg injuries that would effectively end his Indy car career. Meanwhile, Michael was again out front, with seemingly no one able to catch him. Except for a fuel drive belt that failed with 26 miles remaining, he would have won Indy. With his injuries, Mario wasn't able to race at Detroit.

CART Points 1992

		Points	Wins
1.	Bobby Rahal	196	4
2.	Michael Andretti	192	5
3.	Al Unser Jr.	169	1
4.	Emerson Fittipaldi	151	4
5.	Scott Goodyear	108	1
6.	**Mario**	**105**	
7.	Danny Sullivan	99	1
8.	John Andretti	94	
9.	Raul Boesel	80	
	Eddie Cheever	80	

Fans and participants will remember the 1992 Indy 500 as one of the coldest on record. Cold tires were to blame for Mario's wreck. *David Nearpass*

Mario Andretti 1992 Record

Date	Event/Track	Qual	Finish	Entrant/Car/Number	Type Track	Sanction & Division	Distance	Laps Compl	Race Winner	Comments
3/22/92	Surfers Paradise	6	7	Newman-Haas Kmart/ Havoline Lola T91/00 #2	Street course 2.8 miles	CART	181.5 Miles	65	Emerson Fittipaldi	Led 1 lap, running
4/5/92	Phoenix International Raceway	3	17	Newman-Haas Kmart/ Havoline Lola T92/00 #2	Oval 1 mile	CART	200 Miles	111	Bobby Rahal	Transmission broke
4/12/92	Long Beach Grand Prix Long Beach	7	23	Newman-Haas Kmart/ Havoline Lola T92/00 #2	Road course 1.59 miles	CART	167 Miles	0	Danny Sullivan	Accident on first lap
5/24/92	Indianapolis 500 Indianapolis Motor Speedway	3	23	Newman-Haas Kmart/ Havoline Lola T92/00 #2	Oval 2.5 miles	USAC	500 Miles	78	Al Unser Jr.	Led 1 lap, wreck turn four
6/21/92	Portland International Raceway	8	6	Newman-Haas Kmart/ Havoline Lola T92/00 #2	Road course 1.915 miles	CART	200 Miles	101	Michael Andretti	Running (Missed Detroit race because of injures suffered at Indianapolis)
6/28/92	Wisconsin State Fair Park	10	6	Newman-Haas Kmart/ Havoline Lola T92/00 #2	Oval 1 mile	CART	200 Miles	197	Michael Andretti	Running
7/5/92	New Hampshire International Speedway	8	7	Newman-Haas Kmart/ Havoline Lola T92/00 #2	Oval 1 mile	CART	200 Miles	196	Bobby Rahal	Running
7/19/92	Molson Indy Toronto	5	4	Newman-Haas Kmart/ Havoline Lola T92/00 #2	Road course 1.78 miles	CART	167.3 Miles	102	Michael Andretti	Running
8/2/92	Michigan 500 Michigan International Speedway	1	15	Newman-Haas Kmart/ Havoline Lola T92/00 #2	Oval 2 miles	CART	500 Miles	122	Scott Goodyear	Led 38 laps, engine failure
8/9/92	Burke Lakefront Airport	8	5	Newman-Haas Kmart/ Havoline Lola T92/00 #2	Road course 2.369 miles	CART	201.4 Miles	84	Emerson Fittipaldi	Running
8/23/92	Road America	5	5	Newman-Haas Kmart/ Havoline Lola T92/00 #2	Road Course 4 miles	CART	200 Miles	50	Emerson Fittipaldi	Led 2 laps, running
8/30/92	Vancouver	4	6	Newman-Haas Kmart/ Havoline Lola T92/00 #2	Road Course 1.7 miles	CART	167.7 Miles	97	Michael Andretti	Running
9/13/92	Mid-Ohio	4	5	Newman-Haas Kmart/ Havoline Lola T92/00 #2	Road Course 2.25 miles	CART	200 Miles	88	Emerson Fittipaldi	Running
10/3/92	Marlboro Challenge Nazareth Speedway	7	9	Newman-Haas Kmart/ Havoline Lola T92/00 #2	Oval 1 mile	Special event	100 Miles	53	Emerson Fittipaldi	Engine failure
10/4/92	Nazareth Speedway	5	5	Newman-Haas Kmart/ Havoline Lola T92/00 #2	Oval 1 mile	CART	200 Miles	199	Bobby Rahal	Running
10/18/92	Laguna Seca	5	2	Newman-Haas Kmart/ Havoline Lola T92/00 #2	Road Course 2.2 miles	CART	186 Miles	84	Michael Andretti	Running

Mario and Michael relax during a practice day at Indy. Raceday would be one of the worst of Mario's career as both he and Jeff were injured, and Michael's car broke while leading with 27 miles to go. *David Nearpass*

1993

*I'd won 30 races and I was still thought of in terms of being Mario's son.
I still am—but that's a fact of life. Michael Andretti, RACER*

When Michael left Newman-Haas to compete in Formula One with the McLaren team, the previous season's Formula One champion, Nigel Mansell, replaced him. While Mansell was brilliant behind the wheel of a racing machine, rising friction within the team soon made Mario begin contemplating retirement.

The CART season started strong at Surfers Paradise in Queensland, Australia, as Mansell scored his first series victory and Mario had his best finish, fourth, on the street circuit. The next race was on the 1-mile oval at Phoenix, and Mario scored his first victory in four seasons. Starting second, Mario led the opening 10 laps and the last 19 to earn what would be the final on-track victory of his racing career.

Mario held the pole at Indianapolis until Arie Luyendyk out-qualified him later in the day on a cooler track. Yet it was the third consecutive year Mario would start on the front row. He led five times for 73 laps, but his last set of tires didn't perform as he expected and he finished a disappointing fifth, just five seconds behind Fittipaldi. At Michigan, Mario earned the pole with a spectacular 234.275 miles per hour lap that was more than a track record: It was a record for any car on a closed race course. After leading the first 27 laps, Mario finished second to Mansell.

While Mansell went on to win four more races and the CART title, Mario finished sixth in points. He completed 13 of the 16 races and suffered just two mechanical failures. Only Emerson Fittipaldi and Raul Boesel completed more laps during the season, and only Mansell, Fittipaldi and Paul Tracy led more laps. As the season concluded, Mario was frustrated with Mansell's apparent self-elevation to the number one driver on the team. The summer had done nothing to increase the little respect he had for the British driver. Mario decided to retire following the 1994 campaign.

Mario thought he had a good shot at another Indy victory in 1993, but his final set of tires threw the balance of the car off in the closing stages and Mario slipped to fifth. *David Nearpass*

After Mario set a new world closed-course record while qualifying, he and Nigel Mansell run side-by-side at Michigan. They finished one-two, with Mario behind by 9.4 seconds at the finish. *David Nearpass*

CART Points 1993

		Points	Wins
1.	Nigel Mansell	191	5
2.	Emerson Fittipaldi	183	3
3.	Paul Tracy	157	5
4.	Bobby Rahal	133	
5.	Raul Boesel	132	
6.	**Mario**	**117**	**1**
7.	Al Unser Jr.	100	1
8.	Arie Luyendyk	90	
9.	Scott Goodyear	86	
10.	Robby Gordon	84	

Mario Andretti 1993 Record

Date	Event/Track	Qual	Finish	Entrant/Car/Number	Type Track	Sanction & Division	Distance	Laps Compl	Race Winner	Comments
1/31/93	24 Hours of Daytona Daytona International Speedway	7	60	TWR Bud Light Jaguar XJR-12D #3	Road course 3.3 miles	IMSA	24 Hours	18	P. J. Jones/ Mark Dismore/ Rocky Moran	Co-drivers John Nielsen, David Brabham, oil leak
3/21/93	Surfers Paradise	6	4	Newman-Haas Kmart/ Texaco-Havoline Lola T93/06 #6	Street course 2.8 miles	CART	181.5 Miles	65	Nigel Mansell	Running
4/4/93	Phoenix International Raceway	2	1	Newman-Haas Kmart/ Texaco-Havoline Lola T93/06 #6	Oval 1 mile	CART	200 Miles	200	Mario	Led 39 laps
4/18/93	Long Beach Grand Prix Long Beach	6	18	Newman-Haas Kmart/ Texaco-Havoline Lola T93/06 #6	Road course 1.59 miles	CART	167 Miles	94	Paul Tracy	Electrical
5/30/93	Indianapolis 500 Indianapolis Motor Speedway	2	5	Newman-Haas Kmart/ Texaco-Havoline Lola T93/06 #6	Oval 2.5 miles	USAC	500 Miles	200	Emerson Fittipaldi	Led 73 laps, stop and go penalty for entering pits while closed
6/6/93	Wisconsin State Fair Park	5	18	Newman-Haas Kmart/ Texaco-Havoline Lola T93/06 #6	Oval 1 mile	CART	200 Miles	176	Nigel Mansell	Running
6/13/93	Detroit Grand Prix	9	3	Newman-Haas Kmart/ Texaco-Havoline Lola T93/06 #6	Street course 2.1 miles	CART	161.7 Miles	77	Danny Sullivan	Running
6/27/93	Portland International Raceway	5	6	Newman-Haas Kmart/ Texaco-Havoline Lola T93/06 #6	Road course 1.915 miles	CART	200 Miles	101	Emerson Fittipaldi	Led 1 lap, running
7/11/93	Burke Lakefront Airport	11	5	Newman-Haas Kmart/ Texaco-Havoline Lola T93/06 #6	Road course 2.369 miles	CART	201.4 Miles	84	Paul Tracy	Running
7/18/93	Molson Indy Toronto	13	8	Newman-Haas Kmart/ Texaco-Havoline Lola T93/06 #6	Road course 1.78 miles	CART	183.3 Miles	102	Paul Tracy	Running
8/1/93	Michigan 500 Michigan International Speedway	1	2	Newman-Haas Kmart/ Texaco-Havoline Lola T93/06 #6	Oval 2 miles	CART	500 Miles	250	Nigel Mansell	Led 27 laps, running
8/8/93	New Hampshire International Speedway	6	20	Newman-Haas Kmart/ Texaco-Havoline Lola T93/06 #6	Oval 1 mile	CART	200 Miles	137	Nigel Mansell	Wreck with Scott Goodyear
8/22/93	Road America	3	15	Newman-Haas Kmart/ Texaco-Havoline Lola T93/06 #6	Road Course 4 miles	CART	200 Miles	47	Paul Tracy	Blown engine
8/29/93	Vancouver	14	5	Newman-Haas Kmart/ Texaco-Havoline Lola T93/06 #6	Road Course 1.7 miles	CART	173.8 Miles	102	Al Unser Jr.	Running
9/12/93	Mid-Ohio	10	7	Newman-Haas Kmart/ Texaco-Havoline Lola T93/06 #6	Road Course 2.25 miles	CART	200 Miles	89	Emerson Fittipaldi	Running
9/19/93	Nazareth Speedway	6	13	Newman-Haas Kmart/ Texaco-Havoline Lola T93/06 #6	Oval 1 mile	CART	200 Miles	188	Nigel Mansell	Running
10/3/93	Laguna Seca	6	9	Newman-Haas Kmart/ Texaco-Havoline Lola T93/06 #6	Road Course 2.2 miles	CART	186 Miles	83	Paul Tracy	Running

1994

He was the consummate leader in the sense that he knew how to motivate a team to his way of thinking. We had our run-ins, certainly, but I always felt he was the guy you measured yourself against. *Bobby Rahal, RACER*

Preparing for his last Michigan 500, where he started fifth but only lasted 121 laps. The "Arrivederci, Mario" tour honored Mario at each venue as he competed in his final season of competition. *David Nearpass*

After running fourth, Mario's final Indy lasted only 23 laps. *Ken Coles*

"**A**rrivederci, Mario" was the theme for Mario's last season in Indy car racing. The Penske PC23/94s of Al Unser Jr., Fittipaldi, and Tracy were dominant and together they won a dozen races, finishing 1–2–3 in the final points. Michael had returned from Formula One to drive for Chip Ganassi's Target/Scotch Video team. He scored two of the four victories that weren't claimed by the Penske cars.

Numerically, it was Mario's worst season since Clint Brawner hired him 30 years earlier. Uncharacteristically, he didn't lead a lap all season. After finishing third, behind Michael and Fittipeldi at Surfer's Paradise, Mario had just three more finishes in the top 10 all season. He was only running at the finish of half of the races. Following his final CART race, where the engine let go just four laps from the finish, he was 14th in the point standings.

CART Points 1994

		Points	Wins
1.	Al Unser Jr.	225	8
2.	Emerson Fittipaldi	178	1
3.	Paul Tracy	152	3
4.	Michael Andretti	118	2
5.	Robby Gordon	104	
6.	Jacques Villeneuve	94	1
7.	Raul Boesel	90	
8.	Nigel Mansell	88	
9.	Teo Fabi	79	
10.	Bobby Rahal	59	
14.	**Mario**	**45**	

Mario Andretti 1994 Record

Date	Event/Track	Qual	Finish	Entrant/Car/Number	Type Track	Sanction & Division	Distance	Laps Compl	Race Winner	Comments
3/20/94	Surfers Paradise	19	3	Newman-Haas Kmart/Texaco-Havoline Lola T94/00 #6	Street course 2.8 miles	CART	153.7 Miles	55	Michael Andretti	Running
4/10/94	Phoenix International Raceway	4	21	Newman-Haas Kmart/Texaco-Havoline Lola T94/00 #6	Oval 1 mile	CART	200 Miles	156	Emerson Fittipaldi	Wreck with Michael
4/17/94	Long Beach Grand Prix Long Beach	6	5	Newman-Haas Kmart/Texaco-Havoline Lola T94/00 #6	Road course 1.59 miles	CART	167 Miles	104	Al Unser Jr.	Running
5/29/94	Indianapolis 500 Indianapolis Motor Speedway	9	32	Newman-Haas Kmart/Texaco-Havoline Lola T94/00 #6	Oval 2.5 miles	USAC	500 Miles	23	Al Unser Jr.	Fuel system
6/5/94	Wisconsin State Fair Park	13	14	Newman-Haas Kmart/Texaco-Havoline Lola T94/00 #6	Oval 1 mile	CART	192 Miles	185	Al Unser Jr.	Running, race shortened to 192 miles because of rain
6/12/94	Detroit Grand Prix	9	18	Newman-Haas Kmart/Texaco-Havoline Lola T94/00 #6	Street course 2.1 miles	CART	161.7 Miles	75	Paul Tracy	Running
6/26/94	Portland International Raceway	16	9	Newman-Haas Kmart/Texaco-Havoline Lola T94/00 #6	Road course 1.915 miles	CART	200 Miles	100	Al Unser Jr.	Running
7/10/94	Burke Lakefront Airport	9	27	Newman-Haas Kmart/Texaco-Havoline Lola T94/00 #6	Road course 2.369 miles	CART	201.4 Miles	31	Al Unser Jr.	Broken suspension
7/17/94	Molson Indy Toronto	10	4	Newman-Haas Kmart/Texaco-Havoline Lola T94/00 #6	Road course 1.78 miles	CART	174.4 Miles	98	Michael Andretti	Running
7/31/94	Michigan 500 Michigan International Speedway	5	18	Newman-Haas Kmart/Texaco-Havoline Lola T94/00 #6	Oval 2 miles	CART	500 Miles	121	Scott Goodyear	Engine failure
8/14/94	Mid-Ohio	15	10	Newman-Haas Kmart/Texaco-Havoline Lola T94/00 #6	Road Course 2.25 miles	CART	185.7 Miles	82	Al Unser Jr.	Running, race finished 6 laps early because of television schedule
8/21/94	New Hampshire International Speedway	5	19	Newman-Haas Kmart/Texaco-Havoline Lola T94/00 #6	Oval 1 mile	CART	200 Miles	107	Al Unser Jr.	Accident
9/4/94	Vancouver	10	11	Newman-Haas Kmart/Texaco-Havoline Lola T94/00 #6	Road Course 1.7 miles	CART	171 Miles	101	Al Unser Jr.	Running
9/11/94	Road America	7	16	Newman-Haas Kmart/Texaco-Havoline Lola T94/00 #6	Road Course 4 miles	CART	200 Miles	47	Jacques Villeneuve	Engine failure
9/18/94	Nazareth Speedway	5	25	Newman-Haas Kmart/Texaco-Havoline Lola T94/00 #6	Oval 1 mile	CART	200 Miles	40	Paul Tracy	Wreck with Cheever
10/9/94	Laguna Seca	12	19	Newman-Haas Kmart/Texaco-Havoline Lola T94/00 #6	Road Course 2.2 miles	CART	186 Miles	80	Paul Tracy	Engine failure

1995·2000

When we were up there on the podium, I guarantee you that, us three, I certainly could say for myself, 'We were the ones who had the most fun today.' Because we were just, I mean, really balls-out. And I love that. God, I love that. Mario, after finishing second at LeMans in 1995, RACER

It was totally different, the conditions and everything else. I second-guessed the situation and made the rear bar too soft. I underestimated how dry the infield was going to get, watching the F1 practice. It was a mistake. I felt it the first lap. I just couldn't get it to turn. Mario, IMS press release following the Porsche SuperCup events

The 24 Hours of LeMans is an event that naturally appealed to Mario. With his technical interest and love of competition, it was a challenge that he relished. Joining Bob Wollek and Eric Helary in a Courage Porsche, he came closest to winning in 1995. After racing more than 2,500 miles, they finished less than 6 miles behind the winning McLaren despite a variety of incidents and language-exacerbated problems. One stop to repair damaged bodywork took nearly 25 minutes.

In 1996 and 1997, Mario again raced a Courage Porsche. In 1996, Mario, Jan Lammers, and Derek Warrick finished 13th, about 330 miles behind the winner. The next year, he was teamed with Michael and French racing veteran Olivier Grouillard. They completed more than 1,600 miles before being eliminated by mechanical failure.

For the 2000 LeMans, Mario was teamed with David Brabham and Jan Magnussen in the Panoz. They struggled through a variety of mechanical problems to register a 15th-place result, still less than 500 miles behind the winning Audi after the 24 hours.

Mario's final racing events (as of this writing) came in conjunction with the inaugural United States Grand Prix at Indianapolis in September 2000. Mario drove a Porsche 911 in the Porsche SuperCup races that were held on Saturday and Sunday after qualifying and before the Grand Prix. Mario, with Al Unser Jr. and Derek Hill, started near the rear of the field in both races. It gave him an opportunity to compete on the new 2.606-mile Indianapolis road course and to return to the stage where he was a central player for so many years.

The Courage in the pits at LeMans; Mario is ready to climb in. In 1995, he teamed with the late Bob Wollek and Eric Helary to finish second. *Aysedasi*

During the prerace driver's parade in 1997, Mario rides between Michael and codriver Olivier Grouillard. *Aysedasi*

Mario Andretti 1995 - 2000 Record

Date	Event/Track	Qual	Finish	Entrant/Car/Number	Type Track	Sanction & Division	Distance Compl	Laps	Race Winner	Comments
6/18/95	24 Hour of Le Mans	3	2	Courage C34 Porsche #13	Road Course 8.45 Miles	ACO	24 Hours	297	Yannick Dalmas/ Masanori Sekiya/J. J. Lehto	Codrivers Bob Wollek and Eric Helary
6/16/96	24 Hours of Le Mans	11	13	Courage C36 Porsche #4	Road Course 8.45 Miles	ACO	24 Hours	315	Davy Jones/ Alexander Wurz/ Manuel Reuter	Codrivers Jan Lammers and Derek Warrick
6/15/97	24 Hours of Le Mans	13	DNF	Courage C36 Porsche #9	Road Course 8.45 Miles	ACO	24 Hours	197	Michele Alboreto/ Stefan Johansson/ Tom Kristensen	Codrivers Michael Andretti and Olivier Grouillard
6/18/00	24 Hours of Le Mans	4	15	Panoz LMP-1 Roadster	Road Course 8.45 Miles	ACO	24 Hours	315	Frank Biela/ Tom Kristensen/ Emanuele Pirro	Codrivers David Brabham and Jan Magnussen
9/23/00	Porsche Pirelli SuperCup Indianapolis Motor Speedway		17	Infineon Technologies Porsche 900 GT3 Cup #15	Road Course 2.6 Miles	PSC			Bernd Maylander	
9/24/00	Porsche Pirelli SuperCup Indianapolis Motor Speedway		18	Infineon Technologies Porsche 900 GT3 Cup #15	Road Course 2.6 Miles	PSC			Jorg Bergmeister	

In 1996, Mario had a shunt at the Indianapolis corner shortly after 11 a.m., just into the 21st hour of the race. Here the course marshals work the Courage C36 Porsche free, and after a loss of several minutes, Mario headed back to the pits where the front bodywork was repaired. *Aysedasi*

CHAPTER 5

Finishing Touches

I think that I am basically a very optimistic person by nature anyway. And I always feel a lot better when I give a positive interview. Not every interview can be positive, unfortunately life is not that sweet. Again it's just a matter of expressing your views, and sometimes maybe there wouldn't be so much controversy if you would be totally politically sensitive, but there are times when I have a tendency to really say it like it is. Not all of my interviews have been perfect, as far as being politically correct. *Mario*

Two of the best of a generation, Mario and Emmo accumulated a total of five Indy car titles, three Formula One championships and three Indy victories. Here they exchange notes at California Speedway in 2001. *Howard Koby*

In 1996, Mario helped make an IMAX movie about CART racing. Here he dices with Robby Gordon at Michigan with a special IMAX camera mounted on his machine. *Ken Coles*

Since retirement, Mario has remained busy. He has business interests in a variety of successful endeavors, including auto dealerships and car washes. Andretti Winery, located in Napa Valley, produces a variety of popular wines that are nationally distributed. Mario has also become a frequent and popular speaker for businesses and conferences. Grandchildren also keep Mario busy (Michael has three children, and Jeff two) and he enjoys time with his expanding family.

A number of projects have also attracted Mario's attention. One that has received national acclaim is the IMAX movie, "Super Speedway," that Mario helped develop and that focuses on Michael's 1996 racing effort. Mario worked with director Stephen Low to create a realistic look into the world of championship racing. He drove a Lola with an IMAX camera, created specially for the film, mounted on the car under racing conditions.

Mario stays in touch with racing by continuing to follow Michael's efforts. He is frequently invited to participate in special tributes. On May 18, 2000, Mario was honored at the Indianapolis Motor Speedway as part of their annual legends program. Thousands of fans came out, and the autograph line was one of the longest ever seen at the Speedway.

A late night pit stop for the Panoz LMP-1 roadster at LeMans. When Mario raced at LeMans in 2000, he became one of the few drivers to compete in six different decades. *Aysedasi*

Standing between the track and pit lane, Mario has the stopwatch on Michael. After a five-year absence, Michael returned to Indy in 2001, led 16 laps and finished third. *Ken Coles*

Mario tested the road course at Indy during the Porsche SuperCup race as part of the inaugural U.S. Grand Prix. *Photo courtesy of Indianapolis Motor Speedway.*

Focus on Indy

CHAPTER 6

As a driver you cannot rank a title higher than a single race. Career-wise, Indianapolis arguably has to be one of the most meaningful, if not the most meaningful event, in any professional driver's career if you can put it under your belt, because it can technically change your life overnight. Mario, Gamenight, ESPN Radio

Mario Andretti's history at Indianapolis is as much a part of American racing lore as Barney Oldfield's Peerless Green Dragon and Ralph DePalma pushing his Mercedes in the second 500 mile race. In the 29 times he rolled off the starting line at Indy, Mario experienced some of the highest peaks as well as the lowest valleys of his racing career. Two thoughts generally overshadow most people's recollections of Mario's performances at Indy. His win in 1969 is foremost. Then we remember his many close attempts at a second victory, only to be denied by seemingly the cruelest tricks of Lady Luck.

Mario came to Indianapolis for the first time in 1965, under the guidance of veterans Clint Brawner and Jim McGee. After starting fourth, he ran steadily all day and trailed Jim Clark and Parnelli Jones at the finish. This effort earned Mario the Rookie of the Year award, which would also be won by both of his sons, Michael and Jeff, in their first attempts at Indy.

When Mario won at Indy in 1969, the popular opinion was that it was only the first of many victories on Memorial Day weekend. But as is so often the case, Mario's "month of May" was truly unique. First he had a new machine, a tricky four-wheel drive machine designed and built by Colin Chapman's Lotus factory. Then, days before the opening of qualifying, the Lotus broke. An improperly machined hub failed and the Lotus was destroyed. Chapman withdrew the rest of the Lotus cars after Mario's wreck. Brawner and McGee unloaded the trusty Hawk and with just two days to set the car up, Mario qualified 2nd fastest.

In the race there were concerns about keeping the turbocharged Ford cool, and Mario ran a patient pace. Foyt led early, but ran into problems. Lloyd Ruby appeared headed for the win until he pulled out of his pits while his fuel hose was still connected and ripped a gash in the side of his fuel tank. Mario led from lap 106 to the finish and a jubilant victory lane celebration.

Mario's record at Indy is impressive. He started on the pole three times, 1966, 1967, and 1987. He is second to A. J. Foyt with 29 starts in the 500. His 556 laps led are the third most in history and his total miles completed, 7,625, ranks fourth.

But in the years after 1969, Mario came so darned close to winning again that a separate chapter of racing legend has grown up around his luck at the Brickyard. It seems that Mario has experienced almost every method of mechanical failure, incident, and fate to take him out of contention. Here are just a handful of excerpts from Mario's Indianapolis story:

The only injuries that Mario suffered when the Lotus wrecked in 1969 were painful facial burns. *John Mahoney*

A tradition at Indy is that the picture of the previous year's winner is printed on all of the tickets. Mario's photo made the 1970 Indy tickets a collectors' item. *Jim Graybeal collection*

1967 – lost a wheel in turn one and spun into the infield.

1971 – caught up in a multicar wreck when Steve Krisiloff blew an engine in turn three.

1975 – a mechanical failure caused the Viceroy Eagle to spin down the back straight and hit the inside wall.

1981 – finished second to Bobby Unser. After the race, officials penalized Unser one lap for passing under the yellow and declared Mario the winner. But an appeals panel reversed the ruling and reinstated Unser months later.

1982 – In the middle of the front row, Kevin Cogan lost control of his car when the field accelerated onto the main straightaway for the start. Cogan ricocheted into Mario, taking both of them out of the race before they crossed the starting line.

1983 – Johnny Parsons Jr. spun in front of him and both cars hit the wall.

1985 – led 107 laps until Danny Sullivan caught up and tried to pass. Sullivan spun in front of Mario, but saved the car. Sullivan then came back to outrun Mario to the finish by two seconds.

1987 – dominated the race, handily leading all but seven laps when his engine failed. Engineering tests later determined that by taking it easy and not running at top rpm, Mario probably initiated the failure.

1993 – was in the lead late in the race, but the set of tires mounted on the last pit stop didn't perform as predicted, and Mario dropped to fifth while fighting a poorly-handling car.

Mario at speed in the 1973 Parnelli. This was Maurice Phillippe's second design for the Vel's Parnelli Jones Racing team and it was more orthodox than the first. *Ken Coles*

Date	SP	FP	Entrant/Car/Number	Laps Compl	Race Winner	Comments
5/31/65	4	3	Dean Van Lines Brawner/Hawk #12	200	Jim Clark	Rookie of the Year
5/30/66	1	18	Dean Van Lines Brawner/Hawk #1	27	Graham Hill	Led 16 laps, engine
5/30/67	1	30	Dean Van Lines Brawner/Hawk #1	58	A. J. Foyt	Lost wheel in turn 1
5/30/68	4	33	Andretti Overseas National Airways Brawner/Ford #2	2	Bobby Unser	First race with turbocharged Ford engine - burned piston, relieved Larry Dickson for 10 laps - finished 28, piston
5/30/69	**2**	**1**	**Granatelli STP Oil Treatment Hawk III #2**	**200**	**Mario**	**Wrecked Lotus in practice, led 116 laps**
5/30/70	8	6	Granatelli STP Oil Treatment McNamara #1	199	Al Unser	Running
5/29/71	9	30	Granatelli STP Oil Treatment McNamara #5	11	Al Unser	Accident
5/27/72	5	8	Vel's Parnelli Jones Viceroy Parnelli #9	194	Mark Donohue	Ran out of fuel with five laps remaining
5/30/73	6	30	Vel's Parnelli Jones Viceroy Parnelli #11	4	Gordon Johncock	Burned piston
5/26/74	5	31	Vel's Parnelli Jones Viceroy Eagle #5	2	Bobby Unser	Engine valve
5/25/75	27	28	Vel's Parnelli Jones Viceroy Eagle #21	49	Bobby Unser	Mechanical failure, wreck
5/30/76	19	8	Penske CAM-2 McLaren #6	101	Johnny Rutherford	Running, stopped by rain
5/29/77	6	26	Penske CAM-2 McLaren #9	47	A. J. Foyt	Broken header
5/28/78	33	12	Penske Gould Charge Penske #7	185	Al Unser	Qualified 8th by Mike Hiss, running
5/25/80	2	20	Penske Essex PC9/80 #12	70	Johnny Rutherford	Engine seized
5/24/81	32	2	STP Oii Treatment Wildcat #40	200	Bobby Unser	Mario ruled winner when Unser was penalized 1 lap, decision reversed by appeal panel
5/29/82	4	31	STP Intermedics Wildcat 8B #40	0	Gordon Johncock	Wreck at start
5/29/83	11	23	Newman-Haas Budweiser Lola T700 #3	79	Tom Sneva	Wreck with Johnny Parsons Jr.
5/27/84	6	17	Newman-Haas Budweiser Lola T800 #3	153	Rick Mears	Led 29 laps, broken nose cone
5/26/85	4	2	Newman-Haas Beatrice Lola T900 #3	200	Danny Sullivan	Led 107 laps, trailed by 2.47 seconds
6/1/86	30	32	Newman-Haas Lola T86/00 #2	19	Bobby Rahal	Ignition, race delayed one week by rain
5/24/87	1	9	Newman-Haas Hanna Car Wash Lola T87/00 #5	180	Al Unser	Led 170 laps, broken valve spring
5/29/88	4	20	Newman-Haas Amoco/Kmart Lola T87/00 #6	118	Rick Mears	Electrical failure
5/28/89	5	4	Newman-Haas Kmart/Havoline Lola T89/00 #5	193	Emerson Fittipaldi	Led 1 lap, running
5/27/90	6	27	Newman-Haas Kmart/Havoline Lola T90/00 #6	60	Arie Luyendyk	Engine failure
5/26/91	3	7	Newman-Haas Kmart/Havoline Lola T91/00 #6	187	Rick Mears	Led 22 laps, engine failure, stalled at pit entrance
5/24/92	3	23	Newman-Haas Kmart/Havoline Lola T92/00 #2	78	Al Unser Jr.	Led 1 lap, wreck turn four
5/30/93	2	5	Newman-Haas Kmart/Texaco-Havoline Lola T93/06 #6	200	Emerson Fittipaldi	Led 73 laps, stop and go penalty for entering pits while closed
5/29/94	9	32	Newman-Haas Kmart/Texaco-Havoline Lola T94/00 #6	23	Al Unser Jr.	Fuel system

Indy 500 Winners

Year	Winner		Year	Winner
1911	Ray Harroun		1959	Rodger Ward
1912	Joe Dawson		1960	Jim Rathmann
1913	Jules Goux		1961	A. J. Foyt
1914	Rene Thomas		1962	Rodger Ward
1915	Ralph DePalma		1963	Parnelli Jones
1916	Dario Resta		1964	A. J. Foyt
1917 – 1918	No race		1965	Jim Clark
1919	Howdy Wilcox		1966	Graham Hill
1920	Gaston Chevrolet		1967	A. J. Foyt
1921	Tommy Milton		1968	Bobby Unser
1922	Jimmy Murphy		**1969**	**Mario**
1923	Tommy Milton		1970	Al Unser
1924	L. L. Corum/Joe Boyer		1971	Al Unser
1925	Peter DePaolo		1972	Mark Donohue
1926	Frank Lockhart		1973	Gordon Johncock
1927	George Souders		1974	Johnny Rutherford
1928	Lou Meyer		1975	Bobby Unser
1929	Ray Keech		1976	Johnny Rutherford
1930	Billy Arnold		1977	A. J. Foyt
1931	Lou Schneider		1978	Al Unser
1932	Fred Frame		1979	Rick Mears
1933	Lou Meyer		1980	Johnny Rutherford
1934	Bill Cummings		1981	Bobby Unser
1935	Kelly Petillo		1982	Gordon Johncock
1936	Lou Meyer		1983	Tom Sneva
1937	Wilbur Shaw		1984	Rick Mears
1938	Floyd Roberts		1985	Danny Sullivan
1939	Wilbur Shaw		1986	Bobby Rahal
1940	Wilbur Shaw		1987	Al Unser
1941	Floyd Davis/Mauri Rose		1988	Rick Mears
1942 – 1945	No races		1989	Emerson Fittipaldi
1946	George Robson		1990	Arie Luyendyk
1947	Mauri Rose		1991	Rick Mears
1948	Mauri Rose		1992	Al Unser Jr.
1949	Bill Holland		1993	Emerson Fittipaldi
1950	Johnnie Parsons		1994	Al Unser Jr.
1951	Lee Wallard		1995	Jacques Villeneuve
1952	Troy Ruttman		1996	Buddy Lazier
1953	Bill Vukovich		1997	Arie Luyendyk
1954	Bill Vukovich		1998	Eddie Cheever
1955	Bob Sweikert		1999	Kenny Brack
1956	Pat Flaherty		2000	Juan Montoya
1957	Sam Hanks		2001	Helio Castroneves
1958	Jimmy Bryan		2002	Helio Castroneves

I think it was huge for everybody. It was the first time any of us won it. Clint had been there for 25 years and hadn't won it. And myself, I had seen 10 or 12, and Mario was there for 5 races. We had been close a lot of times, we had dominant cars for two or three years, but we still couldn't put it together. That year, the way it all started out, it looked like there was no way we could do it. Where in other years, we could sit on the pole and lead the race easily, but we just couldn't finish. So it was a big victory.

Jim McGee on the 1969 Indianapolis 500

For the second year, the Vel's Parnelli Jones team ran Eagles at Indy in 1975. The cars built by Dan Gurney's All-American Racers were among the most successful during the 1970s. *John Mahoney*

The Newman/Haas Lola started fourth at Indy in 1988, but Mario spent nearly as long in the pits with a gearbox problem as he did on the track. Eventually, an electrical ignition problem proved unsolvable. *Ken Coles*

Mario at speed in the four-wheel-drive Lotus at Indy in 1969 before the wheel hub failed. Colin Chapman withdrew the other Lotus before qualifying. *Ken Coles*

In addition to the Lotus team, Essex Petroleum sponsored Mario's Penske machinery through the first half of 1980. After starting on the front row at Indy, the Cosworth engine let go while Mario was running fourth. *Ken Coles*

Mario was the fastest car 24 hours before pole qualifying in 1978, but rain washed out the entire first weekend. While Mario was racing at Monaco the next weekend, Mike Hiss qualified the Penske in eighth and Mario started last. *Ken Coles*

Mario worked with many of the most successful mechanics and designers during his career. In 1972, he chats with George Bignotti before climbing into the Parnelli at Indy. The dihedral wings were an idea that didn't work as well as Maurice Phillippe expected. *Ken Coles*

Focus on Formula One

These guys on this side of the Atlantic, all the horror stories from Formula 1 and how they're treated – true or not true – it's all a matter of frame of mind. It all boils down to how badly do you want to do it – the hell with everything else.
Mario, RACER

Mario has always been very proud of his Italian heritage. Through his career it is easy to see that other Italians, including George Bignotti and Enzo Ferrari, had a big influence on the decisions he made. Likewise, the Italian racetrack known as Monza had a lasting affect on Mario's life. When he saw Alberto Ascari's victory in the 1954 Italian Grand Prix, he decided he wanted to be a racing driver. And not just any racing driver, but a Grand Prix racing driver. Up to 1975, everything was a step toward this goal.

In 1968, Mario was set to make his Grand Prix debut at Monza, and in fact had qualified seventh, but was prevented from starting the race by politics. Yet this taste only whetted Mario's appetite for Formula One, and it served notice to everyone at Monza that weekend that he would be back.

When Mario finally clinched the World Championship, on a day that he will remember both for its satisfaction and its tragedy, it was at the same Italian Grand Prix, and at the same venue that he had visited 24 years earlier. In his racing career, he had accomplished his most personal goal. Yet after Mario had left Formula One, there was one final hurrah, one more triumph. This also came at Monza, when Ferrari asked Mario to sub for the injured Didier Pironi. When the news was announced, the fans welcomed Mario everywhere he went. It was a magical week, and Mario put the Ferrari on the pole one last time.

Mario takes the Parnelli through a turn at the first Long Beach Grand Prix in 1975. This F-5000 race was the inaugural event on the Long Beach street course, and its success led to a 1976 U.S. Grand Prix West date. *Howard Koby*

Mario edged teammate Ronnie Peterson for the pole by 0.09 second at Hockenheim in 1978. He went on to claim his fifth victory of the season. A potential 1 - 2 finish for Lotus was dashed when Peterson suffered a gearbox failure eight laps from the finish. *Ken Coles*

Formula One Fastest Laps (through 2001)

		Fastest Laps
1.	Michael Schumacher	44
2.	Alain Prost	41
3.	Nigel Mansell	30
4.	Jim Clark	28
5.	Mika Hakkinen	25
6.	Niki Lauda	24
7.	Juan Manuel Fangio	23
	Nelson Piquet	23
9.	Gerhard Berger	21
10.	Stirling Moss	19
	Ayrton Senna	19
	Damon Hill	19
13.	David Coulthard	17
14.	Jackie Stewart	15
	Clay Regazzoni	15
16.	Jacky Ickx	14
17.	Alan Jones	13
	Riccardo Patrese	13
19.	Alberto Ascari	12
	Jack Brabham	12
	Rene Arnoux	12
22.	John Surtees	11
23.	**Mario**	**10**
	Graham Hill	10

Formula One Career Poles (through 2001)

		Poles
1.	Ayrton Senna	65
2.	Michael Schumacher	43
3.	Jim Clark	33
	Alain Prost	33
5.	Nigel Mansell	32
6.	Juan Manual Fangio	29
7.	Mika Hakkinen	26
8.	Niki Lauda	24
	Nelson Piquet	24
10.	Damon Hill	20
11.	**Mario**	**18**
	Rene Arnoux	18
13.	Jackie Stewart	17
14.	Stirling Moss	16
15.	Alberto Ascari	14
	Ronnie Peterson	14
17.	James Hunt	14
18.	Jack Brabham	13
	Graham Hill	13
	Jacky Ickx	13
	Jacques Villeneuve	13

Mario won the 1977 Long Beach Grand Prix in the Lotus 78 Ford Cosworth DFV. Here he comes up to overtake Peterson in the six-wheeled Elf Tyrrell. *Howard Koby*

Mario in the first outing for the Parnelli Formula One design at Mosport Park in the 1974 Canadian Grand Prix. He battled with Denny Hulme before finishing seventh. *Ken Coles*

Formula One Summary

		All-time Rank	Notes
Seasons	14	-	
Races	128	29	
Races Not Qualified	1	-	
Championships	1	14	Tied with Farina, Hawthorne, D. Hill, P. Hill, Hunt, Hulme, Mansell, Rindt, Rosberg, Scheckter, Surtees, J. Villeneuve
Victories	12	18	Tied with Alan Jones and Carlos Reutemann
Winning Percentage	9.2	23	
Points	180	34	Tied with John Surtees
Wins In A Season	6	15	Ascari, Fangio, Clark, Stewart, Hunt, Mansell, Senna, D. Hill and M. Schumacher also have six wins in a season
Pole Positions	18	11	Tied with Rene Arnoux
Fastest Laps	10	23	Tied with Graham Hill
Podium Finishes	19	38	Tied with Patrick Depailler and Dan Gurney
Front Row Starts	24	23	Tied with James Hunt
Laps Completed	5,278	40	
Miles Completed	15,189.4	44	
Races Led	22	23	Tied with Alberto Ascari
Laps Led	798	16	
Miles Led	2220	17	

Driving the Lotus 77, Mario finished third at Mosport Park behind James Hunt and Patrick Depailler in 1976. *Ken Coles*

First turn of Grand Prix racing is electric. At Long Beach in 1978, Gilles Villeneuve grabbed the lead when John Watson pushed Carlos Reutemann wide. Mario started fourth, but only trailed Reutemann's Ferrari at the finish. *Howard Koby*

Formula One Race Victories (through 2001)

		Victories
1.	Michael Schumacher	53
2.	Alain Prost	51
3.	Ayrton Senna	41
4.	Nigel Mansell	31
5.	Jackie Stewart	27
6.	Jim Clark	25
	Niki Lauda	25
8.	Juan Manual Fangio	24
9.	Nelson Piquet	23
10.	Damon Hill	22
11.	Mika Hakkinen	20
	Stirling Moss	16
	Jack Brabham	14
	Graham Hill	14
15.	Emerson Fittipaldi	14
16.	Alberto Ascari	13
17.	**Mario**	12
	Carlos Reutemann	12
19.	Alan Jones	12
20.	David Coulthard	11
	Jacques Villeneuve	11

Mario Andretti Formula One Record

Date	Event/Track	Qual	Finish	Entrant/Car/Number	Laps Compl	Comments
9/8/68	Italian Grand Prix, Monza	7	-	Lotus Cosworth 49B #18	0	Not permitted to start because of racing in Indianapolis the previous day
10/6/68	United States Grand Prix, Watkins Glen	1	DNF	Lotus Cosworth 49B #12	32	Clutch failure
3/1/69	South African Grand Prix, Kyalami	6	DNF	Lotus-Cosworth 49B #3	31	Gearbox failure while running third
8/3/69	German Grand Prix Nurburgring	12	DNF	Gold Leaf Lotus 63 Ford Cosworth #3	0	Accident on lap 1
10/5/69	United States Grand Prix Watkins Glen	13	DNF	Gold Leaf Lotus 63 Ford Cosworth #9	3	Suspension
3/7/70	South African Grand Prix, Kyalami	11	DNF	STP March Ford #8	26	Overheating
4/19/70	Spanish Grand Prix, Jarama	16	3	STP March Ford #18	89	Running
7/18/70	British Grand Prix Brands Hatch	9	DNF	STP March Ford #26	29	Suspension
8/2/70	German Grand Prix Hockenheim	9	DNF	STP March Ford #26	15	Gearbox failure
8/16/70	Austrian Grand Prix Österreichring	18	DNF	STP March Ford #5	13	Accident
3/6/71	**South African Grand Prix Kyalami**	**4**	**1**	**Ferrari 312B/2 #6**	**70**	**Led final four laps**
4/18/71	Spanish Grand Prix Montjuich Park	8	DNF	Ferrari 312B/2 #6	50	Fuel pump failed
5/23/71	Monaco Grand Prix Monaco	-	-	Ferrari 312B/2 #6	0	Did not qualify
6/20/71	Dutch Grand Prix Zandvoort	18	DNF	Ferrari 312B/2 #4	5	Fuel pump failed
8/1/71	German Grand Prix Nurburgring	11	4	Ferrari 312B/2 #5	12	Running
1/23/72	Argentine Grand Prix Buenos Aires	9	DNF	Ferrari 312B2-72 #10	20	Engine misfire
3/4/72	South African Grand Prix Kyalami	6	4	Ferrari 312B2-72 #7	79	Running
5/1/72	Spanish Grand Prix Jarama	5	DNF	Ferrari 312B2-72 #7	23	Engine
9/10/72	Italian Grand Prix Monza	7	7	Ferrari 312B2-72 #3	54	Running
10/8/72	United States Grand Prix Watkins Glen	10	6	Ferrari 312B2-72 #9	58	Running
9/22/74	Canadian Grand Prix Mosport Park	16	7	Vel's Parnelli Jones Viceroy Parnelli VPJ4 Cosworth #55	79	Running
10/6/74	United States Grand Prix Watkins Glen	3	DQ	Vel's Parnelli Jones Viceroy Parnelli VPJ4 Cosworth #55	4	Electrical problems on the grid, disqualified when he was push started
1/12/75	Argentine Grand Prix Buenos Aires	10	DNF	Vel's Parnelli Jones Viceroy VPJ4 Cosworth #27	27	Transmission failure
1/26/75	Brazilian Grand Prix Interlagos	18	7	Vel's Parnelli Jones Viceroy VPJ4 Cosworth #27	40	

Date	Event/Track	Qual	Finish	Entrant/Car/Number	Laps Compl	Comments
3/1/75	South African Grand Prix Kyalami	6	17	Vel's Parnelli Jones Viceroy VPJ4 Cosworth #27	70	CV joint broke
4/27/75	Spanish Grand Prix Montjuich Park	4	DNF	Vel's Parnelli Jones Viceroy VPJ4 Cosworth #27	16	Ran fastest lap of the race on lap 14, suspension/accident
5/11/75	Monaco Grand Prix Monaco	13	DNF	Vel's Parnelli Jones Viceroy VPJ4 Cosworth #27	9	Oil leak
6/8/75	Swedish Grand Prix, Anderstorp	15	4	Vel's Parnelli Jones Viceroy VPJ4 Cosworth #27	80	
7/6/75	French Grand Prix Paul Ricard	15	5	Vel's Parnelli Jones Viceroy VPJ4 Cosworth #27	54	Running
7/19/75	British Grand Prix Silverstone	12	12	Vel's Parnelli Jones Viceroy VPJ4 Cosworth #27	54	Race stopped by rain, finishers 2 through 5 involved in an accident on lap 56, order reverted to start of lap 56
8/3/75	German Grand Prix Nurburgring	13	10	Vel's Parnelli Jones Viceroy VPJ4 Cosworth #27	12	Out of fuel
8/17/75	Austrian Grand Prix Österreichring	19	DNF	Vel's Parnelli Jones Viceroy VPJ4 Cosworth #27	1	Accident in rain, race halted after 29 laps
9/7/75	Italian Grand Prix Monza	15	DNF	Vel's Parnelli Jones Viceroy VPJ4 Cosworth #27	1	Multicar accident
10/5/75	United States Grand Prix Watkins Glen	5	DNF	Vel's Parnelli Jones Viceroy VPJ4 Cosworth #27	9	Suspension
1/25/76	Brazilian Grand Prix, Interlagos	16	DNF	John Player Lotus 77 Cosworth #6	6	Accident
3/6/76	South African Grand Prix, Kyalami	13	6	VPJ American Racing Wheels VPJ4B Cosworth #27	77	Running
3/28/76	United States Grand Prix West Long Beach	15	DNF	VPJ American Racing Wheels VPJ4B Cosworth #27	15	Water leak
5/2/76	Spanish Grand Prix Jarama	9	DNF	John Player Lotus 77 Cosworth #5	34	Gearbox failure
5/16/76	Belgian Grand Prix Zolder	11	DNF	John Player Lotus 77 Cosworth #5	28	CV joint
6/13/76	Swedish Grand Prix, Anderstorp	2	DNF	John Player Lotus 77 Cosworth #5	45	Led 45 laps, was to be penalized one minute for jumping the start, engine failure
7/4/76	French Grand Prix Paul Ricard	7	5	John Player Lotus 77 Cosworth #5	54	Running
7/18/76	British Grand Prix Brands Hatch	3	DNF	John Player Lotus 77 Cosworth #5	4	Engine problems.
8/1/76	German Grand Prix Nurburgring	12	12	John Player Lotus 77 Cosworth #5	14	Running

Date	Event/Track	Qual	Finish	Entrant/Car/Number	Laps Compl	Comments
8/15/76	Austrian Grand Prix					
	Österreichring	9	5	John Player Lotus 77 Cosworth #5	54	Running
8/29/76	Dutch Grand Prix					
	Zandvoort	6	3	John Player Lotus 77 Cosworth #5	75	
9/12/76	Italian Grand Prix, Monza	14	DNF	John Player Lotus 77 Cosworth #5	23	Accident
10/3/76	Canadian Grand Prix					
	Mosport Park	5	3	John Player Lotus 77 Cosworth #5	80	Running
10/10/76	United States Grand Prix East					
	Watkins Glen	11	DNF	John Player Lotus 77 Cosworth #5	23	Suspension
10/24/76	**Japanese Grand Prix**					
	Mt. Fuji	**1**	**1**	**John Player Lotus 77 Cosworth #5**	**73**	**Led 10 laps, first Japanese Grand Prix**
1/9/77	Argentine Grand Prix					
	Buenos Aires	8	5	John Player Lotus 78 Cosworth #5	51	Wheel bearing failure while running second
1/23/77	Brazilian Grand Prix, Interlagos	3	DNF	John Player Lotus 78 Cosworth #5	19	Ignition
3/5/77	South African Grand Prix, Kyalami	6	DNF	John Player Lotus 78 Cosworth #5	43	Accident, front suspension damage
4/3/77	**United States Grand Prix West**					
	Long Beach	**2**	**1**	**John Player Lotus 78 Cosworth #5**	**80**	**Led 4 laps**
5/8/77	**Spanish Grand Prix**					
	Jarama	**1**	**1**	**John Player Lotus 78 Cosworth #5**	**75**	**Dominating performance – led all 75 laps from the pole**
5/22/77	Monaco Grand Prix					
	Monaco	10	5	John Player Lotus 78 Cosworth #5	76	Running
6/5/77	Belgian Grand Prix					
	Zolder	1	DNF	John Player Lotus 78 Cosworth #5	1	Tangled with John Watson in the rain
6/19/77	Swedish Grand Prix, Anderstorp	1	6	John Player Lotus 78 Cosworth #5	72	Led 68 laps, fuel metering problem while leading with three laps to go, fastest lap
7/3/77	**French Grand Prix**					
	Dijon-Prenois	**1**	**1**	**John Player Lotus 78 Cosworth #5**	**80**	**Passed John Watson on last lap for victory, led one lap**
7/16/77	British Grand Prix					
	Silverstone	6	14	John Player Lotus 78 Cosworth #5	62	Engine failure
7/31/77	German Grand Prix					
	Hockenheim-Ring	7	DNF	John Player Lotus 78 Cosworth #5	34	Engine failure
8/14/77	Austrian Grand Prix					
	Österreichring	3	DNF	John Player Lotus 78 Cosworth #5	11	Led 11 laps, engine failure while leading
8/28/77	Dutch Grand Prix					
	Zandvoort	1	DNF	John Player Lotus 78 Cosworth #5	75	Engine failure
9/11/77	**Italian Grand Prix, Monza**	**4**	**1**	**John Player Lotus 78 Cosworth #5**	**52**	**Led 43 laps, set fastest lap**
10/2/77	United States Grand Prix East					
	Watkins Glen	4	2	John Player Lotus 78 Cosworth #5	59	Running
10/9/77	Canadian Grand Prix					
	Mosport Park	1	9	John Player Lotus 78 Cosworth #5	80	Led 76 laps, engine failure while leading
10/23/77	Japanese Grand Prix					
	Mt. Fuji	1	DNF	John Player Lotus 78 Cosworth #5	1	Accident with Laffite
1/15/78	**Argentine Grand Prix**					
	Buenos Aires	**1**	**1**	**John Player Lotus 78 Cosworth #5**	**52**	**Led every lap from the pole**
1/29/78	Brazilian Grand Prix					
	Jacarepagua	3	4	John Player Lotus 78 Cosworth #5	63	Running, jammed in fourth gear for last 6 laps
3/4/78	South African Grand Prix, Kyalami	2	7	John Player Lotus 78 Cosworth #5	77	Led 20 laps, had fastest race lap, lost 1 lap because of a late race fuel stop

Date	Event/Track	Qual	Finish	Entrant/Car/Number	Laps Compl	Comments
4/2/78	United States Grand Prix West Long Beach	4	2	John Player Lotus 78 Cosworth #5	80	Running
5/7/78	Monaco Grand Prix Monaco	4	11	John Player Lotus 78 Cosworth #5	69	Fixed fuel leak, running, 6 laps behind
5/21/78	**Belgian Grand Prix Zolder**	1	1	**John Player Lotus 79 Cosworth #5**	70	**Led all 70 laps, first race for new Lotus 79**
6/4/78	**Spanish Grand Prix Jarama**	1	1	**John Player Lotus 79 Cosworth #5**	75	**Led 70 laps, fastest lap**
6/17/78	Swedish Grand Prix, Anderstorp	1	DNF	John Player Lotus 79 Cosworth #5	46	Led 38 laps, engine failure
7/2/78	**French Grand Prix Paul Ricard**	2	1	**John Player Lotus 79 Cosworth #5**	54	**Passed John Watson on first lap, led all 54 laps**
7/16/78	British Grand Prix Brands Hatch	2	DNF	John Player Lotus 79 Cosworth #5	28	Led 23 laps, flat tire, engine failure
7/30/78	**German Grand Prix Hockenheim**	1	1	**John Player Lotus 79 Cosworth #5**	45	**Led 41 laps**
8/13/78	Austrian Grand Prix Österreichring	2	DNF	John Player Lotus 79 Cosworth #5	0	Accident with Reutemann on first lap
8/27/78	**Dutch Grand Prix Zandvoort**	1	1	**John Player Lotus 79 Cosworth #5**	75	**Led all 75 laps from pole**
9/10/78	Italian Grand Prix, Monza	1	6	John Player Lotus 79 Cosworth #5	40	Led last 6 laps, penalized 1 minute for jumping restart
10/1/78	United States Grand Prix East Watkins Glen	1	DNF	John Player Lotus 79 Cosworth #5	59	Led 2 laps, engine failure
10/8/78	Canadian Grand Prix Montreal	9	10	John Player Lotus 79 Cosworth #5	69	Spun on lap 6, running
1/21/79	Argentine Grand Prix Buenos Aires	7	5	Martini Racing Team Essex Lotus 79 Cosworth #1	52	Running
2/4/79	Brazilian Grand Prix Interlagos	4	DNF	Martini Racing Team Essex Lotus 79 Cosworth #1	2	Fuel leak, fire
3/3/79	South African Grand Prix, Kyalami	8	4	Martini Racing Team Essex Lotus 79 Cosworth #1	78	Running
4/8/79	United States Grand Prix West Long Beach	6	4	Martini Racing Team Essex Lotus 79 Cosworth #1	80	Running
4/29/79	Spanish Grand Prix Jarama	4	3	Martini Racing Team Essex Lotus 80 Cosworth #1	75	Running
5/13/79	Belgian Grand Prix Zolder	5	DNF	Martini Racing Team Essex Lotus 79 Cosworth #1	27	Brakes
5/27/79	Monaco Grand Prix Monaco	13	DNF	Martini Racing Team Essex Lotus 80 Cosworth #1	21	Rear suspension

Date	Event/Track	Qual	Finish	Entrant/Car/Number	Laps Compl	Comments
7/1/79	French Grand Prix Dijon-Prenois	12	DNF	Martini Racing Team Essex Lotus 80 Cosworth #1	51	Brakes, suspension
7/14/79	British Grand Prix Silverstone	9	DNF	Martini Racing Team Essex Lotus 79 Cosworth #1	3	Wheel bearing failure
7/29/79	German Grand Prix Hockenheim	11	DNF	Martini Racing Team Essex Lotus 79 Cosworth #1	16	Transmission
8/12/79	Austrian Grand Prix Österreichring	15	DNF	Martini Racing Team Essex Lotus 79 Cosworth #1	0	Clutch
8/26/79	Dutch Grand Prix Zandvoort	17	DNF	Martini Racing Team Essex Lotus 79 Cosworth #1	9	Rear suspension
9/9/79	Italian Grand Prix, Monza	10	5	Martini Racing Team Essex Lotus 79 Cosworth #1	50	Running
9/30/79	Canadian Grand Prix Montreal	10	10	Martini Racing Team Essex Lotus 79 Cosworth #1	66	Ran out of fuel
10/17/79	United States Grand Prix East Watkins Glen	17	DNF	Martini Racing Team Essex Lotus 79 Cosworth #1	59	Gearbox
1/13/80	Argentine Grand Prix Buenos Aires	6	DNF	Team Essex Lotus 81 Cosworth #11	20	Fuel system metering
1/27/80	Brazilian Grand Prix Interlagos	11	DNF	Team Essex Lotus 81 Cosworth #11	1	Spin
3/1/80	South African Grand Prix, Kyalami	15	12	Team Essex Lotus 81 Cosworth #11	76	Running
4/30/80	United States Grand Prix West Long Beach	15	DNF	Team Essex Lotus 81 Cosworth #11	0	Accident with Jarier
5/4/80	Belgian Grand Prix Zolder	17	DNF	Team Essex Lotus 81 Cosworth #11	41	Gear linkage
5/18/80	Monaco Grand Prix Monaco	19	7	Team Essex Lotus 81 Cosworth #11	73	Running
6/1/80	Spanish Grand Prix Jarama	8	DNF	Team Essex Lotus 81 Cosworth #11	28	Engine failure, ruled to be a non-point race
6/29/80	French Grand Prix Paul Ricard	12	DNF	Team Essex Lotus 81 Cosworth #11	18	Gearbox failed
7/13/80	British Grand Prix Brands Hatch	9	DNF	Team Essex Lotus 81 Cosworth #11	57	Gearbox failed
8/10/80	German Grand Prix Hockenheim	9	7	Team Essex Lotus 81 Cosworth #11	45	Running
8/17/80	Austrian Grand Prix Österreichring	17	DNF	Team Essex Lotus 81 Cosworth #11	6	Engine failure
8/31/80	Dutch Grand Prix Zandvoort	10	8	Team Essex Lotus 81 Cosworth #11	70	Ran out of fuel
9/14/80	Italian Grand Prix, Imola	10	DNF	Team Essex Lotus 81 Cosworth #11	40	Engine failure
9/28/80	Canadian Grand Prix Montreal	18	DNF	Team Essex Lotus 81 Cosworth #11	11	Involved in multicar accident on start, restarted backup car, engine failure

Date	Event/Track	Qual	Finish	Entrant/Car/Number	Laps Compl	Comments
10/5/80	United States Grand Prix East Watkins Glen	11	6	Team Essex Lotus 81 Cosworth #11	58	Running, only point scored during season
3/15/81	United States Grand Prix West Long Beach	6	4	Marlboro Team Alfa Romeo 179C #22	80	Running
3/29/81	Brazilian Grand Prix Interlagos	9	DNF	Marlboro Team Alfa Romeo 179C #22	0	Involved in first lap wreck
4/12/81	Argentine Grand Prix Buenos Aires	17	8	Marlboro Team Alfa Romeo 179C #22	52	Running
5/3/81	San Marino Grand Prix, Imola	12	DNF	Marlboro Team Alfa Romeo 179C #22	26	Gearbox
5/17/81	Belgian Grand Prix Zolder	18	10	Marlboro Team Alfa Romeo 179C #22	53	Running
5/31/81	Monaco Grand Prix Monaco	12	DNF	Marlboro Team Alfa Romeo 179C #22	0	Accident at start with Elio de Angelis
6/21/81	Spanish Grand Prix Jarama	8	8	Marlboro Team Alfa Romeo 179C #22	80	Running
7/5/81	French Grand Prix Dijon-Prenois	10	8	Marlboro Team Alfa Romeo 179C #22	79	Running
7/18/81	British Grand Prix Silverstone	11	DNF	Marlboro Team Alfa Romeo 179C #22	59	Throttle cable broke
8/2/81	German Grand Prix Hockenheim	12	9	Marlboro Team Alfa Romeo 179C #22	44	Running
8/16/81	Austrian Grand Prix Österreichring	13	DNF	Marlboro Team Alfa Romeo 179C #22	46	Running
8/30/81	Dutch Grand Prix Zandvoort	7	DNF	Marlboro Team Alfa Romeo 179C #22	62	Blown tire, accident
9/13/81	Italian Grand Prix, Monza	13	DNF	Marlboro Team Alfa Romeo 179C #22	41	Engine failure
9/27/81	Canadian Grand Prix Montreal	16	7	Marlboro Team Alfa Romeo 179C #22	62	Running
10/17/81	USA Las Vegas Grand Prix Las Vegas	10	DNF	Marlboro Team Alfa Romeo 179C #22	29	Suspension failure
4/4/82	United States Grand Prix West Long Beach	14	DNF	TAG Saudia Williams FW07D #5	19	Accident
9/12/82	Italian Grand Prix, Monza	1	3	Ferrari 126C2 #28	52	Running
9/25/82	USA Las Vegas Grand Prix Las Vegas	7	DNF	Ferrari 126C2 #28	26	Suspension failure

CHAPTER 8

Focus on Champ Cars

The only thing that has saved CART is its product. The series, with its combination of street races and road races along with ovals, is still incredibly viable. It is a very attractive series and that is why so many foreign drivers come from all over the world to race with CART. Mario, LA Times, March 29, 2002

Mario is seen here at the 1974 Ontario Grand Prix. Earlier that season his Vel's Parnelli Jones team switched to the Eagle chassis. *Howard Koby*

Even if you ignore the Formula One championship, don't count the Daytona 500 victory and forget about the sports car and F-5000 wins, Mario Andretti remains one of the greatest racers of all time. Only A. J. Foyt has more victories in the National Championship series.

Mario's achievements in championship cars span several very dynamic eras that can be illustrated by the changes in racing venues. When he first joined the circuit, it consisted of a mixture of tough dirt tracks, like the Indiana State Fairgrounds and Springfield, with paved ovals that included Indianapolis, Langhorne, Atlanta, Hanford, and Trenton. The Pikes Peak Hill Climb was scored as part of the series. Then various road courses were added to the mix. Mario's first win came the first time the champ cars visited Indianapolis Raceway Park. Riverside, St. Jovite, Castle Rock, Mosport, Kent, Las Vegas, and the Meadowlands were all on the trail at one time or another.

As the cars changed with advances in technology, the championship circuit adjusted to increased demands of speed, competition, and safety. Michigan International and Pocono added high-speed ovals to the mix. Modern road racing venues like Portland, Long Beach, and Elkhart Lake became staples of the series.

An amazing fact that demonstrates Mario's prowess is that he has won at every track named.

When Mario won the USAC national championship as a rookie in 1965, it hadn't been accomplished since Johnnie Parsons claimed the title in 1949. Mario started fourth and finished 13th at Trenton in September. *Ken Coles*

National Championship Record

Date	Event/Track	Qual	Finish	Entrant/Car/Number	Laps Compl	Comments
4/19/64	Trenton Speedway	16	11	Stearly Motor Freight Elder #28	92	Running
6/21/64	Langhorne Speedway	8	9	Glessner Windmill Trucking Silnes #74	95	Running
7/19/64	Trenton Speedway	8	11	Dean Blum Roadster #7	134	Running
8/22/64	Illinois State Fairgrounds	9	6	Dean Kuzma Offy #7	99	Running
8/23/64	Wisconsin State Fair Park	9	3	Dean Blum Roadster #7	196	Highest finishing roadster
9/7/64	DuQuoin State Fairgrounds	11	15	Dean Kuzma Offy #7	45	Wreck T3
9/26/64	Indiana State Fairgrounds	6	10	Dean Kuzma Offy #7	97	Running
9/27/64	Trenton Speedway	6	22	Dean Blum Roadster #7	54	Spin T3
10/25/64	California State Fairgrounds	16	8	Dean Kuzma Offy #7	99	Running
11/22/64	Phoenix International Raceway	3	18	Dean Blum Roadster #7	72	Broken torque arm
3/28/65	Phoenix International Raceway	3	6	Dean Blum Roadster #12	148	Running, led 63 laps
4/25/65	Trenton Speedway	5	2	Dean Blum Roadster #12	87	Race stopped, rain
5/31/65	Indianapolis 500					
	Indianapolis Motor Speedway	4	3	Dean Van Lines Brawner/Hawk #12	200	Rookie of the Year
6/6/65	Wisconsin State Fair Park	12	4	Dean Van Lines Brawner/Hawk #12	99	Running
6/20/65	Langhorne Speedway	1	2	Dean Van Lines Brawner/Hawk #12	100	Led 33 laps
7/18/65	Trenton Speedway	-	-	Dean Van Lines Brawner/Hawk #12	0	Wrecked in practice
7/25/65	**Indianapolis Raceway Park**	**1**	**1**	**Dean Van Lines Brawner/Hawk #12**	**80**	**First USAC Championship victory**
8/1/65	Atlanta Motor Speedway	8	2	Dean Blum Roadster #12	167	
8/8/65	Langhorne Speedway	3	4	Dean Blum Roadster #12	125	
8/14/65	Wisconsin State Fair Park	2	2	Dean Van Lines Brawner/Hawk #12	150	Led 1 lap
8/21/65	Illinois State Fairgrounds	6	3	Dean Kuzma Offy #12	99	Running
8/22/65	Wisconsin State Fair Park	3	16	Dean Van Lines Brawner/Hawk #12	127	Led 98 laps until mechanical failure
9/6/65	DuQuoin State Fairgrounds	7	15	Dean Kuzma Offy #12	14	Engine
9/18/65	Indiana State Fairgrounds	6	2	Dean Kuzma Offy #12	100	
9/26/65	Trenton Speedway	4	13	Dean Van Lines Brawner/Hawk #12	168	Running
10/24/65	California State Fairgrounds	2	3	Dean Kuzma Offy #12	100	Led 25 laps
11/21/65	Phoenix International Raceway	1	2	Dean Van Lines Brawner/Hawk #12	200	Led 183 laps, won championship
3/20/66	Phoenix International Raceway	1	15	Dean Van Lines Brawner/Hawk #1	48	Accident with Foyt
4/24/66	Trenton Speedway	1	4	Dean Van Lines Brawner/Hawk #1	101	Running, Led 64 laps, stopped after 102 laps because of rain
5/30/66	Indianapolis 500					
	Indianapolis Motor Speedway	1	18	Dean Van Lines Brawner/Hawk #1	27	Led 16 laps, engine
6/5/66	**Wisconsin State Fair Park**	**1**	**1**	**Dean Van Lines Brawner/Hawk #1**	**100**	**Led all 100 laps**
6/12/66	**Langhorne Speedway**	**1**	**1**	**Dean Van Lines Brawner/Hawk #1**	**100**	**Led all 100 laps**
6/26/66	**Atlanta Motor Speedway**	**1**	**1**	**Dean Van Lines Brawner/Hawk #1**	**200**	**Led all 200 laps**
7/24/66	**Indianapolis Raceway Park**	**2**	**1**	**Dean Van Lines Brawner/Hawk #1**	**80**	**Spun on first lap, came back to lead 38 laps and win**
8/7/66	Langhorne Speedway	20	21	Robbins Vollstedt #66	33	Set new track record on first qualifying lap, wrecked on second lap; reassigned to Jim Robbins backup car
8/20/66	Illinois State Fairgrounds	4	2	Dean Kuzma Offy #1	100	Running
8/27/66	**Wisconsin State Fair Park**	**1**	**1**	**Dean Van Lines Brawner/Hawk #1**	**200**	**Led 159 laps**
9/5/66	DuQuoin State Fairgrounds	5	15	Dean Kuzma Offy #1	28	Engine
9/10/66	**Indiana State Fairgrounds**	**2**	**1**	**Dean Kuzma Offy #1**	**100**	**Led 3 laps**
9/25/66	**Trenton Speedway**	**1**	**1**	**Dean Van Lines Brawner/Hawk #1**	**200**	**Led 199 laps, set new 200 mile track record**
10/9/66	Mt. Fuji International Speedway	-	-	Dean Van Lines Brawner/Hawk #1	0	Burned piston in practice
10/23/66	California State Fairgrounds	3	10	Dean Kuzma Offy #1	95	Contact with Snider while leading – broke gears, Led 64 laps
11/20/66	**Phoenix International Raceway**	**1**	**1**	**Dean Van Lines Brawner/Hawk #1**	**200**	**Led 153 laps**
4/9/67	Phoenix International Raceway	-	-	Dean Van Lines Brawner/Hawk #1	0	Wrecked in practice, then wrecked Robbins car after qualifying
4/23/67	**Trenton Speedway**	**1**	**1**	**Dean Van Lines Brawner/Hawk #1**	**150**	**Led all 150 laps, set new qualifying and 150 mile race records**

Date	Event/Track	Qual	Finish	Entrant/Car/Number	Laps Compl	Comments
5/30/67	Indianapolis 500					
	Indianapolis Motor Speedway	1	30	Dean Van Lines Brawner/Hawk #1	58	Lost wheel in turn 1
6/4/67	Wisconsin State Fair Park	-	-	Dean Van Lines Brawner/Hawk #1	0	Wrecked in practice
6/18/67	Langhorne Speedway	6	3	Dean Van Lines Brawner/Hawk #1	100	
6/25/67	Pikes Peak Hill Climb	6	14	Leader Cards/Rislone Lotus 24 Chevy #1	1	First Pikes Peak attempt
7/1/67	Mosport Park	15	21	Dean Van Lines Brawner/Hawk #1	3	Broke half shaft
7/1/67	Mosport Park	20	11	Dean Van Lines Brawner/Hawk #1	6	Halted at 6 laps, rain
7/23/67	Indianapolis Raceway Park	2	1	Dean Van Lines Brawner/Hawk #1	80	Led 66 laps, set new race record
7/30/67	Langhorne Speedway	2	1	Dean Van Lines Brawner/Hawk #1	150	Led all 150 laps
8/6/67	St. Jovite, Le Circuit Mt. Tremblant	3	1	Dean Van Lines Brawner/Hawk #1	36	Led all 36 laps
8/6/67	St. Jovite, Le Circuit Mt. Tremblant	1	1	Dean Van Lines Brawner/Hawk #1	36	Led all 36 laps
8/19/67	Illinois State Fairgrounds	3	2	Dean Kuzma Offy #1	100	Running
8/20/67	Wisconsin State Fair Park	2	1	Dean Van Lines Brawner/Hawk #1	200	Led 199 laps, new race record
9/4/67	DuQuoin State Fairgrounds	11	2	Dean Kuzma Offy #1	100	
9/9/67	Indiana State Fairgrounds	2	1	Dean Kuzma Offy #1	100	Led 86 laps
9/24/67	Trenton Speedway	1	25	Dean Van Lines Brawner/Hawk #1	5	Led 4 laps; broke suspension and spun
10/1/67	California State Fairgrounds	2	2	Dean Kuzma Offy #1	100	
10/22/67	Hanford Speedway	4	24	Dean Van Lines Brawner/Hawk #1	18	Wreck
11/19/67	Phoenix International Raceway	2	1	Dean Van Lines Brawner/Hawk #1	200	Led 20 laps
11/26/67	Riverside International Raceway	6	3	Dean Van Lines Brawner/Hawk #1	116	Led 38 laps
3/17/68	Hanford Speedway	3	23	Andretti Brawner/Ford #2	40	Half shaft
3/31/68	Stardust International Raceway	3	2	Andretti Brawner/Ford #2	50	Led 41 laps
4/7/68	Phoenix International Raceway	2	15	Andretti Brawner/Ford #2	80	led 24 laps, wrecked
4/21/68	Trenton Speedway	1	2	Andretti Overseas National Airways Brawner/Ford #2	150	Led 8 laps
5/30/68	Indianapolis 500					
	Indianapolis Motor Speedway	4	33	Andretti Overseas National Airways Brawner/Ford #2	2	First race with turbocharged Ford engine - burned piston, relieved Larry Dickson for 10 laps - finished 28, piston
6/9/68	Wisconsin State Fair Park	9	2	Andretti Overseas National Airways Brawner/Ford #2	150	Led 23 laps
6/15/68	Mosport Park	2	2	Andretti Overseas National Airways Brawner/Ford #2	40	Running
6/15/68	Mosport Park	2	2	Andretti Overseas National Airways Brawner/Ford #2	40	Running
6/23/68	Langhorne Speedway	5	17	Andretti Overseas National Airways Brawner/Ford #2	44	Valve
6/30/68	Pikes Peak Hill Climb	4	4	Andretti Overseas National Airways Brawner/Hawk #2	1	
7/7/68	Continental Divide Raceway	5	15	Andretti Overseas National Airways Brawner/Ford #2	25	Coil
7/13/68	Nazareth National Speedway	4	2	Andretti Overseas National Airways Kuzma #2	89	First USAC championship race run at night under lights
7/21/68	Indianapolis Raceway Park	1	2	Andretti Overseas National Airways Brawner/Ford #2	40	Led 16 laps
7/21/68	Indianapolis Raceway Park	2	2	Andretti Overseas National Airways Brawner/Ford #2	40	
7/28/68	Langhorne Speedway	14	23	Leader Cards Zecol-Lubaid Watson #90	-	Blown engine in practice, switched to Leader Cards entry, did not compete in second heat race
8/4/68	St. Jovite, Le Circuit Mt. Tremblant	1	1	Andretti Overseas National Airways Brawner/Ford #2	38	Led 26 laps
8/4/68	St. Jovite, Le Circuit Mt. Tremblant	1	1	Andretti Overseas National Airways Brawner/Ford #2	38	Led all 38 laps
8/17/68	Illinois State Fairgrounds	6	18	Andretti Overseas National Airways Kuzma #2	12	Engine
8/18/68	Wisconsin State Fair Park	6	2	Andretti Overseas National Airways Brawner/Ford #2	200	Running
9/2/68	DuQuoin State Fairgrounds	6	1	Andretti Overseas National Airways Kuzma #2	100	Led 94 laps
9/7/68	Indiana State Fairgrounds	1	2	Andretti Overseas National Airways Kuzma #2	100	Set new qualifying track record
9/22/68	Trenton Speedway	2	1	Andretti Overseas National Airways Brawner/Offy #2	200	Led 172 laps, first race with turbo Offy
9/29/68	California State Fairgrounds	1	4	Andretti Overseas National Airways Kuzma #2	100	
10/13/68	Michigan International Speedway	1	2	Andretti Overseas National Airways Brawner/Offy #2	124	Led 1 lap – First race on track
11/3/68	Hanford Speedway	2	3	Andretti Overseas National Airways Brawner/Offy #2	167	Led 11 laps
11/17/68	Phoenix International Raceway	1	24	Andretti Overseas National Airways Brawner/Offy #2	6	Led 4 laps, wreck, relieved Snider for 190 laps-finished 3rd

Date	Event/Track	Qual	Finish	Entrant/Car/Number	Laps Compl	Comments
12/1/68	Riverside International Raceway	2	18	Andretti Overseas National Airways Brawner/Ford #2	59	Engine, relieved Leonard for 1 lap, relieved Ruby for 44 laps-finished 3rd
3/30/69	Phoenix International Raceway	4	16	Granatelli STP Oil Treatment Hawk III #2	38	Led 27 laps, half shaft
4/13/69	Hanford Speedway	1	1	Granatelli STP Oil Treatment Hawk III #2	134	Led all 134 laps
5/30/69	**Indianapolis 500**					
	Indianapolis Motor Speedway	2	1	Granatelli STP Oil Treatment Hawk III #2	200	Wrecked Lotus in practice, led 116 laps
6/8/69	Wisconsin State Fair Park	1	7	Granatelli STP Oil Treatment Hawk III #2	141	Led 89 laps, ran out of fuel and wouldn't restart in pits
6/15/69	Langhorne Speedway	1	5	Granatelli STP Oil Treatment Hawk III #2	147	Running, led 41 laps
6/29/69	Pikes Peak Hill Climb	-	1	Granatelli STP Oil Treatment Special King #2	1	Margin of victory was 21 seconds
7/6/69	Continental Divide Raceway	2	10	Granatelli STP Oil Treatment Hawk III #2	33	Oil leak
7/12/69	Nazareth National Speedway	2	1	Granatelli STP Oil Treatment Kuzma #2	89	Led 78 laps
7/19/69	Trenton Speedway	1	1	Granatelli STP Oil Treatment Hawk III #2	134	Led 58 laps
7/27/69	Indianapolis Raceway Park	2	9	Granatelli STP Oil Treatment Hawk III #2	39	Running
7/27/69	Indianapolis Raceway Park	9	2	Granatelli STP Oil Treatment Hawk III #2	40	Running
8/17/69	Wisconsin State Fair Park	2	4	Granatelli STP Oil Treatment Hawk III #2	196	Running
8/18/69	Illinois State Fairgrounds	2	1	Granatelli STP Oil Treatment Kuzma #2	100	Sidelined by mechanical problem on original race date. When the race was delayed two days by rain, able to repair the car and lead 80 laps.
8/24/69	Dover Downs	3	11	Granatelli STP Oil Treatment Hawk III #2	137	Led 19 laps, wreck
9/1/69	DuQuoin State Fairgrounds	2	2	Granatelli STP Oil Treatment Kuzma #2	100	Running
9/6/69	Indiana State Fairgrounds	2	6	Granatelli STP Oil Treatment Kuzma #2	100	Led 54 laps, running
9/14/69	Donnybrooke Raceway	3	4	Granatelli STP Oil Treatment Hawk III #2	34	Running
9/14/69	Donnybrooke Raceway	4	3	Granatelli STP Oil Treatment Hawk III #2	34	Running
9/21/69	Trenton Speedway	6	1	Granatelli STP Oil Treatment Hawk III #2	200	Led 59 laps
9/28/69	California State Fairgrounds	3	15	Granatelli STP Oil Treatment Kuzma #2	83	Oil pressure
10/19/69	Seattle International Raceway	2	1	Granatelli STP Oil Treatment Hawk III #2	45	Led all 45 laps
10/19/69	Seattle International Raceway	1	2	Granatelli STP Oil Treatment Hawk III #2	45	Raced in rain, first time in history of USAC
11/15 - 16/69	Phoenix International Raceway	2	21	Granatelli STP Oil Treatment Hawk III #2	73	Tangled with Bobby Unser, accident. Race halted after 83 laps because of rain, completed next day (11/16)
12/7/69	Riverside International Raceway	3	1	Granatelli STP Oil Treatment Hawk III #2	120	Led 5 laps
3/28/70	Phoenix International Raceway	1	13	Granatelli STP Oil Treatment Hawk/Ford #1	78	Led 14 laps, valve
4/4/70	Sears Point	2	2	Granatelli STP Oil Treatment Hawk/Ford #1	60	Led 3 laps, running
4/26/70	Trenton Speedway	3	2	Granatelli STP Oil Treatment Hawk/Ford #1	134	Led 23 laps, running
5/30/70	Indianapolis 500					
	Indianapolis Motor Speedway	8	6	Granatelli STP Oil Treatment McNamara #1	199	Running
6/7/70	Wisconsin State Fair Park	1	5	Granatelli STP Oil Treatment McNamara #1	149	Running
6/14/70	Langhorne Speedway	4	8	Granatelli STP Oil Treatment Hawk/Ford #1	147	Running
6/28/70	Continental Divide Raceway	2	1	Granatelli STP Oil Treatment McNamara #1	57	Led 41 laps, first victory for McNamara chassis
7/4/70	Michigan International Speedway	2	21	Granatelli STP Oil Treatment Hawk/Ford #1	9	Blew RR tire
7/26/70	Indianapolis Raceway Park	1	18	Granatelli STP Oil Treatment McNamara #1	14	Wrecked
8/22/70	Illinois State Fairgrounds	5	24	Granatelli STP Oil Treatment King #1	5	Broken suspension
8/23/70	Wisconsin State Fair Park	4	24	Granatelli STP Oil Treatment McNamara #1	4	Dropped valve
9/6/70	California 500					
	Ontario Motor Speedway	8	10	Granatelli STP Oil Treatment McNamara #1	182	Engine
9/7/70	DuQuoin State Fairgrounds	2	17	Granatelli STP Oil Treatment King #1	0	Engine
9/12/70	Indiana State Fairgrounds	14	11	Granatelli STP Oil Treatment King #1	96	Running
9/19/70	Missouri State Fairgrounds	2	2	Granatelli STP Oil Treatment King #1	99	Led 4 laps, ran out of fuel on backstretch on last lap
10/3/70	Trenton Speedway	2	21	Granatelli STP Oil Treatment McNamara #1	69	Broken suspension
10/4/70	California State Fairgrounds	3	14	Granatelli STP Oil Treatment King #1	69	Led 1 lap, wrecked
11/21/70	Phoenix International Raceway	24	8	Granatelli STP Oil Treatment Hawk/Ford #20	146	Running, wrecked McNamara in practice, took over car qualified by Steve Krisiloff

Date	Event/Track	Qual	Finish	Entrant/Car/Number	Laps Compl	Comments
3/27/71	Phoenix International Raceway	8	9	Granatelli STP Oil Treatment McNamara #5	147	Running
4/25/71	Trenton Speedway	3	18	Granatelli STP Oil Treatment McNamara #5	35	Led 26 laps, turbocharger bearing failed while leading
5/29/71	Indianapolis 500					
	Indianapolis Motor Speedway	9	30	Granatelli STP Oil Treatment McNamara #5	11	Accident
6/6/71	Wisconsin State Fair Park	5	11	Granatelli STP Oil Treatment McNamara #5	142	Running
7/3/71	Pocono 500					
	Pocono International Raceway	5	4	Granatelli STP Oil Treatment McNamara #5	198	Running
7/18/71	Michigan International Speedway	3	12	Granatelli STP Oil Treatment McNamara #5	74	Turbocharger failure
8/15/71	Wisconsin State Fair Park	5	19	Granatelli STP Oil Treatment McNamara #5	92	Fuel leak
9/5/71	California 500					
	Ontario Motor Speedway	8	33	Granatelli STP Oil Treatment McNamara #5	0	Electrical
10/3/71	Trenton Speedway	13	2	Granatelli STP Oil Treatment McNamara #5	198	Running
10/23/71	Phoenix International Raceway	9	4	Granatelli STP Oil Treatment McNamara #5	149	Led 8 laps, running
3/18/72	Phoenix International Raceway	4	2	Vel's Parnelli Jones Viceroy VPJ Colt #9	150	Led 3 laps, running
4/23/72	Trenton Speedway	4	22	Vel's Parnelli Jones Viceroy Parnelli #9	1	Broken piston
5/27/72	Indianapolis 500					
	Indianapolis Motor Speedway	5	8	Vel's Parnelli Jones Viceroy Parnelli #9	194	Ran out of fuel with five laps remaining
6/4/72	Wisconsin State Fair Park	8	8	Vel's Parnelli Jones Viceroy Parnelli #9	148	Led 14 laps, running
7/16/72	Michigan International Speedway	6	12	Vel's Parnelli Jones Viceroy Parnelli #9	80	Led 12 laps, broke ring and pinion while leading
7/29/72	Pocono 500					
	Pocono International Raceway	3	7	Vel's Parnelli Jones Viceroy Parnelli #9	188	Led 105 laps, running
8/13/72	Wisconsin State Fair Park	1	11	Vel's Parnelli Jones Viceroy Parnelli #9	108	Led 107 laps, locked wheel in pits while leading
9/3/72	California 500					
	Ontario Motor Speedway	5	27	Vel's Parnelli Jones Viceroy Parnelli #9	52	Blown engine
9/24/72	Trenton Speedway	2	28	Vel's Parnelli Jones Viceroy Parnelli #9	0	Broken half shaft
11/4/72	Phoenix International Raceway	2	3	Vel's Parnelli Jones Viceroy Parnelli #9	149	Led 53 laps, running
4/7/73	Texas World Speedway	3	25	Vel's Parnelli Jones Viceroy Parnelli #11	10	Broken piston
4/15/73	Trenton Speedway	8	4	Vel's Parnelli Jones Viceroy Parnelli #11	100	Led 2 laps, running; event run in two 100 lap heats, starting order of second heat based on finish of first heat
4/15/73	**Trenton Speedway**	**4**	**1**	**Vel's Parnelli Jones Viceroy Parnelli #11**	**100**	**Led 52 laps, received a $1,000 bonus for leading overall points**
5/30/73	Indianapolis 500					
	Indianapolis Motor Speedway	6	30	Vel's Parnelli Jones Viceroy Parnelli #11	4	Burned piston
6/10/73	Wisconsin State Fair Park	11	8	Vel's Parnelli Jones Viceroy Parnelli #11	145	Running
7/1/73	Pocono 500					
	Pocono International Raceway	3	7	Vel's Parnelli Jones Viceroy Parnelli #11	184	Led 10 laps, dropped valve
7/15/73	Michigan International Speedway	7	5	Vel's Parnelli Jones Viceroy Parnelli #11	99	Running
8/12/73	Wisconsin State Fair Park	9	19	Vel's Parnelli Jones Viceroy Parnelli #11	93	Broken suspension
8/26/73	Ontario Motor Speedway	2	12	Vel's Parnelli Jones Viceroy Parnelli #11	28	Broken shift link, qualification heat for 500 mile race
9/2/73	California 500					
	Ontario Motor Speedway	15	2	Vel's Parnelli Jones Viceroy Parnelli #11	200	Led 28 laps, running
9/16/73	Michigan International Speedway	8	5	Vel's Parnelli Jones Viceroy Parnelli #11	63	Running
9/16/73	Michigan International Speedway	3	2	Vel's Parnelli Jones Viceroy Parnelli #11	62	Led 4 laps, running
9/23/73	Trenton Speedway	5	7	Vel's Parnelli Jones Viceroy Parnelli #11	131	Running
10/6/73	Texas World Speedway	1	17	Vel's Parnelli Jones Viceroy Parnelli #11	39	Led 19 laps, broken valve
11/3/73	Phoenix International Raceway	17	7	Vel's Parnelli Jones Viceroy Parnelli #11	148	Running
3/3/74	Ontario Motor Speedway	3	9	Vel's Parnelli Jones Viceroy Parnelli #5	37	Led 30 laps, ran out of fuel while leading
3/10/74	California 500					
	Ontario Motor Speedway	14	25	Vel's Parnelli Jones Viceroy Parnelli #5	91	Blown engine
3/17/74	Phoenix International Raceway	7	5	Vel's Parnelli Jones Viceroy Eagle #5	150	Running
4/7/74	Trenton Speedway	1	9	Vel's Parnelli Jones Viceroy Parnelli #5	73	Led 33 laps, burned piston

Date	Event/Track	Qual	Finish	Entrant/Car/Number	Laps Compl	Comments
5/26/74	Indianapolis 500					
	Indianapolis Motor Speedway	5	31	Vel's Parnelli Jones Viceroy Eagle #5	2	Engine valve
6/9/74	Wisconsin State Fair Park	11	17	Vel's Parnelli Jones Viceroy Parnelli #5	65	Turbocharger failed
6/30/74	Pocono 500					
	Pocono International Raceway	8	17	Vel's Parnelli Jones Viceroy Eagle #5	132	Wrecked
7/21/74	Michigan International Speedway	3	18	Vel's Parnelli Jones Viceroy Eagle #5	48	Led 1 lap, broken piston
8/11/74	Wisconsin State Fair Park	12	8	Vel's Parnelli Jones Viceroy Eagle #5	197	Running
9/15/74	Michigan International Speedway	5	10	Vel's Parnelli Jones Viceroy Eagle #5	82	Broken piston
11/2/74	Phoenix International Raceway	5	3	Vel's Parnelli Jones Viceroy Eagle #5	148	Running
3/9/75	California Grand Prix					
	Ontario Motor Speedway	18	28	Vel's Parnelli Jones Viceroy Eagle #21	15	Broken connecting rod
5/25/75	Indianapolis 500					
	Indianapolis Motor Speedway	27	28	Vel's Parnelli Jones Viceroy Eagle #21	49	Mechanical failure, wreck. 435 miles – rain
6/29/75	Pocono International Raceway	10	25	Vel's Parnelli Jones Viceroy Eagle #21	79	Engine, 425 miles – rain
11/9/75	Phoenix International Raceway	3	3	O'Connell Sugaripe Prune Eagle #12	149	Led 40 laps, running
5/30/76	Indianapolis 500					
	Indianapolis Motor Speedway	19	8	Penske CAM-2 McLaren #6	101	Running, stopped by rain
6/27/76	Pocono 500					
	Pocono International Raceway	3	5	Penske CAM-2 McLaren #6	198	Led 45 laps, running
10/31/76	Texas World Speedway	4	4	Penske Norton Spirit McLaren #68	99	Led 1 lap, running
11/7/76	Phoenix International Raceway	3	3	Penske Norton Spirit McLaren #68	150	Led 1 lap, running
3/27/77	Phoenix International Raceway	-	-	Penske CAM-2 McLaren #9	0	Blew engine in practice
4/30/77	Trenton Speedway	2	16	Penske CAM-2 McLaren #9	37	Led 29 laps, engine
5/29/77	Indianapolis 500					
	Indianapolis Motor Speedway	6	26	Penske CAM-2 McLaren #9	47	Broken header
6/26/77	Pocono 500					
	Pocono International Raceway	3	2	Penske CAM-2 McLaren #9	200	Led 30 laps, Penske 1 – 2 finish
9/4/77	Ontario Motor Speedway	2	4	Penske CAM-2 McLaren #9	197	Led 12 laps, running
9/17/77	Michigan International Speedway	2	20	Penske CAM-2 McLaren #9	21	Clutch failure
10/29/77	Phoenix International Raceway	5	4	Penske CAM-2 McLaren #9	149	Running
3/26/78	Ontario Motor Speedway	2	15	Penske Gould Charge Penske #7	35	Led 18 laps, engine
4/15/78	Texas World Speedway	2	5	Penske Gould Charge Penske #7	98	Led 23 laps, running
4/23/78	Trenton Speedway	3	13	Penske Gould Charge Penske #7	92	Engine
5/28/78	Indianapolis 500					
	Indianapolis Motor Speedway	33	12	Penske Gould Charge Penske #7	185	Qualified 8th by Mike Hiss, running
6/25/78	Pocono 500					
	Pocono International Raceway	6	23	Penske Gould Charge Penske #7	73	Led 1 lap, gearbox
9/16/78	Michigan International Speedway	4	20	Penske Gould Charge Penske #7	0	Engine problem
9/23/78	**Trenton Speedway**	**3**	**1**	**Penske Gould Charge Penske #7**	**100**	**Led 33 laps**
10/28/78	Phoenix International Raceway	5	7	Penske Gould Charge Penske #7	148	Running
9/2/79	California 500					
	Ontario Motor Speedway	4	3	Penske Gould Charge PC6/78 #99	200	Running
9/15/79	Michigan International Speedway	0	0	Penske Gould Charge PC6/78 #99	0	Wrecked in practice
5/25/80	Indianapolis 500					
	Indianapolis Motor Speedway	2	20	Penske Essex PC9/80 #12	70	Engine siezed
6/22/80	Pocono 500					
	Pocono International Raceway	3	17	Penske Essex PC9/80 #12	105	Led 4 laps, transmission failure
9/20/80	**Michigan International Speedway**	**1**	**1**	**Penske AB Dick Pacemaker PC9/80 #12**	**75**	**Led 53 laps**
11/8/80	Phoenix international Raceway	1	2	Penske AB Dick Pacemaker PC9/80 #12	150	Led 1 lap, running
3/22/81	Phoenix International Raceway	4	11	STP Oil Treatment Wildcat #40	139	Led 30 laps, fuel pump failure

Date	Event/Track	Qual	Finish	Entrant/Car/Number	Laps Compl	Comments
5/24/81	Indianapolis 500					
	Indianapolis Motor Speedway	32	2	STP Oil Treatment Wildcat #40	200	Mario ruled winner when Unser was penalized 1 lap, decision reversed by appeal panel
6/7/81	Wisconsin State Fair Park	6	3	STP Oil Treatment Wildcat #40	148	Led 6 laps, running
6/28/81	Atlanta Motor Speedway	3	3	STP Oil Treatment Wildcat #40	83	First race of twin 125's, running
6/28/81	Atlanta Motor Speedway	3	2	STP Oil Treatment Wildcat #40	83	Second race of twin 125's, running
9/20/81	Michigan International Speedway	3	2	STP Oil Treatment Wildcat #40	74	Led 24 laps, running
10/4/81	Watkins Glen	1	16	STP Oil Treatment Wildcat #40	25	Led 23 laps, gearbox failure
10/31/81	Phoenix International Raceway	4	4	STP Oil Treatment Wildcat #40	150	Led 4 laps, running
3/28/82	Phoenix International Raceway	5	2	STP Oil Treatment Wildcat 8B #40	150	Led 8 laps, running
5/1/82	Atlanta Motor Speedway	2	11	STP Oil Treatment Wildcat 8B #40	88	Led 9 miles, engine failure
5/29/82	Indianapolis 500					
	Indianapolis Motor Speedway	4	31	STP Intermedics Wildcat 8B #40	0	Wreck at start
6/13/82	Wisconsin State Fair Park	3	9	STP Intermedics Wildcat 8B #40	143	Brakes
7/4/82	Burke Lakefront Airport	3	2	STP Intermedics Wildcat 8B #40	125	Led 9 laps, running
7/18/82	Michigan 500					
	Michigan International Speedway	3	2	STP Intermedics Wildcat 8B #40	250	Led 35 laps, running
8/1/82	Wisconsin State Fair Park	5	3	STP Intermedics Wildcat 8B #40	199	Running
8/15/82	Pocono 500					
	Pocono International Raceway	4	14	STP Intermedics Wildcat 8B #40	114	Gearbox
8/29/82	Riverside International Raceway	2	23	STP Intermedics Wildcat 8B #40	11	Led first 10 laps until transmission failed
9/19/82	Road America	4	14	STP Intermedics Wildcat 8B #40	29	Led 20 laps, transmission
9/26/82	Michigan International Speedway	25	2	STP Intermedics Wildcat 8B #40	75	Led 17 laps, running
11/6/82	Phoenix International Raceway	2	3	STP Intermedics Wildcat 8B #40	150	Running
4/17/83	Atlanta Motor Speedway	6	5	Newman-Haas Budweiser Lola T700 #3	128	Running
5/29/83	Indianapolis 500					
	Indianapolis Motor Speedway	11	23	Newman-Haas Budweiser Lola T700 #3	79	Wreck with Johnny Parsons Jr.
6/12/83	Wisconsin State Fair Park	12	18	Newman-Haas Budweiser Lola T700 #3	58	Overheated
7/3/83	Burke Lakefront Airport	1	14	Newman-Haas Budweiser Lola T700 #3	56	Led 34 laps, overheating
7/17/83	Michigan 500					
	Michigan International Speedway	18	3	Newman-Haas Budweiser Lola T700 #3	250	Led 21 laps, running
7/31/83	**Road America**	**1**	**1**	**Newman-Haas Budweiser Lola T700 #3**	**50**	**Led 6 laps, first win for Lola in CART**
8/14/83	Pocono 500					
	Pocono International Raceway	9	7	Newman-Haas Budweiser Lola T700 #3	197	Running
8/28/83	Riverside International Raceway	3	16	Newman-Haas Budweiser Lola T700 #3	57	Led 18 laps, transmission failure while leading
9/11/83	Mid-Ohio	4	2	Newman-Haas Budweiser Lola T700 #3	84	Led 4 laps, running
9/18/83	Michigan International Speedway	6	4	Newman-Haas Budweiser Lola T700 #3	99	Led 4 laps, running
10/8/83	**Las Vegas**	**3**	**1**	**Newman-Haas Budweiser Lola T700 #3**	**178**	**Led 112 laps**
10/23/83	Laguna Seca	6	2	Newman-Haas Budweiser Lola T700 #3	98	Led 3 laps, running
10/29/83	Phoenix International Raceway	2	2	Newman-Haas Budweiser Lola T700 #3	150	Led 12 laps, trailed Fabi by .09 second at finish
4/1/84	**Long Beach Grand Prix**					
	Long Beach	1	1	**Newman-Haas Budweiser Lola T800 #3**	112	**Led all 112 laps from the pole, won by more than a minute (63.2 sec.)**
4/18/84	Phoenix International Raceway	3	20	Newman-Haas Budweiser Lola T800 #3	88	Led 7 laps, CV joint failure
5/27/84	Indianapolis 500					
	Indianapolis Motor Speedway	6	17	Newman-Haas Budweiser Lola T800 #3	153	Led 29 laps, broken nose cone
6/3/84	Wisconsin State Fair Park	3	8	Newman-Haas Budweiser Lola T800 #3	196	Running
6/17/84	Portland International Raceway	1	26	Newman-Haas Budweiser Lola T800 #3	13	Led 4 laps, overheating
7/1/84	**Meadowlands**	**1**	**1**	**Newman-Haas Budweiser Lola T800 #3**	**100**	**Led all 100 laps, margin of victory 71.7 seconds**
7/8/84	Burke Lakefront Airport	1	21	Newman-Haas Budweiser Lola T800 #3	49	Led first 28 laps, ignition

Date	Event/Track	Qual	Finish	Entrant/Car/Number	Laps Compl	Comments
7/22/84	**Michigan 500**					
	Michigan International Speedway	1	1	**Newman-Haas Budweiser Lola T800 #3**	250	**Led 51 laps, victory by .14 seconds**
8/5/84	**Road America**	1	1	**Newman-Haas Budweiser Lola T800 #3**	50	**Led 34 laps, victory by more than a minute**
8/19/84	Pocono 500					
	Pocono International Raceway	3	19	Newman-Haas Budweiser Lola T800 #3	163	Engine failure
9/2/84	**Mid-Ohio**	1	1	**Newman-Haas Budweiser Lola T800 #3**	84	**Led 78 laps**
9/9/84	Sanair Super Speedway	4	7	Newman-Haas Budweiser Lola T800 #3	222	Running
9/24/84	**Michigan International Speedway**	3	1	**Newman-Haas Budweiser Lola T800 #3**	100	**Led 37 laps, halted by rain after 33 laps, completed next day**
10/14/84	Phoenix International Raceway	7	12	Newman-Haas Budweiser Lola T800 #3	144	Led 59 laps, tangled with Johncock on frontstretch, running
10/21/84	Laguna Seca	1	2	Newman-Haas Budweiser Lola T800 #3	98	Led 24 laps, running
11/11/84	Las Vegas	2	2	Newman-Haas Budweiser Lola T800 #3	178	Led 10 laps, running
4/14/85	**Long Beach Grand Prix**					
	Long Beach	1	1	**Newman-Haas Beatrice Lola T900 #1**	90	**Led 70 laps, margin of victory more than 1 second**
5/26/85	Indianapolis 500					
	Indianapolis Motor Speedway	4	2	Newman-Haas Beatrice Lola T900 #3	200	Led 107 laps, trailed by 2.47 seconds
6/2/85	**Wisconsin State Fair Park**	1	1	**Newman-Haas Beatrice Lola T900 #1**	200	**Led 196 laps**
6/16/85	**Portland International Raceway**	4	1	**Newman-Haas Beatrice Lola T900 #1**	104	**Led 29 laps**
6/30/85	Meadowlands	1	26	Newman-Haas Beatrice Lola T900 #1	34	Led 19 laps, wreck while leading
7/7/85	Burke Lakefront Airport	3	14	Newman-Haas Beatrice Lola T900 #1	84	Led 75 laps, car caught fire on course while leading
7/28/85	Michigan 500					
	Michigan International Speedway	3	10	Newman-Haas Beatrice Lola T900 #1	241	Led 16 laps, wrecked, race delayed one week because of tire problems
8/18/85	Pocono 500					
	Pocono International Raceway	10	7	Newman-Haas Beatrice Lola T900 #1	198	Led 1 lap, running
9/1/85	Mid-Ohio	4	7	Newman-Haas Beatrice Lola T900 #1	82	Led 1 lap, wrecked
9/8/85	Sanair Super Speedway	8	15	Newman-Haas Beatrice Lola T900 #1	154	Broken hose clamp
9/22/85	Michigan International Speedway	2	21	Newman-Haas Beatrice Lola T900 #1	71	Transmission failure
10/6/85	Laguna Seca	8	11	Newman-Haas Beatrice Lola T900 #1	94	Engine fire
10/13/85	Phoenix International Raceway	7	3	Newman-Haas Beatrice Lola T900 #1	149	Running
11/9/85	Tamiami Park Raceway	9	27	Newman-Haas Beatrice Lola T900 #1	0	Multicar wreck at start
4/6/86	Phoenix International Raceway	1	7	Newman-Haas Lola T86/00 #5	195	Led 17 laps, ran out of fuel
4/13/86	Long Beach Grand Prix					
	Long Beach	3	5	Newman-Haas Lola T86/00 #5	94	Running
6/1/86	Indianapolis 500					
	Indianapolis Motor Speedway	30	32	Newman-Haas Lola T86/00 #2	19	Ignition, race delayed one week by rain
6/8/86	Wisconsin State Fair Park	4	5	Newman-Haas Lola T86/00 #5	198	Running
6/15/86	**Portland International Raceway**	7	1	**Newman-Haas Hanna Car Wash Lola T86/00 #5**	104	**Led 1 lap**
6/29/86	Meadowlands	2	24	Newman-Haas Hanna Car Wash Lola T86/00 #5	8	Led 4 laps, broken water pipe
7/6/86	Burke Lakefront Airport	5	3	Newman-Haas Hanna Car Wash Lola T86/00 #5	88	Running
7/20/86	Molson Indy Toronto	3	3	Newman-Haas Hanna Car Wash Lola T86/00 #5	103	Running
8/2/86	Michigan 500					
	Michigan International Speedway	10	21	Newman-Haas Hanna Car Wash Lola T86/00 #5	69	Wreck
8/17/86	Pocono 500					
	Pocono International Raceway	3	1	**Newman-Haas Hanna Car Wash Lola T86/00 #5**	200	**Led 119 laps**
8/31/86	Mid-Ohio	1	24	Newman-Haas Hanna Car Wash Lola T86/00 #5	13	Led 12 laps, exhaust
9/7/86	Sanair Super Speedway	5	8	Newman-Haas Hanna Car Wash Lola T86/00 #5	219	Led 42 laps, incident with Tony Bettenhausen lap 136, running
9/28/86	Michigan International Speedway	10	10	Newman-Haas Hanna Car Wash Lola T86/00 #5	123	Led 1 lap, engine failure
10/4/86	Road America	6	9	Newman-Haas Hanna Car Wash Lola T86/00 #5	49	Race started on Sept. 21 but stopped after lap 4 because of rain. Completed Oct. 4, running
10/12/86	Laguna Seca	1	4	Newman-Haas Hanna Car Wash Lola T86/00 #5	98	Led 8 laps, running
10/19/86	Phoenix International Raceway	5	4	Newman-Haas Hanna Car Wash Lola T86/00 #5	199	Running

Date	Event/Track	Qual	Finish	Entrant/Car/Number	Laps Compl	Comments
11/9/86	Tamiami Park Raceway	5	11	Newman-Haas Hanna Car Wash Lola T86/00 #5	107	Running
4/5/87	**Long Beach Grand Prix**					
	Long Beach	1	1	**Newman-Haas Hanna Car Wash Lola T87/00 #5**	**95**	**Led all 95 laps**
4/12/87	Phoenix International Raceway	1	5	Newman-Haas Hanna Car Wash Lola T87/00 #5	198	Led 30 laps, running
5/24/87	Indianapolis 500					
	Indianapolis Motor Speedway	1	9	Newman-Haas Hanna Car Wash Lola T87/00 #5	180	Led 170 laps, broken valve spring
5/31/87	Wisconsin State Fair Park	3	17	Newman-Haas Hanna Car Wash Lola T87/00 #5	149	Led 46 laps, lost wing and wrecked while leading
6/14/87	Portland International Raceway	5	10	Newman-Haas Hanna Car Wash Lola T87/00 #5	65	Fuel pickup
6/28/87	Meadowlands	1	2	Newman-Haas Hanna Car Wash Lola T87/00 #5	100	Led 15 laps, running
7/5/87	Burke Lakefront Airport	3	10	Newman-Haas Hanna Car Wash Lola T87/00 #5	75	Engine failure
7/19/87	Molson Indy Toronto	5	15	Newman-Haas Hanna Car Wash Lola T87/00 #5	46	Off course
8/2/87	Michigan 500					
	Michigan International Speedway	3	19	Newman-Haas Hanna Car Wash Lola T87/00 #5	156	Led 118 laps, engine failure while leading
8/16/87	Pocono 500					
	Pocono International Raceway	1	19	Newman-Haas Hanna Car Wash Lola T87/00 #5	88	Led 22 laps, wrecked
8/30/87	**Road America**	1	1	**Newman-Haas Hanna Car Wash Lola T87/00 #5**	**50**	**Led all 50 laps**
9/6/87	Mid-Ohio	4	17	Newman-Haas Hanna Car Wash Lola T87/00 #5	64	Accident
9/20/87	Nazareth Speedway	7	19	Newman-Haas Hanna Car Wash Lola T87/00 #5	106	Contact with Rutherford, wrecked
10/11/87	Laguna Seca	1	17	Newman-Haas Hanna Car Wash Lola T87/00 #5	68	Led 61 laps, engine failure
11/1/87	Tamiami Park Raceway	1	4	Newman-Haas Hanna Car Wash Lola T87/00 #5	102	Led 3 laps, race ended at 103 laps because of heavy rain, running
4/10/88	**Phoenix International Raceway**	3	1	**Newman-Haas Amoco/Kmart Lola T88/00 #6**	**200**	**Led 135 laps**
4/17/88	Long Beach Grand Prix					
	Long Beach	2	15	Newman-Haas Amoco/Kmart Lola T88/00 #6	70	Led 1 lap, mechanical problem
5/29/88	Indianapolis 500					
	Indianapolis Motor Speedway	4	20	Newman-Haas Amoco/Kmart Lola T87/00 #6	118	Electrical failure
6/5/88	Wisconsin State Fair Park	2	17	Newman-Haas Amoco/Kmart Lola T88/00 #6	147	Led 9 laps, broken rear axle
6/19/88	Portland International Raceway	5	5	Newman-Haas Amoco/Kmart Lola T88/00 #6	103	Running
7/3/88	**Burke Lakefront Airport**	3	1	**Newman-Haas Amoco/Kmart Lola T88/00 #6**	**80**	**Led 24 laps**
7/17/88	Molson Indy Toronto	2	25	Newman-Haas Amoco/Kmart Lola T88/00 #6	11	Mechanical failure
7/24/88	Meadowlands	2	2	Newman-Haas Amoco/Kmart Lola T88/00 #6	149	Led 11 laps, broken ring gear while leading
8/7/88	Michigan 500					
	Michigan International Speedway	3	12	Newman-Haas Amoco/Kmart Lola T87/00 #6	180	Led 10 laps, engine failure
8/21/88	Pocono 500					
	Pocono International Raceway	5	17	Newman-Haas Amoco/Kmart Lola T87/00 #6	116	Led 25 laps, wreck with Simon while leading
9/4/88	Mid-Ohio	4	2	Newman-Haas Amoco/Kmart Lola T88/00 #6	84	Led 18 laps, running
9/11/88	Road America	6	3	Newman-Haas Amoco/Kmart Lola T88/00 #6	50	Running
9/25/88	Nazareth Speedway	3	3	Newman-Haas Amoco/Kmart Lola T88/00 #6	199	Running
10/16/88	Laguna Seca	2	3	Newman-Haas Amoco/Kmart Lola T88/00 #6	84	Led 2 laps, running
11/6/88	Tamiami Park Raceway	2	15	Newman-Haas Amoco/Kmart Lola T88/00 #6	43	Led 5 laps, fuel system problem while leading
4/9/89	Phoenix International Raceway	4	8	Newman-Haas Kmart/Havoline Lola T89/00 #5	195	Running
4/16/89	Long Beach Grand Prix					
	Long Beach	5	18	Newman-Haas Kmart/Havoline Lola T89/00 #5	83	Led 8 laps, damage from contact with Unser Jr. while leading
5/28/89	Indianapolis 500					
	Indianapolis Motor Speedway	5	4	Newman-Haas Kmart/Havoline Lola T89/00 #5	193	Led 1 lap, running
6/4/89	Wisconsin State Fair Park	6	7	Newman-Haas Kmart/Havoline Lola T89/00 #5	195	Running
6/18/89	Detroit Grand Prix	4	3	Newman-Haas Kmart/Havoline Lola T89/00 #5	62	Led 2 laps, running
6/25/89	Portland International Raceway	3	25	Newman-Haas Kmart/Havoline Lola T89/00 #5	19	Electrical failure
7/2/89	Burke Lakefront Airport	3	2	Newman-Haas Kmart/Havoline Lola T89/00 #5	80	Running
7/16/89	Meadowlands	2	20	Newman-Haas Kmart/Havoline Lola T89/00 #5	75	Led 1 lap, broken suspension, race halted 5 laps early because of heavy rain

Date	Event/Track	Qual	Finish	Entrant/Car/Number	Laps Compl	Comments
7/23/89	Molson Indy Toronto	7	26	Newman-Haas Kmart/Havoline Lola T89/00 #5	8	Hit Guerrero's disabled car parked on the course
8/6/89	Michigan 500					
	Michigan International Speedway	6	3	Newman-Haas Kmart/Havoline Lola T89/00 #5	249	Led 45 laps, running
8/20/89	Pocono 500					
	Pocono International Raceway	5	5	Newman-Haas Kmart/Havoline Lola T89/00 #5	199	Running
9/3/89	Mid-Ohio	11	7	Newman-Haas Kmart/Havoline Lola T89/00 #5	83	Running
9/10/89	Road America	7	7	Newman-Haas Kmart/Havoline Lola T89/00 #5	49	Ran out of fuel
9/24/89	Nazareth Speedway	9	8	Newman-Haas Kmart/Havoline Lola T89/00 #5	194	Running
10/15/89	Laguna Seca	8	2	Newman-Haas Kmart/Havoline Lola T89/00 #5	84	Led 20 laps, running
4/8/90	Phoenix International Raceway	6	4	Newman-Haas Kmart/Havoline Lola T90/00 #6	199	Running
4/22/90	Long Beach Grand Prix					
	Long Beach	6	5	Newman-Haas Kmart/Havoline Lola T90/00 #6	95	Led 4 laps, running
5/27/90	Indianapolis 500					
	Indianapolis Motor Speedway	6	27	Newman-Haas Kmart/Havoline Lola T90/00 #6	60	Engine failure
6/3/90	Wisconsin State Fair Park	4	21	Newman-Haas Kmart/Havoline Lola T90/00 #6	59	Led 7 laps, radiator
6/17/90	Detroit Grand Prix	3	25	Newman-Haas Kmart/Havoline Lola T90/00 #6	14	Engine failure
6/24/90	Portland International Raceway	4	2	Newman-Haas Kmart/Havoline Lola T90/00 #6	104	Led 3 laps, running
7/8/90	Burke Lakefront Airport	6	4	Newman-Haas Kmart/Havoline Lola T90/00 #6	85	Running
7/15/90	Meadowlands	2	24	Newman-Haas Kmart/Havoline Lola T90/00 #6	41	Led 22 laps, wreck with Rahal
7/22/90	Molson Indy Toronto	3	6	Newman-Haas Kmart/Havoline Lola T90/00 #6	93	Led 6 laps, running
8/5/90	Michigan 500					
	Michigan International Speedway	11	3	Newman-Haas Kmart/Havoline Lola T90/00 #6	249	Running
8/26/90	Denver Grand Prix	4	4	Newman-Haas Kmart/Havoline Lola T90/00 #6	80	Led 2 laps, running
9/2/90	Vancouver	8	3	Newman-Haas Kmart/Havoline Lola T90/00 #6	97	Running
9/16/90	Mid-Ohio	8	2	Newman-Haas Kmart/Havoline Lola T90/00 #6	89	Led 25 laps, running
9/23/90	Road America	3	5	Newman-Haas Kmart/Havoline Lola T90/00 #6	50	Running, race halted for one hour because of Foyt accident
10/7/90	Nazareth Speedway	7	4	Newman-Haas Kmart/Havoline Lola T90/00 #6	198	Running
10/21/90	Laguna Seca	2	26	Newman-Haas Kmart/Havoline Lola T90/00 #6	2	Electrical failure
3/17/91	Surfers Paradise	5	17	Newman-Haas Kmart/Havoline Lola T91/00 #6	41	Wreck with Unser Jr. and Cheever
4/14/91	Long Beach Grand Prix					
	Long Beach	7	19	Newman-Haas Kmart/Havoline Lola T91/00 #6	49	Electrical
4/21/91	Phoenix International Raceway	3	9	Newman-Haas Kmart/Havoline Lola T91/00 #6	197	Led 33 laps, running
5/26/91	Indianapolis 500					
	Indianapolis Motor Speedway	3	7	Newman-Haas Kmart/Havoline Lola T91/00 #6	187	Led 22 laps, engine failure, stalled at pit entrance
6/2/91	Wisconsin State Fair Park	2	3	Newman-Haas Kmart/Havoline Lola T91/00 #6	199	Led 31 laps, running
6/16/91	Detroit Grand Prix	5	7	Newman-Haas Kmart/Havoline Lola T91/00 #6	62	Running. Made contact with an emergency vehicle blocking track on lap 48, race was stopped for 55 minutes
6/23/91	Portland International Raceway	7	5	Newman-Haas Kmart/Havoline Lola T91/00 #6	104	Running
7/7/91	Burke Lakefront Airport	5	6	Newman-Haas Kmart/Havoline Lola T91/00 #6	85	Led 1 lap, running
7/14/91	Meadowlands	5	15	Newman-Haas Kmart/Havoline Lola T91/00 #6	134	Contact with Unser Jr. lap 20, running
7/21/91	Molson Indy Toronto	5	2	Newman-Haas Kmart/Havoline Lola T91/00 #6	103	Running
8/4/91	Michigan 500					
	Michigan International Speedway	3	4	Newman-Haas Kmart/Havoline Lola T91/00 #6	245	Led 14 laps, engine failure
8/25/91	Denver Grand Prix	5	15	Newman-Haas Kmart/Havoline Lola T91/00 #6	50	Wreck with Scott Brayton
9/1/91	Vancouver	10	4	Newman-Haas Kmart/Havoline Lola T91/00 #6	99	Running
9/15/91	Mid-Ohio	6	7	Newman-Haas Kmart/Havoline Lola T91/00 #6	89	Led 1 lap, running
9/22/91	Road America	6	3	Newman-Haas Kmart/Havoline Lola T91/00 #6	50	Running
10/6/91	Nazareth Speedway	4	5	Newman-Haas Kmart/Havoline Lola T91/00 #6	200	Running
10/20/91	Laguna Seca	6	3	Newman-Haas Kmart/Havoline Lola T91/00 #6	84	Running
3/22/92	Surfers Paradise	6	7	Newman-Haas Kmart/Havoline Lola T91/00 #2	65	Led 1 lap, running

Date	Event/Track	Qual	Finish	Entrant/Car/Number	Laps Compl	Comments
4/5/92	Phoenix International Raceway	3	17	Newman-Haas Kmart/Havoline Lola T92/00 #2	111	Transmission broke
4/12/92	Long Beach Grand Prix					
	Long Beach	7	23	Newman-Haas Kmart/Havoline Lola T92/00 #2	0	Accident on first lap
5/24/92	Indianapolis 500					
	Indianapolis Motor Speedway	3	23	Newman-Haas Kmart/Havoline Lola T92/00 #2	78	Led 1 lap, wreck turn four
6/21/92	Portland International Raceway	8	6	Newman-Haas Kmart/Havoline Lola T92/00 #2	101	Running (Missed Detroit race because of injures suffered at Indianapolis)
6/28/92	Wisconsin State Fair Park	10	6	Newman-Haas Kmart/Havoline Lola T92/00 #2	197	Running
7/5/92	New Hampshire International Speedway	8	7	Newman-Haas Kmart/Havoline Lola T92/00 #2	196	Running
7/19/92	Molson Indy Toronto	5	4	Newman-Haas Kmart/Havoline Lola T92/00 #2	102	Running
8/2/92	Michigan 500					
	Michigan International Speedway	1	15	Newman-Haas Kmart/Havoline Lola T92/00 #2	122	Led 38 laps, engine failure
8/9/92	Burke Lakefront Airport	8	5	Newman-Haas Kmart/Havoline Lola T92/00 #2	84	Running
8/23/92	Road America	5	5	Newman-Haas Kmart/Havoline Lola T92/00 #2	50	Led 2 laps, running
8/30/92	Vancouver	4	6	Newman-Haas Kmart/Havoline Lola T92/00 #2	97	Running
9/13/92	Mid-Ohio	4	5	Newman-Haas Kmart/Havoline Lola T92/00 #2	88	Running
10/3/92	Marlboro Challenge					
	Nazareth Speedway	7	9	Newman-Haas Kmart/Havoline Lola T92/00 #2	53	Engine failure
10/4/92	Nazareth Speedway	5	5	Newman-Haas Kmart/Havoline Lola T92/00 #2	199	Running
10/18/92	Laguna Seca	5	2	Newman-Haas Kmart/Havoline Lola T92/00 #2	84	Running
3/21/93	Surfers Paradise	6	4	Newman-Haas Kmart/Texaco-Havoline Lola T93/06 #6	65	Running
4/4/93	**Phoenix International Raceway**	**2**	**1**	**Newman-Haas Kmart/Texaco-Havoline Lola T93/06 #6**	**200**	**Led 39 laps**
4/18/93	Long Beach Grand Prix					
	Long Beach	6	18	Newman-Haas Kmart/Texaco-Havoline Lola T93/06 #6	94	Electrical
5/30/93	Indianapolis 500					
	Indianapolis Motor Speedway	2	5	Newman-Haas Kmart/Texaco-Havoline Lola T93/06 #6	200	Led 73 laps, stop and go penalty for entering pits while closed
6/6/93	Wisconsin State Fair Park	5	18	Newman-Haas Kmart/Texaco-Havoline Lola T93/06 #6	176	Running
6/13/93	Detroit Grand Prix	9	3	Newman-Haas Kmart/Texaco-Havoline Lola T93/06 #6	77	Running
6/27/93	Portland International Raceway	5	6	Newman-Haas Kmart/Texaco-Havoline Lola T93/06 #6	101	Led 1 lap, running
7/11/93	Burke Lakefront Airport	11	5	Newman-Haas Kmart/Texaco-Havoline Lola T93/06 #6	84	Running
7/18/93	Molson Indy Toronto	13	8	Newman-Haas Kmart/Texaco-Havoline Lola T93/06 #6	102	Running
8/1/93	Michigan 500					
	Michigan International Speedway	1	2	Newman-Haas Kmart/Texaco-Havoline Lola T93/06 #6	250	Led 27 laps, running
8/8/93	New Hampshire International Speedway	6	20	Newman-Haas Kmart/Texaco-Havoline Lola T93/06 #6	137	Wreck with Scott Goodyear
8/22/93	Road America	3	15	Newman-Haas Kmart/Texaco-Havoline Lola T93/06 #6	47	Blown engine
8/29/93	Vancouver	14	5	Newman-Haas Kmart/Texaco-Havoline Lola T93/06 #6	102	Running
9/12/93	Mid-Ohio	10	7	Newman-Haas Kmart/Texaco-Havoline Lola T93/06 #6	89	Running
9/19/93	Nazareth Speedway	6	13	Newman-Haas Kmart/Texaco-Havoline Lola T93/06 #6	188	Running
10/3/93	Laguna Seca	6	9	Newman-Haas Kmart/Texaco-Havoline Lola T93/06 #6	83	Running
3/20/94	Surfers Paradise	19	3	Newman-Haas Kmart/Texaco-Havoline Lola T94/00 #6	55	Running
4/10/94	Phoenix International Raceway	4	21	Newman-Haas Kmart/Texaco-Havoline Lola T94/00 #6	156	Wreck with Michael
4/17/94	Long Beach Grand Prix					
	Long Beach	6	5	Newman-Haas Kmart/Texaco-Havoline Lola T94/00 #6	104	Running
5/29/94	Indianapolis 500					
	Indianapolis Motor Speedway	9	32	Newman-Haas Kmart/Texaco-Havoline Lola T94/00 #6	23	Fuel system
6/5/94	Wisconsin State Fair Park	13	14	Newman-Haas Kmart/Texaco-Havoline Lola T94/00 #6	185	Running, race shortened to 192 miles because of rain
6/12/94	Detroit Grand Prix	9	18	Newman-Haas Kmart/Texaco-Havoline Lola T94/00 #6	75	Running
6/26/94	Portland International Raceway	16	9	Newman-Haas Kmart/Texaco-Havoline Lola T94/00 #6	100	Running
7/10/94	Burke Lakefront Airport	9	27	Newman-Haas Kmart/Texaco-Havoline Lola T94/00 #6	31	Broken suspension
7/17/94	Molson Indy Toronto	10	4	Newman-Haas Kmart/Texaco-Havoline Lola T94/00 #6	98	Running

Date	Event/Track	Qual	Finish	Entrant/Car/Number	Laps Compl	Comments
7/31/94	Michigan 500					
	Michigan International Speedway	5	18	Newman-Haas Kmart/Texaco-Havoline Lola T94/00 #6	121	Engine failure
8/14/94	Mid-Ohio	15	10	Newman-Haas Kmart/Texaco-Havoline Lola T94/00 #6	82	Running, race finished 6 laps early because of television schedule
8/21/94	New Hampshire International Speedway	5	19	Newman-Haas Kmart/Texaco-Havoline Lola T94/00 #6	107	Accident
9/4/94	Vancouver	10	11	Newman-Haas Kmart/Texaco-Havoline Lola T94/00 #6	101	Running
9/11/94	Road America	7	16	Newman-Haas Kmart/Texaco-Havoline Lola T94/00 #6	47	Engine failure
9/18/94	Nazareth Speedway	5	25	Newman-Haas Kmart/Texaco-Havoline Lola T94/00 #6	40	Wreck with Cheever
10/9/94	Laguna Seca	12	19	Newman-Haas Kmart/Texaco-Havoline Lola T94/00 #6	80	Engine failure

By the second year with Mario, Clint Brawner and Jim McGee had improved the Brawner Hawk design, eliminating many of the shortcomings found the year before. Mario won both races at Milwaukee in 1966. *Ken Coles*

Most Poles Won in a Season
AAA/USAC/CART National Championship (1930 – 1994)

1.	A. J. Foyt	10	1965
2.	**Mario**	**9**	**1966**
	Danny Sullivan	9	1988
4.	**Mario**	**8**	**1968**
	Al Unser	8	1970
	A. J. Foyt	8	1974
	Danny Ongais	8	1978
	Rick Mears	8	1982
	Mario	**8**	**1984**
	Mario	**8**	**1987**
	Michael Andretti	8	1991
12.	Bobby Unser	7	1971
	Bobby Unser	7	1972
	A. J. Foyt	7	1975
	A. J. Foyt	7	1976
	Tom Sneva	7	1978
	Bobby Unser	7	1979
	Bobby Rahal	7	1985
	Michael Andretti	7	1992
	Nigel Mansell	7	1993

The dirt car races were part of USAC's national championship until the 1970s. Mario is shown at speed during the 1967 Hoosier Hundred.
John Mahoney

National Championship Race Winners
AAA/USAC/CART National Championship (1909 – 1994)

Rank		Wins	Date of First Win	Site of First Win	Time Span of Wins
1.	A. J. Foyt	67	9/5/60	DuQuoin	1960 - 1981
2.	**Mario**	**52**	**7/25/65**	**Indianapolis Raceway Park**	**1965 - 1993**
3.	Al Unser	39	7/4/65	Pikes Peak	1965 - 1987
4.	Bobby Unser	35	7/4/66	Pikes Peak	1966 - 1981
5.	Rick Mears	29	6/18/78	Milwaukee	1978 – 1991
	Michael Andretti	29	4/13/86	Long Beach	1986 – 1994
7.	Johnny Rutherford	27	8/1/65	Atlanta	1965 – 1986
	Al Unser Jr.	27	6/17/84	Portland	1984 – 1994
9.	Rodger Ward	26	6/21/53	Springfield	1953 – 1966
10.	Gordon Johncock	25	4/13/65	Atlanta	1965 – 1983
11.	Bobby Rahal	24	7/4/82	Cleveland	1982 – 1992
	Ralph DePalma	24	9/29/09	Riverhead	1909 – 1921
13.	Tommy Milton	23	9/15/17	Providence	1917 – 1925
14.	Tony Bettenhausen	22	10/6/46	Goshen	1946 – 1959
15.	Emerson Fittipaldi	21	7/28/85	Michigan	1985 – 1994
16.	Earl Cooper	20	7/5/12	Tacoma	1912 – 1926
17.	Jimmy Bryan	19	10/25/53	Sacramento	1953 – 1958
	Jimmy Murphy	19	2/28/20	Beverly Hills	1920 – 1924
19.	Ralph Mulford	17	8/27/10	Elgin	1910 – 1919
	Danny Sullivan	17	7/28/84	Cleveland	1984 - 1993

National Championship Earnings Leaders
AAA/USAC/CART National Championship (1946–1994)

1.	Al Unser Jr.	$15,379,906
2.	Emerson Fittipaldi	13,272,875
3.	Bobby Rahal	13,003,241
4.	**Mario**	**11,552,154**
5.	Michael Andretti	11,332,566
6.	Rick Mears	11,050,807
7.	Danny Sullivan	8,254,673
8.	Arie Luyendyk	7,124,771
9.	Al Unser	6,740,843
10.	A. J. Foyt	5,357,589
11.	Raul Boesel	5,273,584
12.	Scott Brayton	4,500,711
13.	Tom Sneva	4,392,993
14.	Roberto Guerrero	4,275,163
15.	Scott Goodyear	4,212,298

National Championship Lap Leaders
AAA/USAC/CART National Championship (1946–1994)

1.	**Mario**	**7,587**
2.	A. J. Foyt	6,621
3.	Al Unser	5,812
4.	Bobby Unser	4,862
5.	Michael Andretti	4,460
6.	Rick Mears	3,506
7.	Gordon Johncock	3,417
8.	Bobby Rahal	2,965
9.	Rodger Ward	2,955
10.	Tony Bettenhausen	2,869
11.	Johnny Rutherford	2,703
12.	Emerson Fittipaldi	2,508
13.	Al Unser Jr.	2,491
14.	Tom Sneva	1,781
15.	Parnelli Jones	1,589

Emulating Monaco, more downtown street circuits were adopted by CART in the 1980s. Mario led two laps and finished behind Emerson Fittipaldi and Scott Pruett at Detroit in 1989. *Ken Coles*

National Championship Pole Position Winners
AAA/USAC/CART National Championship (1930–1994)

1.	**Mario**	**67**
2.	A. J. Foyt	53
3.	Bobby Unser	49
4.	Rick Mears	38
5.	Al Unser	27 (tie)
	Michael Andretti	27 (tie)
7.	Johnny Rutherford	23
8.	Gordon Johncock	20
9.	Rex Mays	19 (tie)
	Danny Sullivan	19 (tie)
11.	Bobby Rahal	18
12.	Emerson Fittipaldi	17
13.	Tony Bettenhausen	14 (tie)
	Don Branson	14 (tie)
	Tom Sneva	14 (tie)

Mario was busy during the 1970s, frequently flying back and forth between practicing, qualifying, and racing at different tracks on the same weekend. Here he's climbing into a helicopter after a day's work at Ontario in 1975. *Howard Koby*

This interesting shot shows most of drivers in the field waiting for the driver's meeting to start before the USAC National Championship race at Sacramento in 1965. Sitting on folding chairs are (back row, l - r) George Snider (with the hat), Carl Williams, Bob Harkey, Jud Larson, Al Unser, Arnie Knepper; (middle row, l - r) Johnny Rutherford, A. J. Foyt, Don Branson, Bob Tattersall, Roger McCluskey, Dick Atkins, Bud Tingelstad; (front, l - r) Larry Dickson, Bobby Unser, Gary Congdon, and a relaxed Mario. *John Mahoney*

The Record

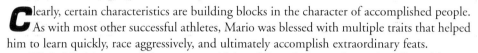

Desire is the key to motivation, but it's the determination and commitment to an unrelenting pursuit of your goals—a commitment to excellence—that will enable you to attain the success you seek. Mario, *www.andrettiwinery.com*

On the road to a second consecutive USAC National Championship in 1965. Mario is shown here before the start of an October race in Sacramento. *John Mahoney*

Clearly, certain characteristics are building blocks in the character of accomplished people. As with most other successful athletes, Mario was blessed with multiple traits that helped him to learn quickly, race aggressively, and ultimately accomplish extraordinary feats.

While Mario's accomplishments are widely publicized, the attributes that allowed him to excel in such a wide array of motorsports disciplines have not been as well known. One characteristic that separated Mario from other drivers of the time was a solid, seat-of-the-pants grasp of the technical side of race car engineering. He understood the subtleties of the various elements of a car's structure or suspension and how to fine-tune each to advance the car to the point where he could drive it most effectively.

The first rear-engine car Mario drove was also the first rear-engine car built by Clint Brawner and Jim McGee. Mario was responsible for sorting out the car, even though he only had part of one season on the USAC championship circuit, and that had been in a roadster. He applied himself with the same enthusiasm that characterized all of his efforts: Here was an opportunity, and he was going to make the most of it.

Having mastered the basic racing techniques while driving stock cars, midgets, and sprint cars on dirt ovals, Mario had a lot to learn about road racing. He clearly brought a lot of natural talent, shown by his early successes. He won a race at Lime Rock in a midget and his first champ car victory came on a road course at Indianapolis Raceway Park. As a test driver for Ford and Firestone, he had the opportunity to sharpen his inherent skills.

Looking back, it seems obvious that the elements that led to his growth on road courses were all interconnected. As he began developing the Brawner-Hawk, he was also learning the technical aspects of car setup. Working with Ford and Firestone, he turned more laps on road courses and this led to opportunities to drive for different Ford programs, including stock cars and sports cars. As he continued a demanding regimen of racing and testing, he learned quickly. Others took notice of his talent, and soon he was in demand as an emerging road racing star.

Beginning with Mario's earliest efforts in USAC's championship cars, Jim McGee may have worked more with him than any other chief mechanic. Today, McGee is the team manager for Patrick Racing in CART. He acknowledges that Mario had an approach that was unique and ultimately contributed to his success in many different types of racing. McGee explains, "In those days, the driver was kind of like the engineer of the car. Especially in Mario's case, he picked his own springs and he knew what he wanted in shocks and roll bars, and was very into the setup of the car. Not so much working on the car, but understanding what it took to make it handle. He was very into that. Mario kept his own book or notes of everything he did through the years and he had a good background of what it took to make a car handle."

After the Brawner Hawk, Mario helped develop the McNamara and the various Parnellis (the Indy cars as well as the Formula One and F-5000 machines) into competitive racers. He played a key role in the development of the ground effects advancements in the Lotus 78 and 79. And Mario's testing efforts were critical in the evolution of the Lola T-700, establishing a solid base for future Lola designs. Without a formal engineering education, Mario did it all by the seat of his pants.

McGee also recalls that while Mario possessed many character strengths, the ones that impressed him were his passion for driving and ability to focus. "It continued on throughout his career," said McGee. "Mario demanded a lot of money, but still it wasn't the money that drove him to drive, it was the passion for driving. That was a big part of it, and also the fact that he was so in focus. He could put other things out of his mind. When he was at the race track, the racing is where all of his focus went. The other stuff that went on, he was able to separate that from the racing."

Mario frequently credits his success in life to his passion and determination. Clearly when he was at the track, he didn't worry about what time it was or where they were going to eat. No matter whether they were testing a design modification or getting ready to race, he was focused on what it was going to take to be better. If he got beat, it certainly wasn't going to be because the other guy worked harder.

1987 was the only time Mario and Michael competed together in the International Race Of Champions. Mario finished eighth in this Z28 Camaro at Mid-Ohio. *Ken Coles*

Two of the best on dirt are wheel-to-wheel. This time, A. J. Foyt (1) edged Mario (2) at the Indiana State Fairgrounds in 1968. *John Mahoney*

The Record: Mario Andretti

Year	USAC Champ	Wins	F-1	Wins	CART	Wins	Sports Cars & Endurance	Wins	F-5000	Wins	USAC Open Wheel	Wins	Other	Wins	Milestones
1963											2				
1964	10										24	1			
1965	16	1					2				13	1	5		USAC national championship
1966	15	8					5				20	6	5		USAC national championship
1967	19	8					6	1			4	2	8	2	Daytona 500, Sebring
1968	26	4	2*				5						1		
1969	24	9	3				6				2				Indianapolis 500, USAC national championship Sebring
1970	18	1	5				4	1							
1971	10		5	1			3				3		3	2	First Grand Prix win at South Africa
1972	10		5				5	4							24 Hours of Daytona
1973	15	1					1				3	2			
1974	11		2				2	1	7	3	5	3			USAC Silver Crown championship
1975	4		12						9	4			4		
1976	4		17	1									1		
1977	6		17	4									4		
1978	8	1	16	6									4	2	F-1 World Driving Championship
1979			15		2								7	1	IROC Championship
1980	1		14		3	1	1						2		
1981	1		15		7										
1982	1		3		11		1								
1983	1				12	2	1								
1984	1				15	6	1								CART Championship
1985	1				13	3							2		
1986	1				16	2									
1987	1				14	2							4		
1988	1				14	2	1								
1989	1				14		1								
1990	1				15										
1991	1				16		1								
1992	1				14								1		
1993	1				15	1	1								
1994	1				15										
1995 – 2000							4						2		
Total	211	33	128	12	196	19	52	7	16	7	76	15	53	7	100 Race Victories

Sports Cars & Endurance includes USRRC, WSC, ACO, Can-Am and IMSA. **USAC Open Wheel** includes Silver Crown, sprint cars and midgets. **Other** includes USAC and NASCAR stock cars, IROC and special events. *The 1968 Italian GP, were Mario was prohibited from starting by the organizers, is not generally counted in his Grand Prix total.

Daytona 500 Winners

Daytona Beach Course

1949	Red Byron	Olds (166 miles)
1950	Harold Kite	Lincoln (200 miles)
1951	Marshall Teague	Hudson (160 miles)
1952	Marshall Teague	Hudson (200 miles)
1953	Bill Blair	Olds (160 miles)
1954	Lee Petty	Chrysler (160 miles)
1955	Tim Flock	Chrysler (160 miles)
1956	Tim Flock	Chrysler (160 miles)
1957	Cotton Owens	Pontiac (160 miles)
1958	Paul Goldsmith	Pontiac (160 miles)

Daytona International Speedway

1959	Lee Petty	Olds
1960	Junior Johnson	Chevrolet
1961	Marvin Panch	Pontiac
1962	Fireball Roberts	Pontiac
1963	Tiny Lund	Ford
1964	Richard Petty	Plymouth
1965	Fred Lorenzen	Ford
1966	Richard Petty	Plymouth
1967	**Mario**	**Ford**
1968	Cale Yarborough	Mercury
1969	LeeRoy Yarbrough	Ford
1970	Pete Hamilton	Plymouth
1971	Richard Petty	Plymouth
1972	A. J. Foyt	Mercury
1973	Richard Petty	Dodge
1974	Richard Petty	Dodge
1975	Benny Parsons	Chevrolet
1976	David Pearson	Mercury
1977	Cale Yarborough	Chevrolet
1978	Bobby Allison	Ford
1979	Richard Petty	Olds
1980	Buddy Baker	Olds
1981	Richard Petty	Buick
1982	Bobby Allison	Buick
1983	Cale Yarborough	Pontiac
1984	Cale Yarborough	Chevrolet
1985	Bill Elliott	Ford
1986	Geoff Bodine	Chevrolet
1987	Bill Elliott	Ford
1988	Bobby Allison	Buick
1989	Darrell Waltrip	Chevrolet
1990	Derricke Cope	Chevrolet
1991	Ernie Irvan	Chevrolet
1992	Davey Allison	Ford
1993	Dale Jarrett	Chevrolet
1994	Sterling Marlin	Chevrolet
1995	Sterling Marlin	Chevrolet
1996	Dale Jarrett	Chevrolet
1997	Jeff Gordon	Chevrolet
1998	Dale Earnhardt	Chevrolet
1999	Jeff Gordon	Chevrolet
2000	Dale Jarrett	Ford
2001	Michael Waltrip	Chevrolet
2002	Ward Burton	Dodge

In the haze of the early morning sun, Mario's Viceroy Lola is rolled into its pit stall by a crewman at Ontario, California, in 1974. Mario won at Ontario, but finished second to Brian Redman in the F-5000 championship. *Howard Koby*

In USAC's F-5000 series, Mario won four times in 1975. Here the Vel's Parnelli Jones Viceroy Lola tours Mid-Ohio Raceway. He started on the pole but finished 18th. *Ken Coles*

Niki Lauda (11) claimed the pole and ran the fastest race lap in the U.S. West Grand Prix of 1977, but it was Mario (setting Lauda up for the pass) who claimed the victory by 0.7 of a second over the Ferrari. *Howard Koby*

Mario practiced in George Bignotti's Lola at Riverside in 1968, but mechanical problems kept them from starting the Can-Am event. *Mike Smith*

Appendix

Acronyms and Initials

ACO - Automobile Club de l'Ouest (Race organization for 24 Hours of LeMans)

ARDC -- American Racing Drivers Club

ATQMRA -- American Three-Quarter Midget Racing Association

BRDC – British Racing Drivers Club

CART -- Championship Auto Racing Teams

IMSA -- International Motor Sports Association

IRP – Indianapolis Raceway Park

NART – North American Racing Team

NASCAR – National Association for Stock Car Auto Racing

NHRA -- National Hot Rod Association

USAC – United States Auto Club

URC -- United Racing Club

WSCC – World Sports Car Championship

PSC – Porsche Super Cup

In the first IROC race of his career, Mario finished ninth at Michigan in 1975 – which is actually counted as part of the 1976 series. *Ken Coles*

Race Track Index

Race Track	Location	Type Track	Sanction	Comments
Allentown Fairgrounds	Allentown, PA	.5 mile dirt oval	USAC	
Anderstorp (Scandinavian Raceway)	Anderstorp, Sweden	2.5 mile road course	F-1	
Ascot Park	Gardena, CA	.5 mile dirt oval	USAC	
Astrodome	Houston, TX	1/6 mile dirt indoor oval	USAC	
Atlanta Motor Speedway	Hampton, GA	1.522 mile paved oval	USAC, CART, IROC	
Berlin Raceway	Marne, MI	1/3 mile paved oval	USAC	
Brands Hatch	Fawkham, England	2.65 miles road course 2.614 miles beginning in 1975	F-1	
Bridgehampton	Long Island, NY	2.85 mile road course	USRRC	
Buenos Aires	Buenos Aires, Argentina	Road courses of 2.8 and 3.7 miles	F-1, WSCC	Reportedly this track has had 12 different layouts.
Burke Lakefront Airport	Cleveland, OH	Road course 2.48 miles	CART	
California State Fairgrounds	Sacramento, CA	1 mile dirt oval	USAC	
CNE Exposition Grounds	Toronto, Ontario, Canada	.25 mile paved oval	USAC	
Continental Divide Raceway	Castle Rock, CO	2.66 mile road course	USAC	
Cumberland Speedway	Cumberland, MD	.5 dirt oval	USAC	
Daytona International Speedway	Daytona Beach, FL	2.5 mile paved tri-oval; infield road course 3.81 miles through 2/84, 3.3 miles to present	NASCAR, IROC, WSCC	
Denver Grand Prix	Denver, CO	1.9 mile street circuit	CART	Temporary street circuit located in downtown Denver
Detroit Grand Prix (1)	Street circuit downtown Detroit, MI	2.49 mile street circuit	CART	1989 - 1991
Detroit Grand Prix (2)	Street circuit Belle Isle, Detroit, MI	2.1 mile street circuit	CART	1992 – 2001
Dijon-Prenois	Dijon, France	2.36 mile road course	F-1	
Donington Park	Donington Park, England	1.96 mile road course	Special event	Gunnar Nilsson Memorial Trophy Race
Donnybrooke Raceway	Brainerd, MN	2.833 mile road course	USAC	
Dover Downs	Dover, DE	1 mile paved oval	USAC	
DuQuoin State Fairgrounds	DuQuoin, IL	1 mile dirt oval	USAC	
Eldora Speedway	Rossburg, OH	.5 mile dirt oval	USAC	
Ft. Wayne Memorial Coliseum	Ft. Wayne, IN	1/10 paved indoor oval	USAC	
Hanford International Raceway	Hanford, CA	1.5 mile paved oval	USAC	
Hockenheim	Hamburg, Germany	4.22 miles road course	F-1	
Illinois State Fairgrounds	Springfield, IL	1 mile dirt oval	USAC	
Imola, Autodromo Dino Ferrari	Bologna, Italy	3.1 mile road course	F-1	
Indiana State Fairgrounds	Indianapolis, IN	1 mile dirt oval	USAC	The Hoosier Hundred
Indianapolis Motor Speedway	Speedway, IN	2.5 mile paved oval	USAC	
Indianapolis Raceway Park	Clermont, IN	.686 mile paved oval	USAC	
Indianapolis Raceway Park	Clermont, IN	1.875 mile road course	USAC	Infield road course, converted to 2.5 miles for 1968
Indianapolis Speedrome	Indianapolis, IN	1/5 mile paved oval	USAC	
Interlagos	Sao Paulo, Brazil	4.94 mile road course, modified to 4.89 miles in 1979 – 1980, modified to 3.12 miles for 1981	F-1	
Jacarepagua	Rio de Janeiro, Brazil	3.12 mile road course	F-1	
Jarama	Madrid, Spain	2.115 miles road course, expanded to 2.58 miles beginning in 1979, modified to 2.056 for 1981	F-1	
Kyalami	Johannesburg, South Africa	2.55 miles road course	F-1	

Race Track	Location	Type Track	Sanction	Comments
Laguna Seca	Monterey, CA	1.92 mile road course, expanded to 2.214 miles in 1988	CART, Can-Am	
Lakeside Speedway	Kansas City, KS	.5 mile dirt oval	USAC	
Langhorne Speedway	Langhorne, PA	1 mile paved oval	USAC	Track was dirt in 1964, paved for 1965 season
Las Vegas	Caesar's Palace, Las Vegas	2.27 mile road course, modified to 1.125 miles by 1983	F-1, CART	1981 USA Grand Prix Las Vegas; course constructed in parking lot
St. Jovite, Le Circuit Mt. Tremblant	St. Jovite, Quebec, Canada	2.7 mile road course	USAC	
Le Mans	Le Mans, France	Course has had frequent changes in configuration and length 1966 and 1967 – 8.36 miles 1970 – 8.37 miles 1972 – 8.48 miles 1982 and 1983 – 8.47 miles 1988 – 8.41 miles 1995 and 1996 – 8.45 miles 1997 and 2000 – 8.45 miles	ACO	
Long Beach	Long Beach, CA	2.02 mile road course, expanded to 2.13 miles in 1982, changed to 1.67 miles for 1984, 1.59 miles in 1992	F-1, CART	
Manzanita Park	Phoenix, AZ	.5 mile dirt oval	USAC	
Meadowlands	Meadowlands Sports Complex, East Rutherford, NJ	Road course, 1.8 miles (1984), 1.6 miles (1985 – 1987), 1.217 miles (1988 – 1991)	CART	
Michigan International Speedway	Brooklyn, MI	2 mile paved oval	USAC, CART, IROC	
Minnesota State Fairgrounds	St. Paul, MN	.5 mile paved oval	USAC	
Mid-America Raceways	Wentzville, MO	2.75 mile road course	USAC	
Mid-Ohio Raceway	Lexington, OH	2.4 mile road course, changed to 2.25 miles in 1990	USAC, CART	
Missouri State Fairgrounds	Sedalia, MO	1 mile dirt oval	USAC	
Molson Indy Toronto	Toronto, Ontario, Canada	1.78 mile road course	CART	Street course in Canadian National Expo
Monaco	Monte Carlo	1.954 mile road course until 1973, 2.04 miles through 1975, 2.06 miles until 1986	F-1	
Montjuich Park	Barcelona, Spain	2.35 mile road course through downtown Barcelona	F-1	
Montreal	Ile de Notre Dame, Montreal, Canada	2.8 mile road course, modified to 2.74 miles in 1979	F-1	
Monza	Monza, Italy	3.6 mile road course	F-1	
Mosport Park	Bowmanville, Ontario, Canada	2.459 mile road course	USAC, F-1	
Mt. Fuji International Speedway	Gotemba, Japan	2.7 mile road course	USAC, F-1	
Muskogee Speedway	Muskogee, OK	.5 dirt oval	USAC	
Nazareth Raceway	Nazareth, PA	.5 dirt oval	USAC	
Nazareth Speedway	Nazareth, PA	1.125 mile dirt oval, converted to 1 mile paved tri-oval in 1987	USAC, CART	Also known as Nazareth National Motor Speedway
New Bremen Speedway	New Bremen, OH	.5 mile dirt oval	USAC	

Race Track	Location	Type Track	Sanction	Comments
New Hampshire International Speedway	Loudon, NH	1 mile paved oval	CART	Former site of Bryar Motorsports Park
New York State Fairgrounds	Syracuse, NY	1 mile dirt oval	USAC	
Nurburgring	Nurburg, Germany	14.2 mile road course	F-1	Circuit has changed length several times, is currently 2.8 miles
Ontario Motor Speedway	Ontario, CA	2.5 mile paved oval and 3.19 mile infield road course	USAC	
Orange Show Speedway	San Bernardino, CA	.25 mile paved oval	USAC	
Österreichring	Knittelfeld, Austria	3.673 miles road course, expanded to 3.69 miles in 1977	F-1	
Oswego Speedway	Oswego, NY	.625 mile paved oval	USAC	
Paul Ricard	Marseille, France	3.61 mile road course	F-1	
Phoenix International Raceway	Phoenix, AZ	1 mile paved oval	USAC, CART	
Pikes Peak Hill Climb	Colorado Springs, CO	12.42 mile hill climb	USAC	Part of USAC National Championship through 1969
Pocono International Raceway	Pocono, PA	2.5 mile paved oval	USAC, CART	
Portland International Raceway	Portland, OR	1.915 mile road course	CART	
Reading Fairgrounds	Reading, PA	.25 mile dirt oval	USAC	
Riverside International Raceway	Riverside, CA	2.6 mile road course expanded to 3.3 miles in 1969	NASCAR, LA Times Grand Prix, IROC, Can-Am, CART	
Road America	Elkhart Lake, WI	4 mile road course	CART, Can-Am	
Road Atlanta	Braselton, GA	2.52 mile road course	USAC	
Salem Speedway	Salem, IN	.5 mile paved oval	USAC	
Sanair Super Speedway	St. Pie, Quebec, Canada	.826 mile oval	CART	
Sears Point	Sonoma, CA	2.523 mile road course	USAC	
Seattle International Raceway	Kent, WA	2.25 mile road course	USAC	
Sebring International Raceway	Sebring, FL	5.2 mile road course	WSCC	
Silverstone	Silverstone, England	2.932 mile road course	F-1	
Stardust International Raceway	Las Vegas, NV	3 mile road course	USAC, Can-Am	
Surfers Paradise	Surfers Paradise, Queensland, Australia	2.8 mile street course	CART	Temporary street circuit located in downtown Surfers Paradise
Terre Haute Action Track	Terre Haute, IN	.5 mile dirt oval	USAC	
Texas World Speedway	College Station Texas	2 mile paved oval and 2.75 mile road course	Can-Am	Previously known as Texas International Speedway
Trenton Speedway	Trenton, NJ	1 and 1.5 mile paved oval	USAC	1 mile converted to 1.5 miles in 1969
Tulsa Fairgrounds Speedway	Tulsa, OK	3/8 dirt oval	USAC	
Vancouver	British Colombia Place Stadium, Vancouver, BC, Canada	1.7 mile street course	CART	Temporary street circuit located in downtown Vancouver
Watkins Glen	Watkins Glen, NY	2.3 mile road course, expanded to 3.4 miles in 1971	F-1, CART	
Williams Grove Speedway	Mechanicsburg, PA	.5 mile dirt oval	USAC	
Winchester Speedway	Winchester, IN	.5 mile paved oval	USAC	
Wisconsin State Fair Park	Milwaukee, WI	1 mile paved oval	USAC, CART	
Zandvoort	Haarlem, Holland	2.636 mile road course, modified with a chicane to 2.64 miles for 1979	F-1	
Zolder	Zolder, Belgium	2.65 mile road course	F-1	

Index

Index